HOW *YOU*

CAN SURVIVE

WHEN *THEY'RE*

DEPRESSED

HOW *YOU* CAN SURVIVE WHEN *THEY'RE* DEPRESSED

Living and Coping with Depression Fallout

ANNE SHEFFIELD

Foreword by MIKE WALLACE

Introduction by DONALD F. KLEIN, M.D.

Harmony/New York

To Mary, Howard, and my
daughter Pandora

Copyright © 1998 by Anne Sheffield

All rights reserved. No part of this book may be reproduced or transmitted in any form or by any means, electronic or mechanical, including photocopying, recording, or by any information storage and retrieval system, without permission in writing from the publisher.

Published by Harmony Books, a division of Crown Publishers, Inc., 201 East 50th Street, New York, New York 10022. Member of the Crown Publishing Group.

Random House, Inc. New York, Toronto, London, Sydney, Auckland

http://www.randomhouse.com/

HARMONY and colophon are trademarks of Crown Publishers, Inc.

Printed in the United States of America

Design by Lenny Henderson

Library of Congress Cataloging-in-Publication Data

Sheffield, Anne.

　　How you can survive when they're depressed : living and coping with depression fallout / by Anne Sheffield ; foreword by Mike Wallace ; introduction by Donald F. Klein, M.D. — 1st ed.

　　　　p.　　cm.

　　Includes index.

　　1. Depression, Mental—Popular works.　2. Depressed persons—Family relationships.　I. Title.

RC537.S485　1998

616.8'527—dc21　　　　　　　　　　　　　　　　　97-40281

　　　　　　　　　　　　　　　　　　　　　　　　　　　　　CIP

ISBN 0-517-70866-3

10 9 8 7 6 5 4 3 2 1

First Edition

Contents

Acknowledgments

IN THE COURSE OF WRITING this book, many depression fallout sufferers have shared with me the personal pain and problems that loving and living close to a much-loved depressive or manic-depressive has brought them. Without their honesty and generosity, this book could not have been written, and I am forever in their debt. I thank them not only for sharing their emotions, experience, and solutions to depression fallout, but for their overarching purpose: to help others who suffer without support.

I owe much gratitude to The Mood Disorders Support Group of New York City, which is a model of informed and supportive assistance to both depressives and manic-depressives, and to their families and friends.

My heartfelt thanks go also to the many distinguished psychiatrists, psychopharmacologists, psychotherapists, and researchers who have granted me their wisdom and insights. Above all, I wish to express my appreciation to Dr. Donald Klein for his unflagging encouragement and for the countless hours he devoted to reviewing the manuscript for clarity and accuracy. His help enabled me to transform an idea into a finished product.

Foreword

By Mike Wallace

ONE NOVEMBER DAY IN 1984, I was fidgeting in my chair at the defense table in a Federal courtroom in lower Manhattan, listening to a plaintiff's lawyer do his best to demolish my credibility as a reporter. I was on trial, along with some of my CBS News colleagues, on charges of libeling General William Westmoreland in a *CBS News Reports* broadcast titled "The Uncounted Enemy: A Vietnam Deception."

The broadcast said that General Westmoreland had "cooked the books" in Vietnam in 1967, had failed to tell the American people the truth about how many enemy troops were still out there fighting us, and how many more were coming down from North Vietnam to try to drive us out of the country. That triggered his libel suit.

I knew our reportage had been accurate, which nonetheless made it no easier to sit in that drafty courtroom day after day and listen to the general's lawyer labeling us liars, cheats, and worse.

It was a bitterly draining five-month experience, that trial. I could concentrate on nothing else, I was having trouble sleeping, I'd been losing weight and in general was feeling lower than a snake's belly. My sleeping pills weren't working, but my doctor told me to buck up, that I was strong and resilient. He was wrong; I was feeling whipped. Only Mary Yates, then my companion, now my wife of ten years, knew what was happening to me, that I was sliding into a full-fledged depression. I didn't want to acknowledge to my pals at *60 Minutes* what was going on, nor did I tell my children; I was simply ashamed of having to bear the stigma of that shameful word *depression*.

Finally—finally—Mary persuaded me to see a psychiatrist, who promptly put me on an antidepressant medication, which dried my mouth and made my excretory functions dysfunctional. I was distinctly unpleasant company for just about anyone who came near, but especially for Mary, who had to put up with my unrelieved glumness and short temper. When I went to the office, I did my best to camouflage all that, and thanks to the team I worked with I was able to keep turning out reports for *60 Minutes,* but they had to prop me up to do it. They knew something was wrong, but they weren't sure just what. Meanwhile, I was getting no better.

It's difficult to make others understand how desperate a deep depression can make you feel, how lost, how cope-less, how grim. And no light at the end of the tunnel.

And there is no way properly to describe the anguish that a depressive can put his family through. Gloom, doom, no love, no real communication, short temper, and leave-me-alone fault-finding. Why more marriages don't break up under those desolate circumstances is a puzzle, for you know deep down the damage you're doing to the ones you care about, the ones who have to live through it with you and suffer from depression fallout, and yet you feel somehow incapable of doing anything to lighten the burden for them.

I've been through two more depressive episodes, shorter ones, since that first one back in 1984, which began to lift after General Westmoreland finally withdrew his lawsuit. Both of the later episodes were just as tough on Mary as the first, but at least we knew what was happening the second and third times. That third episode ended almost four years ago, and now I'm on a medication that I intend to stay with for the rest of my life, for to my surprise and delighted bewilderment, I have not felt so whole and so content in years and years.

I recount all this, having just read my friend Anne Sheffield's book. Chances are you wouldn't be reading it unless you or your family or friends have been or are now faced with something similar to what I put Mary through. It's an extraordinary book, full of the insights that come from the fact that Anne herself was a victim of depression fallout. She has written a compassionate and mature account of what can lie in wait for the legions who are captives of the fallout from the depressive's agony; she's got it right, and believe me, she'll help you cope.

Introduction

By Donald F. Klein, M.D.

IT MIGHT HELP THE READER to place Anne Sheffield's book in the historical context of our progressive understanding of psychiatric illness. Her piercing intelligence, feeling heart, and impatience with blather is shown over and over again, but I think it would be a mistake to attribute the novel qualities of this book solely to the author's gifts. What strikes me as overwhelmingly important is that she has developed a unique source of information provided by a remarkable new social invention, which is in turn a spinoff of yet another remarkable new social invention.

The development of support groups for patients with depression is a tale worth telling. Their spinoff, the friends and families support groups, provided the author with an opportunity to plunge as a participant observer into the life histories of many depressives and manic-depressives as told by those who live with them. This gains a detailed picture of the common destructive interactions that fall out from depressive illness.

The average layperson whose knowledge of depression is limited to some of the recent educational efforts probably does not understand the value of this information source, although history may help. The whole idea of depressive illness stemmed from the observations of the "alienists" stationed in the insane asylums of the nineteenth century. These hospital superintendents lived on the grounds of the purposefully isolated asylums and were, all day, every day, in contact with their charges, who often remained for years. Many of those patients had brain syphilis, others the last stages of alcoholism, others pellagra (a nutritional deficiency of the poor), various forms of epilepsy, and brain trauma. It was a bewildering cacophony. Treatment was essentially nursing care and regular meals. Of great importance was the fact that if a patient was discharged and became ill again, he or she would very likely return to the same hospital.

One might wonder at the doctor's plight, given the lack of effective treatments. His job was largely to keep patients as medically healthy as the practices of the day allowed, by prevention of self-starvation and suicide, until the patient might recover. Emil Kraepelin, from his intensive longitudinal contact with his patients, discerned an interesting pattern that, if it did not improve his ability to treat, at least allowed him to predict the patient's outcome with substantial accuracy. He noted that a whole group of patients became ill, often in their teens, showing markedly disorganized thinking and a progressive deterioration in their intellectual and social functioning. This reminded him of the progressive dementias of the elderly. This was a precocious dementia, however, and therefore he named it *dementia praecox*. In more recent times, it has been labeled schizophrenia.

Kraepelin also noted that there were patients who supposedly became severely disordered, usually at a later period in their life, and showed either profound withdrawal and lack of interest and will, or extraordinary energy, hilarity, and flight of ideas. What distinguished these patients, in Kraepelin's mind, was the fact that if kept alive, they often got well and were restored to normal. He also noted that after a period many returned to the hospital with a recurrence of their illness. Kraepelin named this group "manic-depressive."

It should be noted that this term applied to patients who only became depressed as well as to those who became both manic and depressed, because of what appeared to him to be a common outcome. Only recently has there been a distinction between those who have recurrent depressions and those who have both depressions and manias (now referred to as unipolar and bipolar).

Kraepelin's conception of depression was therefore a product of his acute mind and hospital experience. It stamped a certain view of depression onto psychiatry. Depression was an illness that interrupted a person's life and rendered him or her dysfunctional, but after a while would go away with the patient restored to normal. These illnesses were considered brain diseases, although we now know that the crude instruments of the day were not up to the task of detecting subtle physiological changes.

With the development of outpatient psychotherapy, substantially influenced by Freud's views, there were two subtle shifts in our ability to gain knowledge of patients. With the development of the belief that much mental illness was the late manifestation of infantile conflicts, there was a devaluing of the real-life circumstances of the patient, as well as of the effects of the patient's illness on others. Further, the psychotherapist's view of the patient became constricted by the fact that a therapist only saw a very limited aspect of the patient's behavior, at most for several hours a week and often substantially less than that. They had only the patient's reports (and dreams) on which to construct their theories. To be concerned with the real functioning and emotional relatedness of the patient was considered the sure mark of a superficial mind.

The development of the new medications caused a renewed interest in the systematic description of the patient's symptoms which had been dismissed as irrelevant to the real action of unconscious conflict.

The obvious thing for the early psychopharmacologists to focus on was the manifest symptomatic complaints of the patients—for example, their loss of appetite, their inability to sleep, their difficulty in making up their minds. It was shown conclusively that such scales did indeed register the effects of the new medications. They proved these new psychotherapeutic drugs really worked, as compared to placebos. But there remained a constriction of view, since the focus was primarily on what the outpatient could report about feelings and activities. Even measures of social adjustment were made largely on the basis of the patient's testimony concerning how they did in interpersonal relationships, whether they were holding a job and such.

Attempts to gather information from relatives yielded little because the relatives were too poorly trained to be able to discern changes in the patient's behavior that were evident over the short period of time, say six weeks, that most drug trials took. Since the demands by the FDA and the support of industry were narrowly focused on the acute benefits of medication, long-term effects were largely ignored and simple questions, such as how long the patient should be maintained on medication and at what dose, have still gone largely unanswered. The antidepressants have been around now for forty years, and there still has never been a proper long-term study of the proper dose for maintaining patients on medication.

Simply put, there is nobody who is willing to pay for such studies. That includes not only the several federal institutes that support research, but academia and the pharmaceutical industry as well. I'm off on a tangent (one close to my heart, however).

What Anne Sheffield has done is to tap into a deep vein of largely unexplored detailed knowledge of the behaviors and impacts of those afflicted with depression by carefully listening to those who have the most detailed exposure, as well as the strongest of reasons for paying close attention: those who live with the depressive patient. This deep and longitudinal study of the patient is in many ways virgin soil. Such observations are easily dismissed as unsystematic or tainted by self-interest and laden with emotional reactions that distort one's views. That is the way it is with all naturalistic observation. It is such rich observations that provide the jumping-off platform for those who can now see that this unsuspecting source of rich, detailed information is open to systematic, if less creative, investigation.

Is this report an accurate representation of depression and depression fallout? To a clinician working with difficult patients, who uses families as a valuable source of information, these stories ring true. Perhaps my only reservation is that those who attend such a support group may well have to contend with patients who are at the more severe end of the depressive spectrum. Properly speaking, that too is a hypothesis which can be objectively studied. This is not a purely literary debate. The facts are out there, and we know how to get them if we had the resources.

Another acute distinction that this book vividly brings across is the one between depression as an illness and demoralization as a reaction. Though easily confused, they are different and require different treatments. I think it no accident that many of the techniques that have been proposed for the psychotherapy of depression closely resemble techniques that actually work for demoralization, as Jerome Frank originally pointed out as a lone voice in the wilderness. It's not often realized how trenchant a critique Frank's conception of psychotherapy offers, but what he says is that psychotherapy does not treat the illness, but rather demoralization, a secondary complication of the illness.

Finally, we should emphasize the constructive practicality that Anne Sheffield provides, which is an unblinkered and unsentimental view that reveals the pained but often destructive and counterproductive reactions of both patients and relatives. Some of our more enlightened citizens may have trouble with such an unblinkered view, reacting in horror as if this were a callous dismissal of the mentally ill as malingering layabouts who just need a kick in the pants. In contrast, some view them as poor unfortunates whose every action, no matter how shortsighted, pathologically distorted, and destructive, should elicit nothing but sympathy and tolerance.

There is a useful distinction between limitations directly produced by an illness and the miscarried repairs that temporarily raise one's mood and self esteem but nevertheless have long-term destructive consequences. It's not always an easy distinction, but Anne Sheffield will help you see the difference and, further, help you learn that different responses are in order. As a clinician, I am enormously pleased that such a work will inform and help patients and their caregivers of all sorts. As a scientist, I am delighted by this pioneering introduction to a profound source of detailed information that now becomes accessible for future research advances.

1

A PROBLEM SHARED BY

SEVENTEEN MILLION PEOPLE

AT ANY GIVEN MOMENT, APPROXIMATELY 17 million Americans are suffering from a depressive illness. At least the same number, and probably many more, suffer from depression fallout. They are the people closest to those with the illness: the spouses, lovers, parents, and children who experience the consequences of living in close proximity to someone else's despair. Yet most of what one reads and hears about depression fails to look beyond its sufferers, as though they existed in a vacuum. For the intimates of depressives and manic-depressives, this is as puzzling as it is painful. We wonder why no one notices that we are as inexorably drawn into the force field of the illness as iron filings to a magnet. We wonder why no one understands that another's depression directs and colors our lives, our thoughts, our feelings, just as surely as it does those of the depressive.

Living with a husband, wife, lover, parent, or child who views the world through a prism of despair is a daunting task. Proximity to them gives rise to many of the same feelings as does the illness itself: futility, worthlessness, and an inability to enjoy or cope with life. The depressive's outlook is biologically driven, steered by a malfunctioning of the brain's chemicals. Ours is psychologically derived, the by-product of someone else's misery, but no less crippling to the spirit. Depression and depression fallout are mirror images of each other, distinguishable by the fact that the former is a recognizable illness and treatable by medication, while the latter is neither. We have the symptoms but not the illness, and they originate not in our brain's faulty neurotransmitters, but in the other's behavior and our reactions to it.

The many books about depression and its less prevalent but more vicious relative, manic depression, make occasional brief references to what we are expected to do to help the depressive. Typically we are told to be patient and supportive. If and when doctors are willing to speak to family members, they repeat the same advice. Their focus is entirely on the patient. To them we are an appendage—in their language, a "caregiver." But where the doctors and psychotherapists see a patient, we see our wife or husband or lover, our parent or child. That's where our problem begins, out of the public view, in the privacy of our relationship. As we witness a close friend or family member transformed from the familiar to an alien being, we rush to help them, to make them well with our love, our sympathy, our support. As we gradually come to realize our efforts are for naught, we begin to lose our sense of self. Confronted with the unrelenting despondency and negativism of the other's depression, we match it with a painful gloom of our own. And when our love, sympathy, and support are rejected or ignored, we slip into irritability and anger that mimic the depressive's. Guilty and ashamed, we long to escape the source of our black feelings. We do this silently and secretively, persuaded that our aberrant thoughts and feelings are unique to us. Such is the progression of depression fallout. Here is the story of my own.

A Cautionary Tale of Depression Fallout

It is virtually impossible to share life with a depressive and remain free of the miasmic net the illness casts. I grew up in the 1930s and 1940s with a clinically depressed mother, well before we knew what the illness was. Unaware that she was a slave of her faulty neurotransmitters, I made a number of assumptions that shaped both my childhood and my life. I assumed that I was lacking in whatever my mother wanted and expected of me, that my poor performance explained her dissatisfaction with me, and that if I met her expectations I would at last earn her love approval. None of this came to pass.

Nothing I ever did was good enough to please my mother—not my grades, not my accomplishments, not the boys I went out with.

Nothing. As children do, I nonetheless loved her unconditionally when I was young. I accepted her dissatisfaction and lack of affection, and went on trying for approval and love.

My mother was capable of great charm, but she reserved it for friends and acquaintances, not family. Everyone thought she was wonderful except her husbands (all of whom left her), her sister—and, of course, me. When I was really young I don't remember my spirit taking such a battering from her as it did from the age of about sixteen on. Perhaps that was when her depression came into full bloom. The harder I tried, the better I did, the more critical and resentful she became.

As I grew older, I sometimes thought of my mother as consumed by a demon. I even have a photograph of that demon, taken at my wedding. Just as I had always wanted my mother to love me, I had always wanted a father to love, and so, despite years of prohibition on any mention of his existence, I wrote and asked him to give me away. In one of the wedding photographs, the bridesmaids and I are clustered around him, looking up at his handsome face with adoring gazes. Off to one side stands my mother, grim-mouthed, her lovely, long fingers curled up like talons, beaming hatred at us all. That's how I remember her.

Leaving the next day for London, where my husband and I were going to live, was like getting out of reform school. Perhaps that's why I married, to get far away from her. Indeed, life three thousand miles apart was an entirely different proposition. In those days before E-mail, even a long-distance phone call was a rare event. Physically, I was free of her; psychologically, I felt I had at last distanced myself from her. My distress waned.

But the marriage didn't work. In my haste to remove myself from my mother's domain, I had chosen badly. I returned home a scant two years later, minus husband, plus baby daughter, and was immediately sucked back into my mother's sphere of influence. Although an adult with a life of my own, I couldn't seem to escape her pull, and returned to seeking her approbation, her support, her understanding, and her love. In spite of a successful career and social life, I wilted inside. When I returned from my frequent business trips, I would phone her as soon as I got home, stopping only to kiss my daughter. She never asked if the trip had been a success. Indeed, she never asked anything pertaining to me. Instead she complained about her own life in my absence (unsatisfactory), and of how her husband and friends had treated her (badly). Her negativism and disapproval permeated my life once again.

Life went on like that for some ten years. My public existence blossomed while my mother whittled away at the private, essential me. When I talked about my work, of which I was passionately proud, she listened without interest. She casually relegated me to the status of nonperson. When I appeared in a new suit, she asked only how much it had cost. When I went away for a weekend, she reprimanded me for leaving my daughter with the nanny. If I had a new boyfriend, she reminded me I was too fat. When I invited her to dinner, she noted how long it had been since the last dinner. She complained to me of her own friends as well as mine. To their faces she was delightful, and they believed her to be the undeserving victim of an unloving daughter and a string of husbands who did her wrong. At home she was a manipulative bully. And she drank a lot.

My father left my mother when I was one year old. She allowed me to see him only twice, on spring vacations spent with him in Florida during my early teens. Returning home with tales of the fun I'd had resulted in a virtual ban on mention of his name. My first stepfather, who lasted seven years, met with the same fate. My second stepfather, Tony, installed when I returned from London, was a kind and gentle man whose patience with my mother was extraordinary. She came to treat him much as she treated me.

Eventually she drove Tony away, too, but one night, a year before he left, she downed a bottle of sleeping pills, then told him what she had done. He called an ambulance, my aunt, and me. As we stood around her hospital bed, my mother opened her eyes and said, "I did it because Anne doesn't love me." This woman I had spent my life loving, longing for her love in return, in that instant passed such judgment upon me that I was mute, unable to offer some defense of myself, some rejection of her unfounded accusation.

From then on I hated her. I continued to play the dutiful daughter (my own daughter adored her), but behind my facade was an impotent, murderous rage. I wanted her dead and gone from my life. Only my fear of reprisal stood as a barrier between my hatred of her and my imagined solutions to that hatred. Why couldn't I instead have simply walked away? Because it wasn't my body she had hold of, but my psyche. That pernicious bond had been too deeply and too long established to break with mere physical distance. Tony was long gone by then, but I was still trapped—by guilt over my hatred of her, by fear of appearing heartless in the eyes of others, by habit. What I felt for her, I kept profoundly hidden from the rest of the world. That silence was also a form of entrapment.

Following her suicide attempt, my mother had been frequently ill and often in the hospital. I was expected to visit her twice a day; if I didn't, she extracted a price. Her currency was guilt and pity. Perhaps she chose to view the forced visits as a sign of love for her, or perhaps it was just more of her bullying. The illnesses became more frequent until a final one left her exceedingly ill and in great pain. The doctor said the decision whether or not to perform another operation, with only a slim chance of stemming her cancer for a month or two, and with no chance of curing it, was mine. When I said no, he told me I had made the right choice, but I wondered then, and still do, if some black piece of myself wanted her dead, out of my life. Intellectually I understand that was not true, but like everything else about my mother, my understanding remained only in my head, not in my stomach.

In my adult years I had come eventually to tolerate my mother, as one might tolerate chronic back pain. I had learned how to deal with her by strategically maneuvering around her rather than by engaging with her on her terms, which were the only terms she knew, but I had long since given up the unrewarded effort of loving her. Growing up in her domain, I had drawn on a practical instinct for survival, and exercised little or no curiosity about the whys and wherefores of her makeup. She was my mother, and she was what she was. I accepted that I was stuck with her and with my negative feelings toward her.

I viewed my mother as a stroke of bad luck, until a further stroke of chance cast her behavior in a different light. More than ten years after she died, I gradually slipped downward into a depression of my own. The climb back took time, but then, with my own depression consigned to the past and now fully cognizant of its ability to shape its sufferer's experience of the world, I began to reflect on my mother's life, on the enduring dissatisfaction that had rendered her incapable of living with any of her three husbands, of reciprocating the love we so freely offered her, and on her suicide attempt.

It was then, from my new, depression-free vantage point, that my view of my mother and our life together suddenly underwent a kaleidoscopic shift. All the memories and feelings that had composed my lifelong emotional portrait of her instantaneously rearranged themselves in one of those inexplicable epiphanies that clarify and illuminate without any conscious effort or thought. The pieces fit together with such sheer perfection that they left no room for doubt: my mother had spent much of her life in a depression, and I had reaped the consequences. And so was born my concept of depression fallout, a name for the effects of living close to a depressive.

Once I had identified it, I saw it replicated elsewhere. At first I spoke only with a few close friends whom I suspected of sharing my problem, or some version of it. I broached the subject tentatively, clothing it in ellipses and nuances, casting glimpses of my insight like trout flies to see if anyone would nibble. Someone did, a man I had known since my teenage years, almost an adopted brother, who had often dropped hints of the possibility of a divorce in his future. I knew his wife; he had known my mother. It was not the first time we had shared our respective complaints, but this time we did so from a common viewpoint: that of living with someone else's depression. Instead of our usual my-turn-your-turn conversation, we found we were talking about the same problem, that we had the same complaints to voice, that we used the same vocabulary, that the behavior to which we were subjected provoked in us—one as a daughter, the other as a husband—exactly the same reactions: feelings of confusion, self-doubt, demoralization, anger, and, finally, the desire to escape the source of our distress.

Though the particulars of our circumstances differed, my friend's dilemma and my own were the same: we hurt, and we blamed our depressives for the way we felt. We saw them not as stereotypical sad people to whom we owed and offered the expected love and sympathy, but as purveyors of negativity from whom we wished to escape. Instead of being ill and deserving, we thought of them as saboteurs of our well-being. Feeling so made us guilty; unable to shed the guilt, we became angry.

Encouraged by the similarities in our experiences, I looked for others who might share them. Within the space of only a few weeks, my trolling for depression fallout sufferers hooked several more. I decided to broaden my field of research beyond the universe of close friends. Every Friday evening at a New York City hospital, the Mood Disorders Support Group holds meetings for depressives and manic-depressives and, in a separate room, another for friends and families of people with the illness. I began attending this latter group. Once a week, for two hours, between ten and twenty people come and talk about living with someone who has this illness. A few are old hands at coping with their problem; others are newcomers. Their stories of what has transpired in the preceding days or months are composed of love, sadness, frustration, guilt, and anger in equal proportions. They are past pity for their depressives, and deep into their own pain. Protected by the solidarity and confidentiality of the group, they can express their feelings without fear of retribution or judgment. Everyone there is familiar with what everyone else is experiencing, which eliminates the need for pretense and dissimulation.

At first I came only to test my thesis of depression fallout, but I have long since become a regular. We regulars number about six, and are as varied as the changing population of the group. The group facilitator, Howard Smith, was a well-known journalist and an Oscar-winning documentary filmmaker when manic depression abruptly ended that career. Despite the stubborn ferocity of his illness, he has forged another career out of leading support groups both for sufferers of the illness and for their friends and families, and training others to do the same. Like me, he stands with a foot on each side of the problem, since one of his two sons is a manic-depressive. He is committed to his task. If New Year's Eve falls on a Friday night, Howard will be there, doling out his mixture of empathy, humor, and practicality, and drawing on an encyclopedic knowledge of the psychology and pharmacology of depressive illness, which easily surpasses that of the average general practitioner or talk therapist. Howard is not of the 1970s touchy-feely-weepy school, nor does he present himself as a father figure, or as a folksy friend in need. He is simply himself, a super-smart and compassionate manic-depressive and father of another. His personal knowledge of both sides of the equation goes a long way toward stabilizing the lives of all those who turn up at the group sessions, whether they attend on a short-term or a long-term basis.

The other regulars, in addition to myself, include a pair of schoolteachers, a retired businessman, a recovering alcoholic who has gone back to school for a degree in accountancy, and a senior paralegal. We range in age from thirty-four to seventy-five; five of us are white, one black. Our educational and social histories and our financial means are widely varied, as are the outward details of our shared problem of depression fallout. Some of us are parents, some children, and some the spouse or lover of a depressive or manic-depressive. We have different lives, outlooks, and styles. What binds us together is our common problem and our very similar reactions to it.

Many of those who attend the group regularly are friends or family of a manic-depressive, although that version of the illness is far less prevalent than depression. This is because manic-depressives are more volatile and even more taxing to contend with than depressives. They and you must cope not only with their despondent and disagreeable lows, but also with their exaggerated and often disastrous highs. Once this diagnosis is made, their families and friends must face the probability of a longer-term, more overtly dramatic, and harder-to-treat problem than that created by depression. For these members, the group is an indispensable anchor to reality, a way of grounding themselves in a world outside the turbulent illness of the person they love.

Proximity to depression is also difficult and demanding, but this version of the illness usually responds faster and more easily to treatment than does manic depression. Even in this day of relative public awareness about the illness, however, depressives often go undetected and thus untreated for months or even years, just as my mother did. By the time a diagnosis is made, depression fallout within the family, or within the relationship, can be far advanced. These members of the group also need help, and reassurance that their problem is rooted in someone else's illness, not in their own shortcomings or inadequacies.

The more transient group population is made up of people who live with depressives. Their depression fallout lifts when the illness is brought under control, and they disappear back into their lives and are never heard from again, as do the friends and relatives of many manic-depressives. But each week brings new members, the details of whose lives are different, and the cycle starts all over again. In the end it is those details that explain my continuing attendance. People arrive deep in personal and initially inarticulate confusion or pain, but sooner or later they find amazingly moving and varied ways of expression. A number of them have contributed their voices to this book.

So have many who are not group members. That initial tentative conversation, in which I discovered that the daughter of one depressive and the husband of another shared the same experience, has since occurred many times, sometimes with friends but more often with comparative strangers. In writing this book, I have become adept at reading reactions to its subject. About four out of five people organize their faces into an expression of bright attention and tell me how interesting depression fallout sounds. The fifth, who reacts only with polite, expressionless reserve, always turns out to be the one who knows the topic from within. This fifth person says, "My daughter is a manic-depressive," or "My ex-husband was a depressive," or sometimes just "Oh, my God, I know all about that." The overwhelming majority of them have never talked to anyone about what they are feeling and experiencing, but have instead kept it all locked away out of sight, persuaded that their feelings of irritation, impatience, and resentment are aberrant, unique to them, unshared by others. Ashamed of focusing on their own pain when someone they love is ill, they judge themselves selfish and unloving. The realization that their problem is widespread and that their negative reactions are both normal and justifiable unlocks their stories.

Articulating a problem to others who share it always helps unravel tangled emotional threads, but in the case of depression fallout, it also pierces the shroud of stigma surrounding all varieties of mental illness. Stigma breeds shame and silence where neither should exist. There is nothing shameful about mental illness; an illness is an illness, whether of the brain, the heart, or the lung. Where this stigma came from makes interesting reading, and the concluding chapter of this book explores the topic more fully. Its provenance is historical and sociological, but its impact is emotional and increases the burden of both depressive illness and depression fallout. Research has shown that stigma and its natural partner, shame, are internalized by sufferers of depressive illness, producing further demoralization and other negative consequences. Family members also experience these effects. With 17 million depressives and manic-depressives, and at least an equal number of depression fallout sufferers, the total number of persons touched by the illness in this country is at least 34 million. That's a lot of people to stuff into a closet, and the door is beginning to burst open.

Although the tales told by both support group members and nonmembers are similar, the former have something to add to their stories: solutions. The group provides much more than an outlet for pent-up emotions, serving also as an information exchange and a source of practical advice that goes far beyond being patient and supportive of depressives. The information and advice fall into two categories: what you can do to help the depressive or manic-depressive, and what you can do to help yourself. Here again, Howard's influence is evident. A veteran of twenty years with a hard-to-treat depression that is both rare and debilitating, he is also a veteran of psychotherapy, having spent half that many years with its practitioners in the days when it was believed that his illness could be cured by talk alone. As a result, Howard wants to know not just how the members feel, but what they can do about how they feel; he is interested not just in tales about insufficiently knowledgeable doctors, but in how to find a knowledgeable one. While encouraging members to give voice to their problems, he gives equal time to searching for solutions. Howard's favorite question is "What are you going to do about that?" Together we almost always find a way. When people leave at the end of a session, not only do they feel better, but they depart with a strengthened backbone, a sense of purpose, and some measure of control over their lives. No one claims that it's easy to stay centered and loving, but we do think it's possible. Almost every Friday evening brings some further insight, some new piece of information or advice that is useful.

This book is intended as a surrogate support group for those who have no access to one. Among the topics it covers are what you must know about the illness, its symptoms and its treatment; what you can do to help your depressive or manic-depressive; and how you can fight back against depression fallout. You may be inclined to skip over the chapters dealing with diagnosis and treatment to the one that highlights your own particular situation, be it spouse, lover, parent, or child of a depressive. While this is understandable, I urge you to do your technical homework before you indulge in the me-too satisfaction of identification. The book is designed to help you accumulate knowledge and information that will make you far more effective in helping both your depressive and yourself than if you were to plunge into the middle of the fray unarmed.

As you read, it will become apparent that there exists an essential divide between psychiatrists, who, as medical doctors, have come to dominate the biological treatment of the illness, and psychotherapists, who continue to prefer talk therapy as the treatment of choice. Both believe they are right; both want your business. Even within these two camps there are differences of opinion. Further complicating all the decisions facing you and your depressive—decisions in which you must take an active part—is the hard fact that in both disciplines there is a wide range of competence. Some professionals are undertrained and out of date in the rapidly evolving and complex field of brain chemistry; new discoveries and treatment options surface almost daily. Most practitioners are well intentioned and wish to help, but that doesn't mean they are all equally good allies for you and your depressive. A recurring message of this book is that you must be an informed consumer. Learn the facts, check credentials, seek the best, and weigh the evidence before you make definitive choices. When you believe you have made a poor selection, you must not hesitate to regroup, rethink, and change course and treatment provider following the guidelines given here. Many experts have been interviewed for the book; their views and those of others in their field are provided throughout. Ultimately, you and your depressive must listen to what they say, and then make your own decisions.

Also included here are the results of research studies that look at the impact of depressive illness on the behavior and feelings of its primary sufferers, as well as on their families and intimate friends. I refer to them often because they substantiate what you experience and feel. In a very real sense, they are the Good Housekeeping stamp that says, "Yes, you're right, and we have proved it."

The depression fallout stories woven through the book will help you move from your small, closed world of distress to a larger one crowded to overflowing with your peers. Identification with them will take you a long way toward survival and solutions. The storytellers have grappled with depression fallout twenty-four hours a day, sometimes over extended periods. What they have all come to understand is that winning the battle against depression fallout calls for persistence, patience, determination, and courage. These are just the qualities that are placed in jeopardy when someone we love has the illness. It is the nature of depression fallout to render us helpless, hopeless, guilty, and confused. Knowing that you are not alone is a firm foundation from which to launch your battle. Becoming a member of the support group and hearing the members' stories has helped me understand and assuage my guilt for giving up the effort to love my mother, and for substituting instead resentment and anger. I thought the fault was mine. Now I understand that the fault, if fault can be said to exist in such a situation, lies with my mother's depression, with our lack of knowledge and understanding of it, and with the outlook and behavior it provoked in her.

My own experience has taught me what the illness looks like, how it feels, and how it can produce the person my mother was, or became. Had I realized back then that she was clinically depressed, it would not have changed her behavior toward me; only antidepressants could have done that. But knowing the cause of her behavior would have made that part of my life less painful, less damaging. As it was, I had only my mother to blame, and myself.

My feelings toward my mother have lost their immediacy; if I put my mind to it, I can feel sorry for her, for the mess she made of her own life, and for the problems she caused in mine. I know I am not a failure, or any of the other negative self-images she held her mirror up for me to see. I know depression can transform people, and that it wasn't really my mother talking, but her depression. But I also know that my own more recent depression speaks the same language as hers. In down times, I believe I'm not worth much of anything and that I am something of a fraud, just sufficiently clever to keep others from seeing it—that I don't deserve love and happiness and success.

Which seeds did my mother's depression plant in me and which did mine? Is it her voice speaking, or my own? Lacking an answer, I must go on listening to myself. I was the primary target for her despair. I am the product of both her person and her genes, as my own daughter is of mine. We are all three of us depressives, following, I strongly suspect, in the footsteps of my paternal grandmother, who had seven husbands and was considered remarkably eccentric in her day. Depression is often a multigenerational affair.

Of all the negative effects of depression fallout, it is the suspension of an exchange of love between ourselves and those who have the illness that wreaks the greatest damage on all concerned. Lacking that exchange, both we and they fall prey to other, more negative feelings that seep in to fill the vacuum. I did not choose to stop loving my mother; somewhere in time I simply became exhausted by the effort of giving what I never received in return, and so the love lost strength and purpose, and at last died. That is the outcome of depression fallout when allowed to run its full and natural course, as did mine.

I call my story a cautionary tale because, like most cautionary tales, it has a message: Somebody else's depression can be hazardous to your health. But, like depressive illness itself, depression fallout is treatable. The solution lies first in diagnosing what is the matter with you, and then in applying the cure.

2

THE FIVE STAGES OF

DEPRESSION FALLOUT

DEPRESSION FALLOUT IS OUR UNBIDDEN response to someone else's despair. It begins with our first confusing encounter with the other's illness. Unaware of the real source of the problem, we seek it in ourselves, and find it there. Self-doubt accelerates the rise of feelings of helplessness and futility, leaving us demoralized and unable to defend ourselves against the depressive's assault upon our sense of self. Then, shifting course, we blame the way we feel on our depressive or manic-depressive, from whom we receive criticism and hostility in place of the expected love and appreciation. Resentment grows into anger, which leads us to the desire to escape the source of our distress. These stages, five in all, feed into and overlap each other. Together they constitute the circuitous and lonely journey along the continuum of depression fallout.

Depression fallout does not discriminate. Whatever our relationship to the depressive, whether spouse or lover, parent or child, these feelings leave their negative impact on all of us who live next to the illness. Where we differ is in our response to our feelings. The cure for what ails us will come only when we recognize the other's illness as the villain of the piece. Banishing the villain is the task of good medical treatment; encouraging our depressive or manic-depressive to seek it is our responsibility. We bear no responsibility for the presence of the illness, however, nor for our inability to make it go away. Until it does, we must look to ourselves for the patience, determination, and strength to address our own dilemma.

Each of the following stories illustrates one of the five stages of depression fallout. Somewhere in them you will find yourself, even though the contextual relationship of the story may be other than your own. You will hear your own feelings articulated, often in the same words you yourself have used. Only one, Leah, enjoyed access to the friends and family support group, and to the information and reassurance it provides its members; but she attended only two meetings. The others' lack of this resource is evident. Had they understood the patterns of behavior that result from depressive illness, and had they learned from fellow sufferers how to set boundaries to control them (topics that will be covered in this book), their stories would be different. But they are all innocents, driven blindly along the depression fallout continuum with little to guide or sustain them.

Stage One: Confusion

Most tales of depression fallout begin with a mystery. Why is someone you love becoming more remote, as though the connections between you had been uncoupled? Why is he or she so distant and dissatisfied, so lethargic but demanding? You assume some fault on your part, but when you ask what's the matter, you are rebuffed. Far from improving the situation, you soon see yourself cast in the role of intruder and adversary. You look for causes and explanations.

Robert could find none at all for the attitude and behavior he confronted on the day of his wedding to Stephanie. Two years later, after her depression had at last been diagnosed, he still floated in ignorance. "It's only recently that I've understood that depression is biological, not just psychological. I mean, that it's not just a question of will. But in a sense I don't really understand that." This blind spot has left him in perpetual confusion.

Robert's mystery began the day he and Stephanie, an unlikely pair, finally got married. Robert hailed from a small Midwestern town. There was no money to send him to college, so after high school he moved about the country, picking up odd jobs here and there. Eventually he landed in Taos, New Mexico, where he worked as a bartender and an occasional ski instructor. A year later Stephanie arrived, the eldest daughter of moneyed, social parents back East who had twice tried to conceive a son and twice failed. She fled their disappointment in her by choosing a West Coast university. A small bequest from her grandmother coincided with her college graduation, and she took off for Taos to ski and write poetry. There, Robert and Stephanie met, fell in love, and decided to move to California. Giddy with love and optimism, Stephanie spent the last of her grandmother's money on a red BMW and they took off. Three months later they were married.

According to Robert, their wedding night in California was more an end than a beginning. "When the reception was over we went back to our apartment. Steph lay down on the bed and turned her face to the wall and said, 'Don't touch me.' And she went to sleep. True, we'd been living together for quite a while, but it was our wedding night. I couldn't figure out what was going on." Robert's confusion lasted well beyond that night. He recently told me that he really doesn't know the person he married, because Stephanie was already depressed when he met her. "We were so excited about being in love and what we'd do together that I guess it got lost in the shuffle, but here in California, Pandora's box opened up. She fell in and shut the lid behind her, leaving me outside."

Time and reflection have brought Robert no further insights. The sense of alienation that began on his wedding night has continued to grow, even though Stephanie's depression has been diagnosed by her therapist, who believes that talk is better treatment than pills. "My situation is completely out of control," says Robert, "and that's a source of tremendous frustration for me." The logic that serves him well in his successful career as a computer programmer only deepens his confusion at home. "Part of the frustration is the fact that I can't establish any pattern in the way Steph behaves. Most of what I do and the way I think is grounded in logic, but there's none to her depression or what brings it on. Things happen that I just can't fathom. One day the birds were singing and Steph suddenly started crying. She said it made her feel depressed. I couldn't—can't—understand what she means."

Robert's confusion persists because no one has helped him understand its source. Nothing Stephanie does nowadays makes sense to him, including his wife's change from a once sleek and elegant woman to an overweight and sloppy Doppelgänger who trails around all day in an old terrycloth wrapper. "One morning she drove me to the station in her BMW and one of the men I ride the train with asked me why I let the housekeeper use my beautiful expensive car. When I came home that night, I was really upset and we had a big fight. I ended up crying. I felt so frustrated. When I see other women all dressed up and gorgeous, I think, 'I could be with them.' This is a very scary train of thought, because I really love Steph. It makes me feel hateful and guilty."

Stephanie and Robert used to spend hours talking about ideas and feelings, discovering all they had in common, but that easy communication is long gone. "I can't talk to Steph about her depression because I have no idea what we're talking about, like the birds singing can make her cry. And I'm always outside," he adds, and then puts his finger on yet another source of depression fallout distress: "For a depressed person, there is no *you*. It's as though for them you don't exist. I can't count on her. There's no stability in my life anymore. For each brief moment of happiness there's a long period of grief, and I don't know when either is coming."

All this is leading Robert to conclusions he doesn't want to draw. "I never get down about anything that isn't life-threatening. I see silver linings even in nuclear clouds. But if no curtain goes up and no interaction on the level you expected takes place, then big questions come into your head. Steph used to be a beautiful, intelligent, worldly woman. That's who I married. And now she's not. I mean, where does that leave us?"

A good question, to which Robert provides an answer of sorts: "My whole future is up for grabs," he said. Having dabbled in demoralization, he is now well on his way to resentment and anger. Robert is not given to self-doubt, but his need for a controlling logic to his life is just as debilitating in its way. He loves his wife, but his inability to understand why she has slipped from elegance and poetry to tears and housecoats is a trap for his own brand of despair. That Stephanie's therapist is pro-talk and anti-medication doesn't help the situation, but the greatest damage is being done to both by ignorance of what depression is, and what should be done about it.

Stage Two: Self-Doubt

Judith, unlike Robert, is prone to self-doubt. When the father she loved and from whom she had come to expect love in return began, in her early teens, to withhold that love, she asked herself what she had done wrong. Gathering up all the free-floating blame in her parents' home, she set herself on a course of self-destructive behavior that lasted five years. Now she has her life in order, and when a mutual friend told her about the book I was writing, she was confident enough to suggest contributing to it. She blew into the room, arranged herself neatly and expectantly on the sofa, and asked me what I wanted to know. "Anything you want to tell me about your father," I answered. Judith launched into a paean of praise.

"My father was always enormously successful, good at everything he did—his profession, sports, all his various interests. He was brilliant—a genius, really. And a perfectionist." She paused and glowed, as though basking in the warmth of the qualities she assigned to her parent. "He wasn't terribly loving, but he could be very affectionate. And he was tall, and very handsome. My friends used to say they wished they had a father like mine."

I began to think I had misunderstood, and that perhaps it was her mother who had been the depressive, not this brilliant, handsome, and affectionate father. But before I could ask a further question, she blurted out, "And then the shit hit the fan." Her confession seemed to take her by surprise, and the guilt she felt at offering it was obvious. She looked as though she wanted to leave, but instead veered off into a lengthy description of her roommate's behavior.

"It's impossible to live with someone who's depressed. My roommate is depressed, very, very depressed. She's entirely negative and manipulative. And deflating. Nothing I do is right. Everything's always my fault."

"Is she like your father?" I asked.

"I guess," replied Judith, looking at the floor.

Judith is tall and attractive, just as she describes her father. On arrival she carried herself like a dancer, but now she had the sullen droop of a teenager. Urged on by my questioning, she offered what I suspected was a sanitized and truncated description of her father's depression and her reactions to it. Starting when Judith was in her early teens, there were periods, she told me, when he spent days at a time in the bedroom rather than at the office. She remembers arguments between her parents about the family finances, depleted by his periodic inactivity. Something that happened when she was in her senior year at college—she offered no details—sent him to a doctor, who diagnosed depression. "I think my father took his pills for about eight or nine months, but then he stopped. Maybe he didn't like taking them, or maybe he just wouldn't. He certainly didn't seem interested in any long-term solution." These are pale words to describe the condition that provoked three of his four children to seek solace in too much food and alcohol.

"When I was growing up, it was the parents who were perfect and the children who caused the trouble. I couldn't wait to leave the house and go out drinking with my friends. I was a big drinker. And I got very fat. It was my way of handling things at home. I lost all sense of self."

Judith told me she drank her way through college, at one point staying drunk for six weeks. "I lost my job. I felt as though I was invisible to the world," she said.

I asked where her mother stood in her developing years. "I guess she was what you call an enabler," she replied, the description providing evidence of an insight gained at the AA meetings that had helped her to stop drinking four years previously.

That was as close as Judith could come to demolishing the Ideal Father image she had earlier provided, remnants of which she still clung to stubbornly. My further prodding induced little in the way of specific recollections of the past. I could have filled in many of the silences by drawing on my own experience of growing up with a depressed mother. When she did talk, her words were familiar to me. "I was never good enough. The expectation was that I would be perfect, perfectly dressed, perfectly mannered. All the focus was on externals. My father was so good at deflating me." When I asked how, she replied, "Just dirty digs all the time. I never knew where I was with him, never knew what to expect." But in fact she did know what to expect: constant punctures in the balloon of her self-esteem.

Judith's father's largely untreated depression was toxic, infecting first him, then Judith's mother, and then the children. As she observed, "You get sucked in. You lose your focus." When she'd stopped drinking, she broke with her father, and with her mother, too. "Now that I'm back in control of myself, I can allow them into my life some. But my father hasn't changed." Recently she made him a tapestry pillow for his birthday, and he never acknowledged it. Her mother left a message on her answering machine to say he liked it.

Separating from him for a while was a wise choice, because it has permitted Judith's collapsed ego to fatten up, but the parental love denied her by his depression, like the years she lost to alcohol, remains a permanent deficit. Judith is coming slowly to understand that her doubts about herself were misplaced, but like my own they are so deeply rooted that they persist despite self-knowledge.

Stage Three: Demoralization

Demoralization is central to depression fallout, arriving early and staying late. The dictionary defines the verb *demoralize* as to deprive a person of spirit, courage, and discipline; to destroy their morale; and to throw them into disorder or confusion. This is what Jack's depression has done to his wife, Patsy. She knows what's going on, but that offers her little protection from her feelings.

On the surface, Patsy is serene and orderly. A picture-perfect Catholic mother of three and a dutiful, loving wife, she is a typical product of the 1940s and 1950s, taught by society and her parents to defer to men, to subordinate her own desires to her husband's, and to embrace marriage and motherhood as the best of all possible careers. This she has done with grace, good humor, and distinction, neither questioning nor resenting her role. I anticipated that she would tell an elliptical, uncomplaining tale of her husband's second major depression. Instead she said flatly, "I have come to believe there is no solution. Jack is destroying our love."

His first episode came early in their marriage and stayed for two years, eventually cycling its way into remission. Seventeen untroubled years followed. "I thank God for those seventeen wonderful years, because that's all I have to be thankful for now. I love our house, but now I leave it as much as I can. He's invaded it. At night I take my book into another room so as not to have to look at him reading the same Tom Clancy thriller over and over again with the television going. I have very little concentration myself. I hate being home with him because I really hate looking at him. Sometimes I go in the shower just to cry."

Recently, Patsy went to a spa for a week, and had a wonderful time. "When I got away, I found I could still talk to people and have fun. At home I'm getting quieter and quieter because I have no conversation with Jack. But even if I can get away for a little while, I always have to come home, don't I?" For her, home means not only Jack and his depression, but also her own unassailable despondency.

Since Jack's depression came home to roost four years ago, he has stayed in two expensive mental-health clinics, been part of a hospital outpatient program, participated in several therapy groups, seen three different psychotherapists, and been on numerous antidepressant medications, all without any real or lasting improvement. Formerly a top executive in a large company, he has been forcibly retired. Money isn't a problem, but the rest of their life is, and this leaves Patsy feeling depleted and defenseless. Six months ago she took her insomnia, tears, and lethargy to her doctor, who cheerfully told her to play more tennis, absolve herself from guilt, and stop worrying, advice she derides as "profoundly silly," saying, "How can he expect me to do that? How can I stop worrying?"

Like so many depressives, Jack is stubborn, forceful, and unrelenting in his criticism of his wife. "Even though he's depressed," she told me, "he still seems to have this tremendously strong personality. I think he's chosen to be the way he is now." This is a conviction shared by many depression fallout sufferers. "It never seems to make any difference at all what I want," Patsy went on. "He tells me all the time, 'I want you to be happy, I'd do anything for you,' but in fact he only does what he wants and never what I want."

With their three children away at college, Jack and Patsy are planning to move to a smaller house. Their present one has already been sold, but Jack passes negative judgment on every replacement she locates—too big, too small, too expensive, or in the wrong place. "The other day I suggested we take a trip together, get away for a few days and see things more clearly, but he said we couldn't possibly afford to travel. That's not true. Nothing he says is true, but he always makes me feel I'm wrong and he's right.

"I feel absolutely stifled," she continued, "and it comes out as anger. When Jack says he's sorry he upset me, that puts more guilt on me for thinking all these bad thoughts. I used to have hope, but I'm beginning to lose that. I don't know what I'll do. I feel as though I'm being cruel to Jack. I wonder if he'll hold that against me if he ever recovers."

The defining characteristic of the demoralization stage of depression fallout is loss of self-esteem. Patsy's has gone, replaced by a resentment previously foreign to her nature. And she feels ill. Worried by chest pains, she recently visited a cardiologist. When she explained her situation, he was sympathetic to its impact upon her, which fortunately does not show up in her cardiogram. But the doctor had only the same prescription to offer as did her general practitioner: more activity and less guilt.

Now the house is full of her children, home for the summer vacation, and Patsy has no place to hide. She's angry because the kids have invited friends to stay. "Surely they can see that something's wrong, or at least that I'm upset. How could they make everything worse by bringing more people into this house?"

In truth, away at college, they have little understanding of their father's depression and what it has done to both him and their mother. Like many depressives, Jack can put up a good front when he wants to: "Often when one of the children calls home from college, at Jack's request I'll pass him the phone and he raises himself from complete lethargy and chats away as though everything were fine." He can do the same when he and Patsy occasionally see friends. "All of a sudden he's more animated. He gets a little glint back in his eyes, but it's not real improvement. It's the alcohol, and I hate to see that."

Nonetheless, such public behavior reinforces Patsy's latent belief that the explanation for his private behavior to her lies in her own shortcomings. Never having openly discussed Jack's depression with her children, and thinking them capable of inferring it, she is full of apprehension about the summer and what it will bring. "There's so much tension already," she said, "and I dread these coming two months. What will the kids do when they see on a daily basis what their father is like?"

She recounted a dinner to which the kids invited their parents in celebration of their thirtieth wedding anniversary. "I tried to find a card for Jack, but there were only these lovey-dovey ones and I couldn't bring myself to give him anything like that. I just don't feel like that anymore. The kids toasted us and said, 'Here's to thirty more years of happiness.' All I could say was that I didn't know if I could handle all that happiness. I guess I was a little sarcastic."

Patsy would like to leave Jack, but she doesn't know where she would go or what she would do with her life. Her only job has been that of wife and mother. Profoundly demoralized, she lacks the self-assertiveness and courage necessary to strike out on her own. Perhaps eventually some doctor will find a way to medicate Jack's depression; perhaps Patsy will become a regular at spas or spend more time on the tennis court. In the meantime, the behavioral patterns his illness produces and their demolition of her self-esteem will force her to travel back and forth on the depression fallout continuum, visiting and revisiting its various stages.

Stage Four: Anger

In depression fallout, the dividing line between demoralization and anger is sketchy and blurred. Often the two stages fuse, then separate, then come together again, pushing their sufferers about like pawns. Patsy's reticence and upbringing kept her public anger at a well-mannered simmer; privately, it has done her great harm. Robert used his to provoke scenes. Judith turned hers against herself; alcoholism was her weapon of choice. Leah's anger boiled and overflowed like lava. Of the five depression fallout sufferers who speak here, she is the only who has attended the friends and family support group. It was during her second and, as it turned out, final appearance there that she erupted with, "God help me, I cannot stand my son."

The divorced mother of two teenage boys, one a manic-depressive, Leah's days have become a constant treadmill of efforts to control Tommy, protect her other son from the chaos of their home life, and preserve her job as a court stenotypist. She is small and roundly voluptuous, with curly dark hair and creamy skin, and appears to live in a state of perpetual emotion. "I can't believe I'm saying this, it's horrible but it's true. Tommy's ruining my life, and his brother's too. I'm so angry at him all the time. I hate myself. How can a mother say such a thing?" The group leaned toward her in sympathy with her outburst, which had begun in the brief silence following another's story. "Help!" she had pleaded. "Please help me. I hate my son."

Some newcomers to the group that evening pulled back, startled by her honesty. The rest of us leaned forward, understanding how she felt and why. Windmilling her arms, she launched into a rapid-fire listing of Tommy's selfishness and shortcomings, part teenage behavior, part manic-depressive. "It's not just his own room that's messy and dirty and littered with orange peels and uneaten sandwiches, it's the whole house, everywhere he goes, everything he touches. He comes into our bedrooms at three in the morning as though it were seven. He's selfish, destructive, thoughtless, abusive. You wouldn't believe the things he says to us. He acts as though his brother and I weren't real people, as though we were cardboard dummies. I know this must sound so trivial to you, just silly little things, but I want him to leave and I can't throw him out. Where would he go? What would he do? How could he support himself?" Leah's resentment and anger flowed uninterrupted for five minutes, and then she stopped and cried.

Of all the possible permutations of anger in depression fallout, Leah's is perhaps the most traumatic because it has been ignited by her child. She loves her son, but his illness and the way it causes him to behave have left her feeling drained, impotent, and sick with guilt. Leah's dilemma has a primal ring, a sort of Greek or Shakespearean tragedy dressed up in blue jeans and a baseball cap. Her anger is directed not only at her son, but at herself for not being able to cure his illness. We assured her that she was not the first and only parent driven to rage by a child with the illness. We talked with her about setting boundaries to curb Tommy's behavior (the subject of chapter 9). We asked her questions about his doctor, and suggested she discuss with him Tommy's adverse reactions to a recent drug he had prescribed. We explained how to seek a consultation with a second physician if the first was not responsive. She listened, nodding in seeming agreement, and said she would put our advice into practice.

I would like to think that everything went smoothly from then on, and that that was why she never returned to the group. But for most members, once or twice is not enough. Once entrenched, demoralization numbs our will to fight against it. It can take many months of advice and encouragement to shift from negative to positive, from inaction to action, from rage to rationality.

Like depressive illness, depression fallout digs in; exorcising it takes time. Perhaps Leah was a fast learner, but it's also possible that her first public admission of the rage she felt toward her son frightened her and increased the guilt she already carried for not being able to cure his manic depression. Perhaps that guilt was forced underground again, pushing her back into a more passive state of demoralization. This would be unfortunate, because passivity brings indecisiveness and inactivity, which will only make things worse for Leah and both of her sons.

Stage Five: The Desire to Escape

There is a chasm of difference between separation and abandonment. When depressive illness is an issue, people think in terms of the latter. Decisions to stay or to leave can no longer be taken without guilt. "He/she is ill, so I must stay" is the axiom of depression fallout. The pressures to stay are many. Even had Leah been able to cut herself off from her son, where would he go and who would take care of him? Patsy already feels herself guilty of cruelty to Jack, although the sum total of the distance she has managed to put between them is represented only by a week at a health spa and evenings reading in a separate room. Robert's thoughts of well-coiffed women in high heels and short skirts make him feel guilty and disloyal. Only Judith accomplished true separation, albeit after years of alcoholism and other methods of self-destruction.

Though many marriages between depressives and non-depressives end in divorce, I often wonder what proportion of the latter, if any, acknowledge the former's illness as the cause. Steven did not, because, he told me, he had spoken of Camilla's manic depression only with a small circle of intimate friends. But that indeed is why he asked for a divorce, even though he still loved his wife. "The most difficult thing for a human being to do," he said, "is to turn his back on someone he loves who might be out to harm herself. But now, looking back, I think it is the right thing because at least you've saved one person, yourself."

At fifty, Steven is a major player in the theater world. He's a trendsetter rather than a follower, liked and respected by his peers. In New York City in the mid-1970s, when they fell in love, both he and Camilla were already stars. Camilla is beautiful, vivid, and imaginative, and pursued an eclectic range of interests with an energy and enthusiasm that enchanted her friends, and Steven too. But occasionally she would turn off, sequester herself in her apartment for several days at a time, and refuse to answer her telephone.

"I knew it was odd, but I didn't really focus on it—didn't want to, I suppose. I was very much in love. I chose to see Camilla's behavior as an aspect of her personality, rather fey and Garboesque, but it wasn't that at all, of course. The first seven years were the worst." He explained that Camilla had had a colorfully troubled childhood, much of it spent in foster homes and institutions for abandoned kids. For years her numerous therapists chose to blame her personal history for her unstable behavior, not her undiagnosed manic depression. "Shrinks loved her," said Steven. "For them she was a 'fascinating case.'"

Like so many manic-depressives, when Camilla was up, the force of her personality—dazzling, persuasive, fluidly charming—swept everyone along with it, until the day when everything blew up. "I rushed to call her then-psychiatrist, a man she had been seeing twice weekly for several years. I told him his patient had one foot outside the window, and he said, appallingly, 'Dear me, I didn't realize things were as bad as that. You had better call the police.' He hung up and we never saw or heard from him again." Eventually an excellent psychiatrist diagnosed her correctly and prescribed lithium, but the problems weren't over. Lithium must be taken in precise doses, and requires monitoring through periodic blood tests. Camilla was not precise and resisted control, and so the cycle of ups and downs continued, although now with a name.

"When she was down, she was frightened and wanted to help herself," says Steven. "But when she was up, she was out of reach of reality. Sometimes we'd be awake all night long, talking and talking until dawn. She always seemed better by then. She was like a phoenix rising. But I felt terrible. I thought of it in vampire terms, as though I had no blood, as though she had sucked it all out of me. I would go off to the office drained and miserable, a mess."

In all the time he lived with Camilla, Steven told me, he was forced to occupy two worlds: one in his office and the theater, and the other in the interior world Camilla had created for herself.

"Camilla's world was a completely irrational universe, of which she was the total ruler. I had to try to live in it by virtue of being with her, loving her. People who suffer what she did, and still does, live in a special place. They breathe a special air of their own. And when I went in there, I became ill too. In all that time, I felt terribly alone, completely isolated." Steven knew that he was in jeopardy as surely as was Camilla. His office was a haven. When his wife was in a prolonged down phase, he occasionally tried to go out on his own, but, as he points out, "How often can you go out to the movies or dinner with a friend when you know you may come home and find that your wife has attempted suicide? How can you have fun when someone you love is in such pain?"

Eventually, Steven and Camilla agreed to separate for a year, with the expectation that Steven would move back in if Camilla could manage for twelve months to take her medication religiously and keep her illness under strict control. They went out on a date together every Saturday evening, and spoke often on the phone. By Steven's account, everything seemed wonderful. At the end of the year, with great relief and high hopes, he moved back into their apartment, but it wasn't long before his life again separated into two worlds. "She had grown increasingly animated," he explained. "We were coming out of church one Sunday and she was speeded up, talking and talking about things that were bizarre and unrealistic. It wasn't necessarily anything others would tag as abnormal, but I knew all the signals so well, the ones she never saw herself. She'd gone off her pills and let her mania back in, and I had this sudden visceral response. 'I'm off, Camilla,' I said. 'We have to get a divorce.' At the time she was angry and disdainful, but once, weeks later, she admitted she understood. 'How can I blame you for not being able to live with me when I can't live with myself?' she said then.

"Maybe Camilla didn't blame me, but I certainly blamed myself, even though I knew full well that it had in every sense come down to a choice between her sanity and mine. I couldn't help her, and she wouldn't or couldn't help herself. I couldn't any longer live with that." Most people would view Steven as successful and happy with his life today. As a friend, I know the residue of his years with Camilla persists. However uncertain his sense of self may have been before his marriage, it was eroded yet further by living with Camilla's illness. Existing for twelve years in emotional turmoil, feeling drained of energy and independent will, is an experience not easily discarded.

Somewhere in these five stories of depression fallout you will most likely have recognized yourself. In the chapters that follow, you will find ways to cope with your own situation and your own reactions to it. We are all unique and complex creatures, but depression fallout is a widespread syndrome. You are not alone, and whatever you feel is not aberrant, nor should it be guilt-provoking. Your depression fallout is a natural response to the depressive illness of someone you love. If you are to understand and accept that fully, you need to know what causes their illness and what its symptoms are, both those that are familiar to a doctor, and those experienced only by you as a family member or intimate friend.

3

BEYOND LOVE AND
SYMPATHY

THE BATTLE AGAINST DEPRESSION FALLOUT has to be fought simultaneously on two fronts: yours and the depressive's. If you concentrate solely on keeping your own psyche intact, you will be fighting with one hand tied behind your back, as my experience with my mother bears out. Unaware of what drove her behavior, I dealt blindly with its consequences on me, not with its cause. Her doctor, her husband, and I might have persuaded her to seek the help she needed, had knowledge of depression and its treatment been available back then. But we were all in the dark, and so depression colored her view of life and depression fallout colored mine. If you are to avoid a similar experience, there is much you need to know.

Although your love and sympathy will help the depressive, they are not enough. They provide much-needed support, but they cannot and will not cure this illness. You need to get your depressive or manic-depressive to recognize that illness is present and that treatment is imperative. If you can do that, you have won half the battle. Moreover, it's the more important half, because your depression fallout is a direct result of the depressive's illness. The longer the depression remains untreated, the longer you will struggle with your parallel problem, and the further you will travel into depression fallout, until you, like Steven, may see no option but to cut loose. Although his is a worst-case outcome, it is a very real possibility unless you take a hand in the matter.

Getting your depressive or manic-depressive to accept that something is amiss and to seek a solution is not always easy. Research indicates that only about one-third or fewer of those with depressive illness seek help for what ails them. Some are too mired in their feelings of helplessness and hopelessness to take an active role in their cure. Many others fiercely resist doing so because they cannot countenance being "mentally ill," or because they wrongly believe that depression is a sign of personal weakness that they can overcome through determination alone. The better informed you are about the illness, however, the more you can help the depressive overcome his or her resistance and get the appropriate treatment that will ultimately reward you both.

This section of the book is predicated on the premise that one of the following situations fits your circumstances: your depressive is blackly despairing and doesn't know why; your depressive's ability to seek a cure is seriously impaired; or the search for effective treatment has run into a dead end in which little or no improvement has occurred. If any one of the above situations applies, then you must take the lead. You must become an active participant, if not the principal one, in ensuring that the illness is brought under control. To do that, you need to become an amateur expert.

Since you are reading this book, you probably know or suspect that someone you love is depressed, and it is likely you have already done some homework. You've clipped newspaper and magazine articles, read some books, perhaps collected pamphlets with titles like "Are You Depressed?" and "Depression Is a Treatable Illness: A Patient's Guide." Although they have certainly enhanced your understanding of the illness, they have not left you as informed as you may believe. The information isn't inaccurate, it's just incomplete. The standard list of symptoms doesn't include much of the behavior you witness daily. The usual advice tells you to get your depressive to a doctor, but not how to overcome his or her objections to doing so. There is no warning that professionals may make an inaccurate diagnosis or none at all; that they may not provide alternative treatment if the first attempt fails; or that many nonmedical practitioners won't suggest medication.

Furthermore, these standard reading materials don't factor you into the equation. If they acknowledge your existence, it is under the bloodless rubric of "caregiver"; rarely do they recognize you as an intimate partner in what is going on. When you do come into focus, you are offered such advice as, "Invite the depressed person for walks, outings, to the movies, and other activities," and "Be gently insistent if your invitation is refused." Anyone who is living close to a depressive will be tempted to laugh somewhat derisively at being told that "gentle assertiveness may be required to stand by the depressed person, particularly if the individual is withdrawn and rejecting." The "individual," who more than likely is your wife of twenty years or your child or parent of a lifetime, may need a lot more than gentle assertiveness to get them going, and "rejecting" is probably a pale description of their response to your efforts.

In short, the snippets of advice offered to family members and friends are minimal and not very helpful. They suggest modes of behavior we initially adopt without suggestions from others because doing so is a natural expression of love and concern for someone close to us who is in pain. The trouble—our trouble—starts when we discover that what comes naturally to us isn't working very well. The more relevant advice, which does make its way into some of the materials, urges you to encourage the depressive to seek treatment. But, here again, most of the written materials gloss over the fact that this is not easily accomplished.

In brief, all such advice is written as though the illness, its diagnosis, and its treatment occur in a perfect world. They don't. What you need are some real-life facts about the illness and some street-smart advice from others in similar situations about how to use it to the advantage of the person you love. Please do not skip over this chapter in the mistaken belief that this is all very technical stuff and not relevant to your problem. Knowing what is medically the matter with your depressive is as critical to your own well-being as to theirs, now and in the future. These facts provide the foundation for all your tasks to come (covered in chapter 6): persuading the depressive or manic-depressive to see an expert, and understanding and dealing effectively with what the expert says and does.

Depressive illness travels under many names and, as of this writing, more than sixty drugs are used, either singly or in combination, to treat it. All of this makes it difficult for us laypeople to know what the doctors are talking about. What follows is an overview of what is happening chemically in the depressive's brain; a quick glossary of the various kinds of depression and manic depression to guide you through the terminology a doctor will use; and two lists of symptoms, one official and one unofficial.

The Anatomy of Depressive Illness

The complexity of the human brain is such that although science continues to unveil more and more of its intricate workings, discoveries often lead to yet more unsolved mysteries. We do know for certain that when the brain malfunctions, feelings and behavior change. One result of such malfunction is depressive illness. Drs. Demitri and Janice Papolos, in their book *Overcoming Depression* (Harper & Row, 1987), take the lay reader through the world of neurons and neurotransmitters in a manner relatively easy to understand. A brief summary of their explanation follows.

The number of possible interconnections among the 100 billion cells of the brain is purported to exceed the number of atoms in the universe—quite a feat for a bundle of tissue no bigger than a grapefruit. Near the brain's center lies the limbic system, and it is there that scientists look for answers about mental illness, including depression and manic depression. The limbic system is the mediator of human feelings, receiving and regulating all information of an emotional nature. The most important part of the limbic system is the hypothalamus. Only as big as a walnut, it handles a tremendous workload, regulating appetite, thirst, sleep, sexual desire, and body temperature, handling the fight-or-flight response, and controlling the pituitary gland. The two other major centers of the limbic system are the hippocampus and the amygdala, which gauge emotional reactions such as elation, excitement, anxiety, agitation, rage, and aggression, as well as modulating the capacity to start and stop behaviors associated with these emotions. All of these interconnected areas govern mental activities and bodily functions known to be disrupted during depressive and manic episodes.

Communication among brain cells—or *neurons,* as scientists call them—generates behavior. One cell is separated from the next by an infinitesimal gap; cells communicate by sending an impulse that travels electrically down a narrow tube called an *axon* until it reaches the gap. There, at the brink, little sacks or *vesicles* at the end of the axon spill out chemicals called *neurotransmitters* that ferry the impulse across the gap and then attach themselves to receptors on the neighboring cell that are precisely tailored to receive them.

The gap, or *synaptic cleft,* is about 20 millionths of a millimeter wide, and it takes less than one-five-thousandth of a second to bridge it. Once arrived on the other side, the neurotransmitters rest there for perhaps only the same time it took to cross the cleft. Then they are released and fall back into the synaptic cleft, where they are either deactivated or reabsorbed into the sending cell. This process is called "reuptake."

Back in the 1960s, a deficiency or excess of certain neurotransmitters—serotonin, norepinephrine, and dopamine among them—was thought to be the cause of depression and mania, but although a tremendous amount of effort has gone into trying to measure excess or deficiency of these substances in the brains of those who suffer from this illness, thus far no evidence has been found to support this theory. Another reason scientists have become more cautious in claiming causation is that the effect of the drugs on reuptake occurs in about ten seconds, yet the clinical effects don't occur until three to four weeks later. Obviously, it's more like pushing over the first domino in some tremendous cascade of which little is known. In short, despite all the confident talk, the evidence on just how and why neurotransmitters and the reuptake inhibition are important is none too clear. The safest thing to say is that antidepressants are very effective in controlling depressive illness.

One prominent research psychiatrist suggests that people should leave the neurotransmitter issue to the scientists who will eventually figure it all out. He says he has had patients who ask him if they have a serotonin or a norepinephrine deficiency; when he tells them he doesn't know and there's no way to find out, the patient is horrified. This expert compares the situation to saying, "The cause of headache is the absence of aspirin."

Designing these medications is still in its infancy, as is our understanding of how the brain works. But while ethicists worry about a future in which we may be able to tailor and shape personalities, the rest of us can be grateful for what science has already accomplished.

The Nature-Versus-Nurture Puzzle

Researchers still have no clear answers to why neurotransmitters malfunction in some people but not in others. They have noted that depression and especially manic depression tend to run in families. In order to prove this observation, they turned to studying identical twins. At least seven studies carried out in the United States, England, Germany, Norway, and Denmark found that the rate of concordance for depressive illness in these twins was 76 percent—that is, when one twin of a set was depressed, they found a 76-percent probability that the other twin would be depressed. In fraternal twins, however, the researchers found a concordance rate of only 19 percent, close to the one-in-five incidence prevailing in the general population. Although the results strongly implied a genetic link, they didn't qualify as proof because most of the twins had been raised together in the same family, and so experienced the same social environment. To gauge what role environment might play, researchers tracked down identical twins who had been separated at birth, and discovered that their concordance rate was 67 percent, still far above the norm.

Certainly nature plays a substantial role in determining whether or not someone is going to be vulnerable to depressive illness, but there isn't a way to tease the genetic and the environmental influences apart. Even among identical twins raised together, close to one-fourth were *not* concordant for depressive illness; when raised apart, the rate was 9 percent lower. Other factors clearly play a role.

Stress may be one such factor. About thirty years ago, Dr. Martin Seligman observed that dogs exposed over time to inescapable electric shocks had difficulty learning how to avoid an escapable shock, and called this phenomenon "learned helplessness," in the sense that the dogs had learned they were helpless to change their fate. These dogs stopped grooming themselves, had trouble sleeping, developed eating problems, and lay about a lot. In fact, they behaved as though they were depressed. Unstressed dogs, on the other hand, easily learned how to avoid the shocks and did so.

Later on, Dr. Fritz Henn and his colleagues at Yale University induced depressive behavior in rats using this learned-helplessness model, and discovered that it produced marked changes in the rats' brain functioning. When these rats were given an antidepressant, their functioning returned to normal, and so did their capacity to escape the shock, all in the same time frame as that of a typical human response to antidepressant medication. Then Dr. Henn and his colleagues induced depression in another group of rats, but instead of giving them antidepressants, they taught them how to avoid the shock. Their symptoms abated, too. These and other studies suggest that neurochemistry affects behavior and behavior affects neurochemistry.

But why, for instance, does loss cause some people to become depressed but not others? Loss can be of many kinds: of a child or parent through death, or a spouse through divorce; of income through retirement or improvidence; or perhaps of status or self-esteem through having committed some social, professional, or other stigmatizing transgression. Many face tragedy and deprivation, yet are able, after a period of mourning and adjustment, to recover their equanimity; others cannot seem to do so, and fall into a state of helplessness and hopelessness from which they are unable to emerge without help. The fact is that, once again, nobody has the answer.

The Stress of Being a Caregiver

Recently, researchers have been discovering that a different form of stress can also trigger depression: the stress of taking care of someone who is seriously mentally ill. In an ongoing study under the aegis of the National Institute of Mental Health, one research team is looking at family members or close friends of depressives, manic-depressives, or schizophrenics who have been hospitalized multiple times for their illnesses. The team developed two scales to measure the impact on the caregivers: one a standard depression rating scale, and the other a new scale to measure grief. Since the patients are all living, the grief their intimates feel is the loss of a person to illness rather than death. It is measured by such comments as "I feel sad when I realize how much ———— has changed," and "I feel sad when I think about the future ———— could have had." The depression scale rated caregivers according to the number and severity of the depressive symptoms they displayed.

What the team, headed by Elmer Struening at the New York State Psychiatric Institute, has found in its preliminary conclusions is of particular interest to depression fallout sufferers. At least 40 percent of the caregivers scored 16 or above, exhibiting signs of depression strong enough to qualify them as being seriously depressed. But the mean score of the entire group was 15.84, indicating that many others were depressed to some extent, or at serious risk of becoming so.

This mean score of almost 16 is equal to that of some 1,200 men and women residents of New York City homeless shelters, and is three points higher than a sample of people with multiple sclerosis, both groups that Struening has previously studied. Even more telling, the score was seven points higher than that found in two general population groups used as controls.

The grief scores of the participants varied depending on social and cultural differences among them. African-Americans scored lowest on grief and Hispanics highest, with whites in between. Variances in the depression scores were not correlated to ethnicity, but rather depended on the availability of a support network, the relationship with professionals involved in the treatment of their ill relatives, and with the caregivers' own sense of mastery and self-esteem.

Struening's conclusions bear out the advice in this book: the more you learn about the illness, the better you will be able to cope. Knowledge also enables you to communicate more easily with doctors and other service providers, which, in turn, will give you a sense of mastery, of being in control of the situation and of yourself as well.

Though mastery and self-esteem won't change the behavior of a depressive or manic-depressive, they will help you fight your depression fallout. Caregivers who have little understanding of the illness and the behavior it provokes often try to "control" the ill person, as though he or she were a fractious child. Knowing where the behavior comes from helps, says Struening. "Are you going to take it out on the person by saying, 'You're doing this to give me a hard time,' or do you say, 'He can't help a lot of what he's doing, so I'll have to put up with what's going on?'" But, he adds, "You have to fight, or otherwise you're down under pretty soon. Coping isn't just what you think, it's what you do in the face of these kinds of problems. Eventually you have to act on what's going on, so you'd better be prepared to understand what's causing it. Joining a support group and talking to others in the same boat is a little like saving your life."

The Recent History of Depressive Illness

I used to take it for granted that the highest incidence of depression was here in the United States. Having grown up in an era when psychotherapy flourished, and having endured my share of today's tell-everything-to-everybody talk shows, I accepted the mounting noise about depression as yet another manifestation of our peculiarly American preoccupation with our psyches. Not so. In the last few years, twelve independent studies covering 43,000 people in several countries, including the United States, have shown not only that the same incidence of depression exists everywhere—from Christchurch, New Zealand, to Edmonton, Alberta, from Puerto Rico to Munich and all stops in between—but that it's on the rise.

The researchers who conducted these studies discovered the rate was going up by grouping their subjects into age cohorts, determined by the decade of their birth, starting in 1905 and ending in 1955. In just about every study, people born later in the span were more apt to have become severely depressed at some time in their lives than those born earlier. One of the steepest climbs is in Florence, Italy, where people born after 1945 were found to have a lifetime depression rate of 18 percent, as opposed to the 8-percent rate among their fellow citizens born between the years 1905 and 1915. This sort of odd blip—others appeared elsewhere—has no ready explanation.

Some experts suggest that typically twentieth-century changes, such as the increase in single parents and working mothers, might be responsible for the rise. Others point out that more people know about depression now and can complain of it in recognizable ways, thus making it easier to determine who has it, or think they do; similar shifts have appeared in other illnesses, too. Or that nowadays the younger generation, in particular, talks more openly about feelings their parents and grandparents might have kept hidden. Retrospective analysis is always problematic and often unreliable.

Women everywhere have higher rates of depression than men, by a two-to-one ratio. A lot of the explanations for this hinge on issues of women's traditional place in society, such as loss of power and ineffectuality, all constructs of women's social "inferiority" to men. But recently some epidemiological studies have shown that women are more likely than men to suffer from anxiety early in life, and then go on to develop depression later on. So the mystery recedes one step further because anxiety, say the researchers, fits far less well with loss of power and effectiveness than does depression.

Some psychologists now suggest that women are more readily diagnosed as depressed because they look and behave as the "classic" depressive does—introverted, sad, and withdrawn—while men lash out instead, burying themselves in a frenzy of work and doing a lot of drinking. Perhaps if the researchers were living with those "passively depressed" women, they might discover that they do plenty of lashing out, too. And if oppression, prejudice, and deprivation can cause depression, how can it be that in studies comparing similar populations, African-Americans are found to have a slightly lower rate of depressive illness than their white counterparts?

For every such theory to explain depression, there's a countervailing piece of evidence that questions it. We often slip into the belief that life in a rural setting is less stressful than in a bustling city, yet researchers found that rates of depressive illness were higher in the small Taiwanese towns they looked at than in the big cities. Highly educated people get depressed at the same rate as less educated ones; geniuses suffer the illness equally with people of lower intelligence, as do the famous with the unsung. Neither race, income, nor geography seems to make a measurable difference. The only thing we know for sure about depressive illness is that there's a great deal of it everywhere.

A Glossary of Depressive Illness

The condition as a whole is variously referred to as a psychiatric disorder, an affective or mood disorder, mental illness, or depressive illness. By and large, these terms are used interchangeably. I've chosen to use the term *depressive illness* because *psychiatric* and *mental,* although accurate, carry a lot of baggage. They tweak old prejudices that ought to be long dead but aren't, causing such words as *neurotic, crazy,* and *nutty* to pop into our minds.

Whatever the name or names used, depressive illness has two major subsets. The first, depression, is referred to as clinical or biological depression or, when appropriate, major depression or unipolar depression, *unipolar* meaning that the moods move only on the down side of normal, *normal* being taken to mean free of depression. The second is manic depression, called bipolar disorder, bipolar illness, or bipolar depression, because moods swing back and forth between the polar opposites of high and low. Depression is far more prevalent than manic depression by a ratio of about five to one. People often need constant reminding that manic-depressives almost invariably suffer the downs of depression as well as the highs of mania. That is why much of the experience of those who live with manic-depressives is relevant to those who live with depressives.

Depression

Every depression has its own fingerprints; each will manifest itself differently. Although certain characteristics will turn up with consistency, one depressed person may find it impossible to go to work, instead sitting around the house all day without getting dressed, watching television and eating junk food, and feeling down in the dumps and pessimistic about everything. Another may be anxious and irritable, wake up early and be unable to go back to sleep, but still manage to go to the office and function there, although the self-assured mask assumed during the day in front of others may be put aside at home. Both of these people are clinically depressed. Either of them may sink and stay that way for one, six, or twelve months or longer. Or they may emerge in remission only to sink again, this time even deeper.

No one can predict with complete confidence what's going to happen with any given depression. Some people are consistently depressed for years at a time, while others experience cycles of depression and remission. Among the latter, an average episode, left untreated, lasts from six to nine months. The chances of someone having only one episode are about fifty-fifty, but when a second episode follows the first, the likelihood of a third episode rises to about 80 percent. This finding underscores the importance of treating depression when it first appears, and it explains why there is now close to universal agreement that if the illness does return, it's a very good thing to continue taking antidepressants to make sure it won't come back again and again. When episodes do recur, they tend each time to be more frequent, more severe, and more difficult to treat.

Most depressives will tell you that they feel terrible all the time, but in fact there are variations in their moods. Dr. Jack Gorman of Columbia Presbyterian Hospital in New York often encourages his patients to keep a "psychiatric disorder chart," which turns out to be a depressive's variant on the childhood connect-the-dots game. Each morning and evening at the same hour, patients assess how they feel at that moment and put a dot on a graph at the point, ranging from minus ten to normal, which best represents their mood at that particular moment. Periodically they connect the dots. There are rarely any straight lines on such charts, but only rarely will the fluctuations be near or above normal.

Dysthymia is a chronic form of depression in which the down is a relatively mild one, persisting for two years or more. It is the most undertreated form of depression because people may have had it for years, sometimes the better part of a lifetime, without realizing there was anything the matter with them. They may have forgotten they used to feel different and just accept the way they feel as "normal." A dreary, boring, low-energy person may be suffering from dysthymia. That individual we all know and barely tolerate, who has no sense of humor and a permanently half-empty glass, and who's always gloomy about his own prospects and everyone else's, may have dysthymia. About 80 percent of all dysthymia sufferers eventually fall into a full-fledged depression and are then said to have *double depression.*

Another variety of depression is *atypical depression.* Atypicals overeat (with a particular penchant for carbohydrates) and tend to sleep a great deal. Lack of attention gets them down terribly, and any kind of rejection, which they often infer where it doesn't exist, is for them like being kayoed in the boxing ring. Although the downs vastly prevail, they can have a good time if, for instance, someone persuades them to go to a party, or shows them sympathetic attention and interest, but then they sink back into apathy.

The most recently proposed category of depression is called *mixed anxiety-depression.* Anxiety is as common as morning coffee, and for most of us it seems somewhat absurd to classify it as a serious disorder. But when the anxiety is out of all proportion to reality and combines with depression, it's serious. If your depressive is diagnosed as having mixed anxiety-depression, this is no pop concept, but a real psychiatric illness involving a range of psychological problems that include hypochondria and severe difficulties with personal relationships. The anxiety associated with depression may provoke feelings of paralyzing dread and foreboding, such as being sure one is going to die even though one may be in perfect health at the time. If you have ever felt your heart beat faster because a big date or an important client meeting is in the offing and you fear something may go wrong, imagine that tension and dread multiplied a hundredfold, and you'll have a tiny taste of anxiety-related depression.

Manic Depression

Manic depression, also called bipolar disorder, surely must be the most debilitating and painful of all varieties of depressive illness. Those who suffer from it are forced by their disturbed brain chemistry to undergo not only the dangerous highs of mania, but the downs of depression as well. This illness is harder to live with than unipolar depression, for the primary sufferer and for you too, and is more complicated to treat.

Mania is no more like being excessively happy than depression is like being just excessively sad. The feelings associated with mania—exuberance, exultancy, invincibility—sound extremely appealing. And so they would be if they were motivated by exciting and positive events such as falling in love, or winning the lottery. In a manic state, these feelings surge unbidden and uncontrollably, and are accompanied by wild energy, dramatic psychomotor acceleration, and a flood of inappropriate emotions. As one psychiatrist has observed, "If somebody gives me a million dollars, I will feel terrific, but I won't be sleeping a bare four hours a night and talking incessantly. Mania is not just being happy; it's more like chronic cocaine intoxication." Furthermore, mania produces much more than euphoria; it also brings with it extreme irritability and anger. Trying to control a manic, or steer him or her toward reality, is like standing in the path of a tank. Manics may become extremely aggressive, paranoid, psychotic, and delusional. Afterward they crash into deep, passive downs in which the results of what they have wrought catch up with them: excessive bills, broken relationships, and ruined careers are often the products of mania's extremes and the loss of insight they provoke.

Violence can also be a part of mania, although it is not common. Manics may direct their violent anger at objects. The wife of one friends and family group member has broken many telephones and even wrenched the faucet from her kitchen sink. Or they may sometimes direct it at people, as testified to by the broken arm of another member, the product of her daughter's manic rage.

Like depression, manic depression has a less extreme, chronic form in which its sufferers gyrate between mildish highs and mildish downs. This is known as *cyclothymia*. Or they may suffer from *hypomania,* in which they stay on the up side of normal for days or sometimes weeks at a time, but are spared the more dangerous upper highs and the very deep lows of depression. Hypomanics are often very productive, have a lot of fun, and possess charm and confidence in themselves. They're often successful achievers and good leaders. The trouble is, they run a high risk of spiraling up or down into extremes. The person who figures out how to maintain hypomania without toxicity should win the Nobel Prize.

The most severely afflicted manic-depressives are so-called *rapid cyclers*. Books and pamphlets, if they include any information on rapid cycling, describe rapid cyclers as those who travel through highs and lows on average four times a year. My friends and family group members testify to relatives and friends who cycle monthly, weekly, or even daily, sometimes trapped in both states at the same time. Purely anecdotal evidence suggests that rapid cyclers may be more numerous than the literature indicates.

Here is a sample graph depicting the main categories and their subsets:

	Very low	Normal	Very High
depression	▓▓▓▓▓▓		
atypical depression	▓▓▓▓▓▓		
mixed anxiety-depression	▓▓▓▓▓▓		
dysthymia		▓▓▓	
manic depression	▓▓▓▓▓▓▓▓▓▓▓▓▓		
mania			▓▓▓▓▓
cyclothymia		▓▓▓▓▓▓▓	
hypomania			▓▓▓▓▓

The Symptoms of Depression

Symptoms are the clues to depressive illness, the trail of bread-crumbs that leads to a correct diagnosis. You, the observer, will probably be the first to suspect the presence of the illness, and you should pay careful attention to all symptoms before getting the depressive or manic-depressive to a doctor to confirm or allay your suspicion. Most people have a preformed mental image of a typical sufferer, but when they are asked to provide a questioner with those images, their answers are inaccurate and vague. The depressive, they say, mopes around, is gloomy and negative. The manic-depressive is, well, "crazy." The symptoms of the illness indeed do include gloomy, negative, and sometimes "crazy" behavior, in the sense that the person is irrational and out of control, but that's not the whole story. Here is a typical list of symptoms:

- a persistent sad, "empty," or anxious mood

- loss of interest or pleasure in ordinary activities, including sex

- decreased energy, fatigue, being "slowed down"

- sleep disturbances (insomnia, early-morning waking, or oversleeping)

- eating disturbances (loss of appetite and weight, or weight gain)

- difficulty concentrating, remembering, making decisions

- feelings of hopelessness, pessimism

- thoughts of death or suicide, suicide attempts

- irritability

- excessive crying

- chronic aches and pains that don't respond to treatment

The first two on the list are the preeminent indicators of depression; if neither of them pertain to the person you're worried about, he or she is probably just temporarily bothered and upset. But if one or both apply, accompanied by several of the remaining symptoms, then the trail may lead to depression.

The last symptom on the list, chronic aches and pains that don't respond to treatment, needs further explaining. Often depression is accompanied by headache, backache, or stomach distress for which a doctor, using tests and X rays, can find no explanation. Although I had no inkling of it at the time, such a case of masked depression played itself out in my apartment some fifteen years ago. A boyfriend of mine, a brilliant research biologist, came to spend a weekend and proceeded to behave extremely unpleasantly for no apparent reason. He found fault with everything, refused to have dinner with mutual friends, and was obstreperous to everyone, including me. Between insults and fits of pique, he complained of shooting back pains, bouts of dizziness, and weakness in his legs. Having spent much of his visit sulking in his bathrobe, he stomped out a day early and went back home. A few days later he called, not to apologize, but to say his doctor was sending him for X rays to see if he had cancer of the spine. Apparently he did not, since he is still hale and hearty. I learned from his daughter that he is at last taking antidepressants.

My former boyfriend's problem is a melodramatic example of what can happen when a doctor consulted about aches and pains asks no accompanying questions about the emotional state of the patient. Had such questions been posed, they might have elicited important clues to what turned out to be the underlying cause of the symptoms: depression.

Depression in the Elderly

Failure to diagnose depressive illness is of particular concern when the patient is elderly. People who grew up in an era when the causes and treatment of depression were unknown are inclined to see it as a sign of personal weakness rather than as a serious physical ailment, and so are not forthcoming about what they think of as a "mental problem." Also, doctors and laypeople alike often take it for granted that the social, economic, and health problems faced by the elderly are the source of their pessimism and despondency. But depression is not a natural concomitant to the aging process, and it's just as treatable in older people as in younger ones.

According to Dr. Barry Lebowitz, chief of the branch of the National Institute of Mental Health that deals with aging and mental disorders, of the 32 million Americans sixty-five years of age and older, about 6 million suffer from some level of clinical depression. At least 75 percent of them go undiagnosed and thus untreated, even though they may be seeing one or more doctors for other health problems. Given the links between depression and other diseases, this amounts to giving a national health problem the cold shoulder. Depression among those over sixty-five triples the risk of stroke and has been diagnosed in 50 percent of people hospitalized for a stroke, 90 percent of whom remain depressed six months later.

About 30 percent of all cancer patients will develop depression. Depression also weakens the immune system, making it harder for depressed patients to recover from a hip fracture or from illnesses such as pneumonia.

The strongest correlation of all is between depression and heart disease. While one in five people in the general population will have an episode of serious depression in their lifetime, about half of all those with heart disease do so. Dr. Nancy Frasure-Smith of the Montreal Heart Institute followed a group of patients who had suffered heart attacks and found that those who were depressed were four times as likely to die in the next six months as those who were not depressed. Dr. Robert M. Carney of Washington University in St. Louis has reported that people with newly diagnosed heart disease who were depressed were twice as likely to have a heart attack or require bypass surgery within twelve months as those with similar blockages who were not depressed.

One explanation of the heart-depression connection might lie in the stress hormone cortisol. Dr. Philip Gold of the NIMH notes that many depressed people, although they look lethargic, are actually in a constant state of hyperarousal. "If you're a rat being chased by a cat, you are aroused and anxious," says Gold. "Your biochemical programs that focus attention only on the danger stimulus are activated. Virtually everything else is ignored," such as eating, sleeping, and sex. All that remains is the fight-or-flight response. But, he points out, "the fight-or-flight response is supposed to last for hours, maybe days. In depression the response doesn't turn off for weeks or even years."

If you are still clinging to the position that depression is nothing more than a bad attitude, let it go. In a very real sense, it can, if undetected and untreated, be a killer, so don't allow it to be swept under the rug.

The Unofficial Symptoms of Depression

Aches, pains, and all the other symptoms on the official list cited above do not tell the whole story. Judging from my own experience of my mother and testimonies of other depression fallout victims, it is far from comprehensive. Indeed, it reinforces that fallacious stereotype of people with depression as passive bundles of misery. Although such passive behavior does form part of the depressive's repertoire, it is only one of many roles they play, and probably the easiest to sit through. More typically, they are also actively obstreperous, obnoxious, and hard to live with. So here is my unofficial list of symptoms of depression, to be added to the official list:

- self-absorbed, selfish, unaware or unconcerned about the needs of others, demanding

- unresponsive, uncommunicative, aloof

- fractious, querulous, quarrelsome, contrary; finding fault with everything

- changeable and unpredictable; illogical and unreasonable

- manipulative

- pleasant and charming in public, and the opposite at home

- mean, belittling, and critical

- makes inexplicable and sudden references to separation and divorce

- increased use of alcohol and drugs

The difference between the two lists is not just what symptoms turn up where. When a doctor is making a diagnosis of depressive illness, he asks such questions as, "Do you have low energy, fatigue, or chronic tiredness?"—Not, "Are you self-absorbed and unaware of the needs of others?" Or he asks, "Do you find your concentration poor, or that you have difficulty making decisions?" Again, he doesn't ask, "Are you unpredictable, querulous, and fault-finding?" *Low energy, fatigue,* and *poor concentration* are all cool, emotionless words, the sort that those with the illness can easily use to describe themselves without looking bad. *Selfish, picky,* and *critical* are hot words, full of emotion and very judgmental. They are the vocabulary someone with depression fallout would use to describe the depressive. The fact that the person with the illness can be constantly mean at home but charming in public will not help the physician learn what he needs to know, so that question doesn't get posed. And if it were, it wouldn't be answered accurately by the depressive anyway. In short, the doctor worries about the patient, not about how the patient treats the people he or she lives with, which is one of the many reasons that depression fallout is a phenomenon without recognition.

Increased alcohol and drug use is not on the official list because it is not, strictly speaking, a symptom. Substance abuse by depressives is often a form of self-medication, an effort to counter the wretched way they feel. Undepressed people have wine with dinner because it tastes good and enhances the pleasure of the meal and the company. Depressives drink because they can't take pleasure either in the food or in those they share it with. When the alcohol doesn't cheer them up as they had hoped, they drink some more, and some more. For depressives, alcohol and drugs are anesthetics, not pleasure-provokers. If the person you are worried about is suddenly more interested in stimulants than previously, chalk that up as another suspicious sign. In contrast to depressives, manic-depressives are more apt to drink during their highs than in their downs.

Depressives and manic-depressives alike are given to sudden bizarre references to separation and divorce. Each time this problem is raised by a newcomer in my friends and family support group, the old hands nod and mutter assent. This unofficial symptom will be addressed in chapter 10, but in the meantime, don't be surprised if it occurs, and try not to take it personally.

The Symptoms of Manic Depression

The bread-crumb trail to manic depression is far more scattered and difficult to follow than the one to depression. Many cases of manic depression are initially diagnosed as depression because the sufferer has yet to manifest the upward end of the mood spectrum. Even if mania is in process and would be detectable by an expert, you may remain unaware of it. The official list of symptoms of mania usually looks like this:

- inappropriate elation or irritability

- decreased need for sleep

- increased energy

- increased talking, moving, and sexual activity

- racing thoughts

- disturbed ability to make decisions

- grandiose notions

The trouble with assessing these symptoms in someone you love is that when they are relatively mild—that is, within the broad boundaries of acceptable human behavior—they can add up to an exciting, creative, and attractive person. Almost all manics are full of ideas and schemes for cornering markets, creating companies, making movies or writing books, running for public office, and the like. Endowed as they often are with great charm and considerable powers of persuasion, other people find them fun and spellbinding. Even though such behavior is accompanied by bursts of anger and irritability, especially when someone refuses to be swept along and questions their plans, manics often continue on their merry way undetected until their illness spins out of control.

Manics and Money

Money is life's blood to a manic—and not having it doesn't keep them from spending it boldly. Judging from the experience of the members of the friends and family group, spending deserves a place of its own on the unofficial symptoms list, preferably written in red ink. A typical example is that of Joan, whose husband of six years was recently hospitalized for his first attack of full-blown mania. "We met in Los Angeles," Joan says, "in a climate where spending money was a way of life. My husband never bought a thing that didn't have a designer label and a big price tag attached to it. We were forever taking people out to expensive restaurants and going on extravagant trips. I loved it, took it all for granted. Being with John was always exciting and unpredictable. I just assumed that was the sort of person he was." More accurately, John was a manic-depressive sort of person.

But eventually John's extravagance and obliviousness to the realities of money ballooned totally out of control. Unpaid bills were crammed into out-of-the-way drawers. His employer discovered that supposedly secure contracts with several clients were in fact products of his star salesman's self-deluding imagination. A second mortgage taken on the house had been spent with nothing to show for it but clothes and vacations. Other loans came due, and there were no means of paying them. Joan's story of disillusionment is not an isolated one. The manic money syndrome is certainly at work in some addicted gamblers, and perhaps also in the risk-taking of bond traders, grandiose dealmakers, and others whose professions encourage them to live close to the edge. For many manics, risk is as irresistible as spending. The rational approach to risk is to evaluate it, to look before one leaps, so as to land safely on the far side of the chasm rather than at its bottom. The manic is always sure he's going to have a safe landing. That's part of the illness.

A truly bizarre tale of mania, money, charm, and persuasive talk, reported in *The New York Times* in 1996, illustrates why manic-depressives make perfect con men, or, in this case, con women. We call them con men because they fallaciously instill confidence in their victims by their own show of confidence, and manics have confidence to burn. The subject of this news item—a perfect wife, president of the PTA, the Junior League, and the garden club in her hometown in Florida, and honored at President Nixon's White House as one of the ten outstanding young women in the country—was discovered to have been running a pyramid scheme that had whistled $10 million out of the pockets of her fellow church members. More than a third of this sum had disappeared in cycled loans, huge interest payments, and spending sprees. Although everyone, including the judge and jury, agreed she was a manic-depressive and the product of six generations of mentally unstable relatives, they still tucked her away in prison. If she is still in a manic phase of her illness, she probably wonders why. Denial of the obvious is another unofficial symptom of mania.

Meanwhile, her husband, who worked long hours and left his wife in sole charge of the family finances, has turned over all his assets, including their property, his pension plan, his life insurance, and his income as a doctor to the state in recompense for his wife's manic, and criminal, activities. Let this be a warning: the consequences of manic spending are borne not just by the spender, but by a lot of other people, too.

The woman's extraordinarily cavalier attitude toward money was not her only manic symptom. She also had the extraordinary gift of gab that is typical of manics. One member of the friends and family support group was utterly convinced when her normally modest and reticent husband suddenly announced that he intended to run for the state senate, even though politics was a far cry from his usual interests: football and his automotive supply business. At least she believed him until he whirled off several weeks later into full-blown mania, for which he had to be hospitalized. Manics see no impediments to what they want, as opposed to depressives, whose self-doubt knows no limits.

Even armed with these insights from people who live with a depressive or manic-depressive, always remember that you are not a diagnostic expert. Just because your wife is lazy and lacking in concentration, or your husband has overspent or lost interest in sex, or your son or parent endlessly criticizes you and drinks too much, that does not mean they are of necessity depressed or manic. Other symptoms must also be present. But if you do observe significant changes from what has previously been the person's normal behavior, and the changes persist for at least two weeks without letup, get that person to a doctor. Your job is not to diagnose, but knowledge is power: power to overcome your own sense of helplessness, power to persuade the depressive or manic-depressive to accept that something is badly amiss, and power to ensure they are getting the best diagnosis and treatment. Your role in the latter is the subject of chapter 6, but before tackling these issues, it may help you to have some insight into how depressives and manic-depressives really feel.

4

ON THE OTHER SIDE OF THE WALL

EVERYONE REACHES FOR THE WORD *depressed* to describe annoyance, frustration, or dissatisfaction with what life has to offer. It's a handy catchall: "I'm so depressed," we say, and go on to add a complaint about someone who has let us down or the number of bills waiting to be paid. Everyone does indeed feel down in the dumps from time to time, pessimistic or overwhelmed. Most of us also experience days when we feel wonderfully energetic and alive, full of ideas and assured of our ability to execute them. Those who are free of depression or mania assume such transient moments or days of gloom or elation to be akin to the real thing, and thus believe themselves capable of understanding how its sufferers feel. But they do not. Indeed, they cannot because their understanding is entirely intellectual and rational. Depression and manic depression are neither.

Conveying to others the emotions associated with these mood states is painfully difficult, as I have discovered when occasionally I am asked, in the friends and family group, to describe how I felt back then. I begin easily, saying that I existed in a gray, almost emotionless void, floating alone and cut off from others. With these few words I suddenly find myself back there again, reliving, even in health, the silence, the dreadful immediacy of a depression that filled every atom of my being. Unable to fight its sudden reinvasion, I fight instead against revealing it to others, thus sealing myself in its envelope. Trailing off into silence, I know I am powerless to tear down the wall that stands between us. The members of the group wait expectantly, trying hard to catch a glimpse of where I am, but my words are insufficient to the task. The wall still stands, its opaque surface impervious to their efforts and my own.

Two Tales of Depression

Others have described far better than I their depression, among them William Styron, who documents his descent to the edge of suicide in *Darkness Visible, A Memoir of Madness* (Vintage, 1992). Styron writes that one evening he chose to abandon his room and come downstairs to attend a dinner party his wife had arranged, at which he sat in "catatonic muteness. Then," he says, "after dinner, sitting in the living room, I experienced a curious inner convulsion that I can only describe as despair beyond despair. It came out of the cold night; I did not think such anguish possible." He excused himself and went to get his writer's notebook, which he carefully wrapped in old newspapers and taped securely, then buried in the garbage to be collected the following morning. "Fire would have destroyed it faster," he continues, "but in garbage there was an annihilation of self appropriate, as always, to melancholia's fecund self-humiliation. I felt my heart pounding wildly, like that of a man facing a firing squad, and knew I had made an irreversible decision. . . . I had not as yet chosen the mode of my departure, but I knew that that step would come next, and soon, as inescapable as nightfall."

Styron notes that he, like others in a deep depression, had "the sense of being accompanied by a second self—a wraithlike observer who, not sharing the dementia of his double, is able to watch with dispassionate curiosity as his companion struggles against the oncoming disaster, or decides to embrace it." His words convey the sometimes curiously acquiescent nature of severe depression, in which solitary dread and despair replace what in other, better times one had thought of as emotions. Such feelings are unconnected to cognitive thought; there is no "because" attached to them. They are primal in nature, as though welling up from some eternal, uncontrollable source.

The words that Constance uses to describe her hopelessness and submission to depression's force are far from Styron's gifted prose. She is not a writer but an interior designer, and the record that preserves for us her particular state of despair is a clumsy, staccato diary in which, at the suggestion of her doctor, she noted each day how she felt. The journal was intended as a tool to help her navigate the four to six weeks of bleakness she faced while waiting for her antidepressant to take effect. As it turned out, however, the journal covered much more time than that, because it took more than one antidepressant to beat her illness into submission. The incremental changes for the better, small and not always sequential, are hard to recognize when one is at the bottom of the pit. Daily brief recordings of mood provide a measure of hope by allowing the depressive to identify improvements over time that would otherwise go undetected. Her diary starts in early February and runs through April, during which time the first medication was discarded and another tried in its place.

Like many who fall into the pit of depression, Constance had made previous forays into a soggy swamp of downness, but had always climbed back out again. She thought of such periods not as depressions, but simply as bad times, times when the juices stopped flowing, when clients were harder to please and she had less to offer them. For three months or more after her major descent began, she was unaware that anything was seriously wrong. Previous work successes had bred more of the same, and she had taken on several new jobs, two of them large apartments in the city and the third a country house for a couple whose city duplex she had decorated. When she found herself hard pressed to keep track of the innumerable details involved, she attributed this to stress. More and more frequently she sent her assistant to comb the fabric houses in her stead. She lost patience easily, and when clients vacillated between choices, she allowed her irritation to show.

Her energy reserves depleted, Constance began to spend frequent evenings at home alone, sipping steadily from a bottle of wine and watching hours of television, rather than going out with friends. She told everyone she was overworked, exhausted by her business. She woke up one morning and knew that going to the office was impossible. Claiming the then-current strain of flu as an excuse, she stayed home for a week, sleeping through much of the day, unable to concentrate on business or even on reading popular crime novels. When she watched the evening news on television, she often cried for the bleak state the world was in. Despite her success, Constance felt herself a fraud. How had she acquired clients in the first place, when she was obviously without talent or imagination? Unable to prolong the flu excuse, she returned to work, pasty-faced and brooding. The first phone call from a client reduced her to tears, but it proved to be her salvation because her assistant had a depressive father and knew the signs. Constance agreed to see a doctor, and her three-month climb back to normalcy began a few days later as she left his office with a prescription for an antidepressant.

Here are excerpts from Constance's diary. Many days there were no entries; on others she just made an *X*, or a series of them, *XXXXX*, as if to indicate they were not days at all. After a month, there were occasional blips in the upward direction, one of them a drafted response to a magazine's Personals column, which she never mailed because by the time she judged her letter perfect, she had fallen back into the pit again and saw it as a marvel of hypocrisy. Several weeks later her doctor pronounced her medication a failure and tried a new one, leading to five more weeks of waiting, dragging through the days before it worked its magic.

Constance's Diary of Depression

FEBRUARY

Paranoia is king. I have no friends when most I need them. There is nothing. Just self-doubt, self-hatred, futility, pointless-ness, meaningless, aloneness, death.

I go to a "woman's" movie to have an acceptable reason to cry. Tears overcome me. I don't give a fuck if I stop crying or not. I don't know why I'm crying. I don't know why I'm angry. I don't care if I cry or not because it doesn't make any difference since I don't know why I'm crying in the first place. I don't care about anything because there's nothing to cry about or not cry about. There are no boundaries.

Fill the silence with something, anything other than my thoughts. TV talk is best. Outside there are couples everywhere. Music invites my emotions to emote. STOP THINKING.

Memory: Things drop not into but onto it, and run off its surface like rain off a pane of glass. When I go to look for them they have rinsed themselves away and I hover over the surface of my memory, looking for a glimpse of something. But it's all opaque, impenetrable.

News too depressing so watched documentary on stunt actors. The slightest miscalculation is going to result in death. The expectation is death, negative, down, bad, undesirable. To a depressive, confirmation and thus desirable. I am right.

MARCH

The rollercoaster is paramount. M. said wanted to "see me," not "have dinner with me," thus dismissing me. From minute to minute I have no idea what the future holds. It's SO HARD TO CONCENTRATE. I throw down my pen. It makes me feel so angular, so made of metal, so needle-y.

Examination of the rollercoaster. When I read page 42 of my book my eyes filled with tears. An hour later: I read it again. Why did I cry back then? If I can't match up what I read with my instant tears, how can I hope to know what on earth is going on in my life?

Down—jerked around—dead tears. Roller roller roller coaster.

Feel almost like a real person this morning. There is an evocative taste in my coffee which recalls normality. I woke up with a purpose. Off to outdoors, to moving, to exercise. Felt oddly untroubled when I came back although watched a solid six hours of TV.

False alarm. Down down down again. In response to watching "Washington Week in Review" I say, what shit is this? Life as I have appallingly come to know and define it as of March 17, 1992, is shit. Better understood when hopeless, preferably drunk. The barriers fall. Barriers of hope, expectation, resistance, of tomorrow. GET ME THROUGH THIS DAY.

Response to a personal ad in *New York Magazine* (not sent): I really love laughing and I'd love to laugh with you. I'm funny as well as 5'8" and 128 pounds and *extremely* good looking. I'm an interior designer, okay income. I like movies, Brahms and France. Can ride both horses and bikes, and cook. Just took up tennis again. Goals in life: to go around the world and to meet a good man who wants to stick around. I am a *very* interesting person, a warm and sexy woman and although smiling is great I really long for rib-breaking belly laughs. I am a laugher, a lover, and a giver.

How many people wake up every morning with nine strikes against them? Depression saturates your life, takes over. I must constantly fight against it. It keeps winning. My brain chemicals roil about, leaving me exhausted, at their mercy. They color my life gray, black and purple with pain. It's overwhelming. It consumes me. I spend all that energy plus more to COVER UP. LET NO ONE SEE INSIDE.

Woke up late. Sleepy. Went to studio OK but came home and slept and watched TV, and slept some more. Why? Maybe at last more relaxed? Less anxious? Met L. at movies. Silly film. No substance, ugly men, then when they smiled so beautiful. I thought how beautiful men are when they smile. Very bored writing this. Would rather watch "Cheers." Yawning.

Lousy night. Lousy awakening. So-what day. Eyes swollen as from allergy. Slightly nauseous, headachy.

Doc says stuff not working. Changed me to another kind of pill. Probably pointless, say I. He disagrees. I cried. Six weeks of pain behind me, six more to come. Maybe forever. Will I always feel this way? Days and more days to go and I don't believe. Not in me or him or the pills or life. Nothing. How can this be me?

The scope of this problem is endless. The loss we represent is so great it may be the key to unlocking the stigma closet. The stigma thing: UNBELIEVABLE. So we expend all this agony on dealing with it alone and cover up.

Anything that smacks of success—"best of the lot, best at the game"—brings tears to my eyes. Success is my energy, my reason for being. If I'm not accomplishing anything, well, then I am *not being*.

I saw a big brown butterfly on my way home today, resting on the pavement, silently, movelessly, elegantly dying there, so still. I thought of someone stepping on it, crushing it, leaving it both dead and ugly. I thought it was like me. But I am sleeping better. And I think it's a bit easier to think these days. But I still have to go on and on, filling the minutes, the hours with something, trying to pull the wool over my brain.

Woke up a total slug. Finally made it out of the house. Exhausted at theatre, left early. Bad night. Can't remember dreams but threatened me.

Three weeks on new stuff. Told doc all as godawful as always. Said hang in there. Wait for week four or five or six. Wine and waiting. What if I have to have shock treatment?????? Unbearable to contemplate.

APRIL

Slug again. Long dull night but woke up once again with great start as though from an electric shock. Dissipated instantly. I thought, Is this what shock therapy is like? Better after exercise and coffee. Good day at studio. Even better after nice dinner invitation from C.

Long night but better—better waking up, better day, better better better. Ideas for stuff coming again. Fun dinner with S. and L.

Slightly less better but probably more due to red wine excess than relapse. Great dinner party at C.'s. At studio, A. said twice, you have a sparkle in your eye, a spring in your step. No black or purple anything.

Today I am somebody different. I can do something well. I receive praise. I bloom. I radiate. I hardly remember the other me. This is the in-between me.

Read review of Iranian Shah's chief minister's diaries. Shah must have been a depressive. So contemptuous of everyone. Remembered how I used to think in subway, looking at people around me: how fat, how gross, how ugly those people are, how *lower* than me. How angry they made me.

This morning the curtain went up on my life again. Even before I opened my eyes, I knew life was worth living. My movements are part bounce, part crisp at the edges. I remember to take my new pack of subway tokens as I leave the house, giving it a little toss and catching it, zipping it deftly into my pocket.

Nothing in my real life has happened to effect this change, like job, men, money, etc. I think I am me again.

That Constance had to switch from one antidepressant to another undeniably prolonged her pain. Yet had she not had an experienced and highly knowledgeable psychiatrist in charge of her medication, she might well have remained in its embrace for months or even years. When the first medicine failed to dislodge her depression in six or seven weeks, he suspected she might be an "atypical" depressive and put her on the drug that works best for them. In just over four weeks, the lights in Constance's theater went on again, and some fourteen days later she was back on center stage. My daughter chose the same words as Constance to announce her own return to reality and vitality. "I'm back," she announced gleefully over the telephone one morning four weeks after filling her prescription. "Isn't that great? I'm me again."

Two Tales of Mania

I know my way around the depression map, but mania is still a mystery to me. The two following stories of mania are very different from each other. In the first, mania swept down out of the blue onto William, a thirty-two-year-old media consultant who had been on an antidepressant for seven years. In the second, mania and depression alternated in the life of a woman approaching her forties until, increasing in fury, they blew away her successful career as a journalist. As different as these stories are from each other, they disabuse us of the notion that mania's ups bear any resemblance to enjoyment and enthusiasm as you and I understand those feelings.

William was diagnosed as a depressive seven years before this episode. He took medication for six months and then stopped, only to have the depression revisit less than a year later. Once again he began taking the medication, this time on a permanent basis, and for five untroubled years went about his business, graduating from one job to another until he held a position well beyond his years. One day—"a day," says William, "like any other day in my life"—he was meeting with clients. "I was feeling very busy and incredibly energetic, bursting with ideas that I kept pitching. I was vaguely aware that something was amiss and wondered if somehow the dose of Prozac I was taking had suddenly become too high."

What actually had happened was that his antidepressant, after years of doing its job, had suddenly thrown him into mania. It is not unusual for cases of manic depression to present themselves first as what looks like depression; all signs of mania are missing, but in fact the other half of the illness, the mania, is waiting in the wings for a cue to appear. For no apparent reason that cue is given, and the medication that successfully treated the depression then becomes a trigger for the hidden mania. This in part explains the difficulty of treating manic depression: not one but two mood states must be dealt with, yet what helps one may disturb the other.

William believes he called his prescribing doctor to ask if he should reduce his dose because of the agitation, and that the doctor said it sounded like a good idea. "I have to say that subsequently I've learned from other manic-depressives that perhaps I didn't say that at all, and that indeed many of my recollections of what happened during this period may be inaccurate."

William spent that evening with friends at their apartment, and suspects they thought something was the matter. But, as he explains,

> I wasn't absorbing any feedback, and people are very tolerant of the behavior of those they know and like. I do remember that my plan for the following day was to drive to the country to see my parents, and my friends urged me to take the train. I know also that I wanted to go to the Blooming-

dale's sale and had trouble understanding that that wasn't possible, since it was almost eleven o'clock at night.

When I left my friends and headed back to my apartment, I saw a bunch of homeless people in the park not far from where I live. I sat down with them because it suddenly occurred to me to write a book about them and I realized I should interview them. They were so nice and listened politely to me. I gave ten dollars to one of them for some beer and we all sat around and talked for a couple of hours before I went on home.

By then I had decided to write two more books, the first an autobiography about all the different wounds I had suffered during my upbringing, and another about how to be an organized person. Voices told me what to write down. For my autobiography, for instance, I heard the voices telling me to be sure to mention my relationships with my siblings, and to enumerate various things that have happened to me during my life. They told me to be sure to say that my sister often made me feel like dirt, and that she seemed to have much more leeway than we boys. When I heard the voices telling me this, I thought, "What incredible insights." But what I had thought so insightful was very ordinary.

I began making a lot of notes on lined yellow pads. When I ran out of paper I started writing on the wall with a felt pen, and then on my bed sheets, and then on my legs and arms. I had the radio on all this time, and by now I was taking notes on everything that came over the radio. I began to have a distinct feeling of connection to God; I felt I was doing what God was asking me to do.

Suddenly I knew my brother's house was on fire, so I rushed to the phone to tell him. It was more or less two in the morning by now. He didn't answer his phone. Then I knew with equal certainty that my own house, the apartment house in which I lived, was on fire, so I rushed out into the hallway, yelling, "Fire! Fire! Fire!" The superintendent and his wife came running. I had known them for seventeen years, since I moved into the building. They asked me whom they should call. I suppose I thought they meant about the fire, so I told them to call my brother. They did, and he in turn told them to call 911. The emergency medical people soon came and took me away to the local hospital, where I was given antipsychotic drugs immediately. By the next day I was still high but relatively rational, and I've never had another attack of mania since then.

William's episode sounds like a bad dream concocted by a schlock novelist. But not only is it real; it has changed his relatively carefree former life into one held together by the medication, or sometimes multiple medications, that manic depression demands. He will have to be vigilant for the rest of his life about his diet, his sleep patterns, his every tendency toward charged overactivity. Should he slip even for a few days, he could find himself back in that terrifying Technicolor dream, and then once again in the hospital. Like Kate, whose story follows, William has a lifetime illness.

Kate's experience of manic depression began, she reckons, when she was about twelve years old, but her family, including her father, who was a doctor, interpreted her mood swings otherwise. "I remember his telling me, when I was twelve or so, that I was 'labile'; when I looked it up in the dictionary, I found it meant unstable. When I first got my period, I told Dad that just before it came I often felt way down, suicidal. He reported that to a psychiatrist in the hospital where he worked, and came home to tell me that I just didn't like being a woman. I asked him what I was supposed to do about that, and he didn't answer me."

The swings became more obvious in high school, and by the time Kate was in college she was in a state of hypomania much of the time, meaning that her behavior stayed just within the bounds of the socially acceptable. Then the swings accelerated. The medical term for what was going on is *kindling*, because the heat gets turned up when mania and/or depression go untreated. By then Kate was seeing a psychotherapist, not her first, and had run through all the varieties of antidepressants with poor response. A psychopharmacologist was the first to suggest that Kate was probably a rapid cycling manic-depressive, but neither lithium nor any of the other drugs she received did much good, and she tolerated their side effects very poorly.

Despite the enormous handicap her unsuccessfully treated illness imposed, Kate managed to do well in college, and not long after became a working journalist. Getting hired was easy; keeping jobs was not. "I knew already my life was totally disrupted," Kate told me, "and now I had a name for the reason why. I was a mess, but I still took off for Alaska to work as a reporter. It was a bad time. I was on all the wrong meds for me, and of course it was dark most of the time up there, and that didn't help. I lost my job and decided to go back East again, where I found a doctor who was supposed to be an expert on rapid cyclers, but the bunch of drugs he put me on turned me into a zombie. I was what they call 'over the edge.' At the same time, I kept moving from shrink to shrink. The last one told me I was in an altered state, whatever that's supposed to mean. I told him, 'No, I'm in a state of mania.' "

Frightened and exhausted, Kate went back home to see her parents. "I felt so alone; I needed them. Not long after I arrived, I dove into depression and made a very serious attempt at suicide. My parents tried to have me committed to the state institution on the basis of insanity. Did I tell you my father is a professor of medicine?" But the two doctors her family consulted said she was not insane and refused to commit her. "So my parents threw me out of the house," says Kate, "and told me I was no longer welcome there. Not even my twin sister came to my defense." I was shocked, and asked Kate to elaborate. "I've learned that families are capable of complete denial when confronted with this illness," she said. "Similar things have happened to other manic-depressives, and over time I think I've come to understand why. When my mother knew for certain what was wrong with me, she immediately thought it was her fault, that either her genes or the way she had brought me up was responsible for the pitiable state I was in, and she ran from that self-inflicted responsibility. My presence tugged on her sense of culpability, and her response was to banish me from her sight."

So Kate went wandering again, this time to the West Coast, where she landed yet another journalism job. "The last stage of my saga started in the fall of 1988," she says. "I had lost several jobs that year, and finally I jumped in a river in the middle of winter. The police dragged me out after twenty-five minutes in those freezing waters, and put me in jail. I was in shock, shivering. Finally the ambulance arrived and drove me for five hours to a hospital. I don't know why they chose one so far away; I think it was a state institution." It was from that hospital that Jeffrey, a friend since college days, and her husband-to-be, rescued her from three thousand miles away.

Love has been the salvation of many manic-depressives, and of many depressives, too. While those with the illness are abysmally poor givers of love, and are adept at killing it in those who offer it to them, they respond to its presence and are acutely aware of its absence. Jeffrey had, one suspects, always been in love with Kate, but she was hardly ever there, moving from job to job in different parts of the country. Through the years they had kept in touch, and somehow he managed to locate her in the hospital where her latest suicide attempt had landed her. It took months of red tape to persuade the authorities to release Kate into his care.

The hospital discharged her with nothing, not even a pair of socks, only bus money back to where she had been found. Jeffrey sent a plane ticket, and she arrived at his home just before Christmas. "My Christmas present from him was a diamond ring." She told him they couldn't possibly get married, that she was too ill, that she couldn't do that to him. But he countered by saying she was too sick to be on her own, that she needed someone to take care of her, and that he intended to do that because he loved her.

"We married that February," said Kate. "I was still very ill, could hardly get out of bed for months. I still didn't have the right medication or anything approaching it, but after that there were no more suicide attempts, no more hospitalizations. I can't really explain that part of it, because I know manic depression can only be controlled by medications. But somehow the support he was providing, that reassuring sense that someone loved me and would stand by me no matter what, did something to mitigate the illness. Jeffrey was, and is, very calm, very gentle, very loving. Gradually I got better, and finally I was well enough to go looking for the best person in the world to deal with my illness. With my husband's help, I found him. My parents did nothing, have never done anything, to help me. When I thought of my family, it was with such anger. I had had a lifetime of suffering and agony, years on the wrong meds, five or six suicide attempts, about a dozen hospitalizations. I had lost a quarter of my life, lost productivity and accomplishment, had nothing but fractured friendships and strained family relationships." This was a charitable description of her family's ignorance and cruelty toward her. "Imagine what Jeffrey's love meant for me."

What Jeffrey's love had done for Kate was easier for me to understand than her mania. "What was in your head?" I asked her. "How did it make you feel?" This is how she explained it:

> In an odd way, mania is almost more terrifying than depression. Mania is seamless. I went from coping to some sort of higher realm. I couldn't ever tell when I was up; I simply was what I was. When I was up, I had no judgment. I remember once in mania I went out and bought some marijuana because I thought it would put me to sleep, and I wanted that. There wasn't any gap between the decision to buy it and the act of smoking it. There was no decision, no idea of consequences. That's what I mean by seamless. Something is lacking between thinking and doing, something that has to do with what we think of as judgment. Insight, perhaps. Once I checked into a motel in a West Coast city. I called escort services for sex. This didn't seem a bad thing to do; it was just a thing to do. I remember I had a laptop computer with me. I'd turn the television on and watch some sitcom, typing the dialogue on my computer as I watched and listened. My responses were lightning fast. I could transcribe, word-perfect, an entire show. I never wondered why I was doing that, what the point to it was.
>
> While I just arrived in mania without awareness of getting there or being there, depression was different. I could feel myself sinking, but I always thought to myself that the next time I sank I would see the red flag and jump off the tracks, that I'd get out of the train's way in time. But I never did. Even though I could see it coming, the train ran me over every time. Sinking into depression is more brutal, more heartless.
>
> I've worked out a metaphor that describes what it feels like to me to come in and out of depression. When I'm depressed, I'm walking along in a landscape filled with big holes and craters and tunnels. I try all the time to avoid them, but I keep falling into those pits and tunnels no matter what, and then I can't imagine how I'll ever get out. I'm crying and I'm trapped; I can't think of anything to do. Then something comes and somehow picks me up out of the tun-

nel, and for a minute or two I walk through that pitted landscape again, but then I fall into another hole, and another
and another, over and over and over again. But with medication I fall into a hole and on the way down there's a bench. I
sit on that bench and feel my emotions and my depression
passing through me on down to the bottom, while I sit still.
Then whatever is the "me" comes back up again and I can
climb out, I am in control. Without the medication I can't
cope, I am in total chaos and darkness; they consume me.
For years I was hardly ever out of those benchless tunnels
except for manic interludes. I was just a nonbeing at the bottom of the pit. I was spiritually and emotionally dead.

In both states, whether deepest down or highest up, I was
never aware that anything abnormal was going on. That only
happened as I passed normal on to the other end of the
scale. Only just after crashing, while in recovery, could I see
that what I had been doing or thinking was bizarre. For
instance, when I was very down and thinking about killing
myself, I would often devote a couple of hours to reviewing
the physical location I might select. I'd look for the best
trees, the best limbs on those trees. I'd do a survey of the
basement beams and pick out the one that was the strongest
and the best placed for my purpose. While I was doing my
reviews, my surveys, it never occurred to me that that was
completely aberrant behavior. I liked thinking about death
because death meant release for me, release and peace. Fig-
uring out how and where to kill myself didn't seem extraordinary.

The words Kate uses to describe her two extremes are worthy
of the novelist she hopes to be. But the emotions that run through
us on reading those words were not matched by hers at the time.
It's hard for those without the illness to understand this robotic
detachment of thoughts from the feelings that would normally
accompany them.

I am giving the last word on mania to Howard, the leader of the
friends and family group, because he has his own vivid experience of
what the experts call *psychomotor acceleration,* the endless, excitable

compulsion to talk and the inability to sleep or rest that are giveaway symptoms of mania:

> Whenever I was manic, I just simply couldn't stop talking. I knew I should, but I couldn't. I used to roam around the streets at five in the morning because I was sleeping hardly at all, and I'd attach myself to the cop on the beat. At first he was thrilled because he was bored to tears, nothing happening, no crime, no one to talk to. He was glad to have a stranger come up and start chatting. But I couldn't ever let him speak. He would start to say something like, "Did I ever tell you about this fight I got called to?" And I'd say, "Let me tell you about this fight I was in." Whatever he said, I'd take off on it. I wouldn't let him say a word. After a while, all the cops would move away when they saw me coming.
>
> Hapless foreign tourists were another favorite prey of mine. I would wander around Times Square and look for people puzzling over a map. I'd run up and say, "Here, I'm a real New Yorker. Can I help you?" And I'd be off. I remember one Russian couple, sort of stolid-looking and badly dressed, but I guess they must have been pretty important because back then there weren't many Russian tourists around. They hardly spoke any English at all, but that didn't make any difference to me. I talked and talked and talked. I had them pinned to a bench in Bryant Park. They didn't know how to get away from me. For thirty minutes I talked to them about anti-Semitism in Russia, and they didn't understand a word.
>
> All this time I had this big job in journalism, and I wrote a column. I spent a lot of time on the telephone, of course, getting information for the column. But when I was in a manic state, what should have been a five-minute call would last an hour. I just talked until the person on the other end of the phone insisted on hanging up. I always thought I was fascinating, so everything took forever.

Howard can turn anything into a funny story. When people first meet him, they can't believe he's depressed, but his is a rare, weird form of the illness. He hasn't had a manic attack in years, but his depression immobilizes him, making a return to his former life impossible. The group gets going at seven-thirty in the evening, but Howard starts preparing for it at five, dragging himself out of the pervasive lethargy that is his normal state these days, venturing outside for the first time during the day, acclimatizing himself to the world of people and noise, readying himself for what's to come. Sometimes he can't do it, and one of his circle of close friends has to come around and take charge. Getting his socks and shirts together for the laundry is such a major task that it sometimes takes three days. He hasn't thrown anything out in years; when his apartment gets too cluttered for him to navigate, the friends come and try to pare down the accumulated debris of weeks or months.

Considering the severity of his illness, Howard's achievements are spectacular. He runs our group as well as other groups, trains facilitators, and has even opened a new support group location in the city. I talk to Howard on the phone almost every day, but always after one in the afternoon, because it takes him several hours to get in shape for calls. Often I, too, forget how sick he is, and what he has to cope with. When we talk about what happened at the last group meeting, he always psychs things out just right. He always knows which member needs a follow-up call or special attention at the next session. Sometimes in our conversations he starts slowly, his voice dull and unresponsive, but I've learned that if I keep going, keep pushing him to answer and talk, he'll gradually come out of it and start to dazzle— unless it's one of his really bad times. I used to tell him he was brave, but that embarrasses him. He deals with it better when I just tell him that he's smart and funny and good at what he does, because, thank heaven, he knows that's the truth. But he also knows what he's missing because of his illness, all the things that might have been, although he doesn't choose to dwell on them.

Before he got sick, Howard wrote a column for the *Village Voice*. He knew everyone who was anyone, partied with John Lennon and other famous people. He won an Oscar for his film documentary, *Marjoe*, about an evangelist preacher, long before anybody recognized names like Jerry Falwell. Everything he did, he did well. Howard still does everything well that he is capable of doing, but he can't write anymore; indeed, he has trouble reading. But somehow he's held on to his enormous ability for communicating with people, although he no longer goes out looking for bored policemen and

Russian tourists. I think the world of Howard, and so does everyone else in the group.

So that's a sampling of what may be on the other side of the wall that stands between you and your spouse or lover, parent, sibling, or child. The manic gives away more clues to the presence of the illness: extreme volubility, volatility, frenzied activity, little or no sleep, and schemes to conquer the world in one effortless way or another, but we don't always interpret them accurately. Manics are often amazingly charming and seductive; we often see them as inspired and dynamic, capable of transforming what are unlikely plans into projects we admire and wish to join or support.

Depressives, on the other hand, yield few if any identifiable clues to what is going on inside. They are neither charming nor seductive. Your husband may, like William Styron, sit mutely through your dinner party and then go upstairs, having decided to do away with himself. Styron changed his mind and checked himself into a hospital to make sure he wouldn't do it, but not every depressive takes that precaution. Even though she is not contemplating suicide, that attractive woman in the office who has lost her powers of concentration, who has suddenly become edgy, irritable, and hard to work with, may go home in the evening to pen notes of despair to herself, over multiple glasses of wine.

Depressive illness in any form is destructive to the self in ways that the phrases contained in books, articles, and pamphlets do not make adequately clear. Such statements as "loss of pleasure in activities previously enjoyed" and "a state of mind that interferes with one's ability to function at home or in the office" accurately describe depression from the diagnostic point of view, just as "inappropriate elation," "increased talking," and "grandiose notions" do the same for mania. But for those living inside the illness, such symptomatic descriptions are like kindergarten assessments, meaningless in their vapidity.

Not all depressions and manias attain the depths and heights of those described here by their sufferers, but big oaks from little acorns sometimes grow. Mild depression and dysthymia can sink into deep depression; mild hypomania can ratchet up into full-blown psychotic mania. When they do, their sufferers elicit our love and forbearing sympathy, wiping out previously inflicted hurts. It is before and after such episodes of crisis that depression fallout takes its toll. Being on the receiving end of the behavior generated by the illness—the barbs and slights, the selfishness and willfulness—robs us of patience and self-esteem.

No amount of stories from the other side of the wall can magically erase the effects of such behavior, but they can allow you a glimpse into their source. Few depressives and manic-depressives are able, when in the grip of their illness, to translate their inchoate feelings into words. Depressives are often clever actors, able to assume attitudes that conceal their interior life. The great Victorian author Anthony Trollope, whose manic-depressive father made a misery of his childhood, captures this theatrical bent in one of his novels, *The Way We Live*. He writes of the final downfall of a wicked and ruthless financier, Mr. Melmotte, who at last is facing disclosure and ruin:

> The part which [Melmotte] had to act is one very difficult to any actor. The carrying an external look of indifference when the heart is sinking within,—or has sunk almost to the very ground,—is more than difficult; it is an agonizing task. In all mental suffering the sufferer longs for solitude,—for permission to cast himself loose along the ground, so that every limb and every feature of his person may faint in sympathy with his heart. A grandly urbane deportment over a crushed spirit and ruined hopes is beyond the physical strength of most men;—but there have been men so strong.

There is an unbridgeable gap between you and the person with the illness. Whatever metaphor you choose to describe that separation—abyss, wall, facade, role, or just plain illness—be aware that it exists. The next time you tell your depressive to snap out of it and get a life, or instruct your manic-depressive to calm down and be logical, remember and reread this chapter.

5

CASTING THE "IT" AS
VILLAIN

IF YOU LIVE WITH A Constance or a William, a Kate or a Howard, you come face to face every day with the unpleasant manifestations of their illness, and it's rarely a pretty sight. But what's inside those who suffer from depression and manic depression is far more complex than what lies on the surface. Deep within, their essential being, the part of them you know and love, does battle with their illness. It's like a civil war. The latter fights the former, and often wins. Your task is to root for the home team, and you can't do that if you forget they're there.

The renowned neurobiologist Oliver Sacks, in his remarkable books on the mysterious workings and mis-workings of the human brain, reminds us that a gnat-sized cluster of brain cells or a trace more or less of a neurochemical can make the difference between those we call normal and those we perceive as mentally ill. In *An Anthropologist on Mars* (Vintage, 1996), Sacks opens the story of a surgeon's Tourette's syndrome with a concept entirely relevant to depression fallout. "Any disease," he writes, "introduces a doubleness into life—an 'it,' with all its own needs, demands, limitations." This is what may have happened to you. An "it" has entered your daily life and intruded upon an established relationship with someone you love. The more clearly you can perceive their depressive illness as that newly arrived "it," the better you will grapple with "its" effects upon them, and upon yourself. This is what Clarence learned to do, but not until two unhappy years with his manic-depressive girlfriend, Lina, had come and gone, leaving him an exhausted stage-five depression fallout sufferer, wondering how to disentangle his life from that of a woman whom he continued, against all odds, to love.

Clarence's Encounters with Lina's "It"

I have met Clarence's Lina, and it's easy to see why he fell in love with her. She is tall, leggy, and graceful, and could easily be a model, but she has much more to recommend her than her good looks. Deserted by her husband, before meeting Clarence she had raised four children, all of whom were under the age of twelve, had successfully fought her alcoholism, had finished high school, and had gone on to get a college degree in social work, all despite the turbulent mixture of ups and downs to which she is subject. Like so many manic-depressives, when she's up she's charming and talkative, irresistible to those who, like me, see only her public, best behavior.

The two met at a church picnic and knew right away they had a lot in common. Within weeks they were talking about making a serious commitment to each other. Their love, mutual respect, and shared faith in God should have made the relationship a happy one for both, but the "it" of Lina's illness decreed otherwise. "I had been praying for someone like Lina to come into my life," says Clarence, "but I certainly hadn't prayed for her illness to come with her. But it did; it was part of the package." That negative fellow traveler ultimately proved stronger than all the positives that had drawn them together.

Most of us are rescuers at heart, and Clarence is no exception. When someone we love is in trouble, we hop on our charger and rush into the fray, determined to save them. Although assuming responsibility for fighting another's battles makes us feel good and brave and important, it doesn't always accomplish very much. Indeed, such rescue operations, no matter how well intended, often result in two people in trouble instead of one person saved. Far from solving Lina's problem, which was a serious untreated depressive illness, Clarence soon became a full-fledged participant in the demands of the "it." What Lina needed was a good doctor experienced in treating her illness, and a friend who could persuade her to embark on that treatment. Instead she acquired a devoted lover who willingly accepted fault for her depression and mania-driven behavior, and tried to cure her with the love and romance he thought was missing from her life. Though wholeheartedly offered, neither made a dent in her pain. As he tried harder and harder to accomplish his self-appointed task, Clarence lost his objectivity and so became a vulnerable, powerless, and dependent player in the drama of their love affair.

One evening early in their relationship, Lina told Clarence that she was a difficult person, often hard to be with, and added in an off-hand fashion that she had an illness. She ducked Clarence's questions and gave no further details. He let the allusion slide because he was so attracted to her; he didn't want to "rock the boat," as he puts it. But the boat was badly rocked a month later when Lina created out of nothing a sudden storm of unfounded jealousy, accusing Clarence of spending days and nights drinking and sleeping with other women. He watched dumbfounded as she rushed into the bedroom, slamming the door. Following her a few moments later, he found her facedown on the bed, where she remained unresponsive despite his truthful assurances that she was the only woman in his life. His coaxing at length produced an explanation, this time more fully given, about what exactly her illness was: bouts of deep depression, often followed by periods of anger and agitation. "Wild thoughts" was how she put it.

"As she told me this, she disparaged me," recalls Clarence. "She mocked me for hanging around, called me stupid, and I thought to myself, 'What am I doing here with this crazy woman?'" But then Lina calmed down and told him how her mood changes ruled her— how they had a will of their own, and how difficult they had made her life. "I really liked what I heard. She was being totally honest with me, and I admired her for that. Right then I made a vow to myself that I would stick with her. I wanted to be there for her." Thus the "it" made the first of many appearances in their life together.

Clarence started to worry about Lina all the time. Was she going to get to school that day? Would she do what she had to do for the kids? "Would she be sweet and happy with me, or would I step into a turmoil of anger and suspicion about these fantasy women she kept accusing me of?" Though Clarence is nobody's fool, that didn't keep him from assuming fault for Lina's bizarre behavior instead of placing blame on the "it." He kept trying to prove himself to her. "I said to myself, 'Maybe this relationship isn't working because of me. Maybe there's something wrong with me, that if she isn't completely comfortable around me, it must be my fault.' I decided I had to learn how to be more romantic, more like she wants me to be. I even bought more books so I'd have interesting things to talk to her about."

Sometimes good talk and romance led to happy times together, but they were rare intervals between the irrational explosions and unresponsive downs. "I became so angry with her, and with myself for taking what she doled out. But I had become dependent on her, on our relationship. Even though I was saying to myself, 'Get out, get out, get out,' I was very deep into that relationship. I kept thinking, 'God brought us together, and God is going to keep us together.' "

Clarence's rescue mission wasn't working, but by then he'd lost sight of his goal. Both he and Lina knew she suffered from manic depression, a diagnosis made by the psychotherapist her social worker had sent her to, but the therapist wasn't able to persuade her of the critical need for treatment. For lack of it, she was bound to her rollercoaster, and Clarence went along for the ride. Miserable and angry though he was, he couldn't leave someone who had so much faith. "I'd say to her, 'Ask God to take your illness away,' but He didn't. And the negativity kept coming."

After yet another blowup, Clarence, applying his faulty prescription of more romance for their ailing relationship, invited Lina to Atlantic City for a weekend. Because he was unaware that gambling and risk-taking are life's blood to a manic, the trip for which he had such high hopes was a disaster. Shaken, Clarence finally pried Lina away from the slot machines and got her to the hotel he had so carefully chosen to please her, but she couldn't forget about those machines. "She just went nuts in there, playing two at the same time, yelling, 'I'm gonna win, I'm gonna win,' like a crazy person. When I finally dragged her out of there, she was so angry at me. She went on screaming that she'd been just about to win, that I'd taken her away from the only thing she wanted. She didn't even notice how beautiful the room was, wouldn't even try the whirlpool. It was a real bust."

On the bus back home the next day, Lina turned to Clarence and asked him if there was anything in the world he really, really wanted. "I said, 'Yes, you.' Then she said, 'That's not what I mean, dummy. I mean like I wanted to play those slots and win.' I felt so hurt. I just closed up." But once again Lina apologized, and once again Clarence forgave her.

Now the "it" was on stage more often than not, and Clarence, trying to hold down a job at the same time he was going to night school, found himself in an almost permanent state of demoralization and frustration. Lina would call him at his office, letting loose a barrage of insults and accusations, then call back again to wheedle and coo with promises of candlelit dinners and romance. But the evenings would all break down sooner or later, and Clarence would slope off to his own apartment, vowing never to return. Then would come more calls at three in the morning, with more sweet promises. "I was being turned on and off like a faucet," says Clarence. "She had entered me to such an extent that I wasn't me inside anymore. I wanted to find myself. I knew that for my own sanity I had to let go, give her up. But when she wasn't being crazy, she was so loving, so in need."

One day Lina saw an ad in the paper about a research program on manic depression at a local hospital. Sick at heart and mired in a prolonged period of deep depression, she signed up. A doctor prescribed three medications without explaining what they were or what she might expect of them. Because they made her feel sluggish and uncomfortable, she often skipped taking them, so small improvements would give way to more scenes. Once Clarence went to the doctor's with Lina, and the doctor told him that he was the best thing for her. "That really felt wonderful," says Clarence. "I went on a huge ego trip. 'Take *me*,' I was thinking, 'take *me*. I'm better than whatever pills they're giving you.' That really fixated me on sticking with her, on curing her. But she certainly wasn't getting cured."

Gradually, Clarence spent less time at Lina's and moved most of his books and clothes back to his place. But each time he tried to stay away for good, Lina's siren song would recommence and he'd plunge back into their chaotic life together. "She was always making amends after a bad episode, in a sense stroking me for the next one to come. When she apologized and told me how much she loved me, I felt joyous and happy and free. One moment she was loving and communicative and spiritual, and the next she was almost evil. Meanwhile, I was a mess," admits Clarence.

His friends, blessed with the objectivity that comes with emotional distance, saw that Clarence was following a blueprint for disaster, and urged him to seek help. An understanding social worker suggested he join a group of men and women dealing with issues of codependency. Although none of the group's members knew much about depressive illness, Clarence says it didn't matter because they understood what had happened to him. And they knew what to do about it. From the first weekly meeting, Clarence began to understand that, far from solving Lina's problem, he had become an integral piece of it. Fixated on solutions that could never work, he had invested his own ego in a hopeless rescue mission. "Part of me had always known what was the matter with Lina, that she needed medical treatment. But the rest of me just ignored that. I see now that it was crazy, thinking that if I did this or did that I could coax her into being different." In the worst of times, for him Lina *was* her illness. Unable to distinguish between the two, he had helped neither. Because his ego was at stake, his failure had caused him to lose faith in himself.

Coping Effectively with the "It"

If the "it" inhabiting someone you love has been around for a while, either untreated or unsuccessfully treated, you probably have some version of Clarence's problem. Distraught and feeling put upon, you are so busy blaming your spouse, lover, parent, or child for the way you feel that you've lost sight of the real villain: the illness. Should that be the case, you are in part responsible for your own misery. This unpleasant truth, once recognized and accepted, is the key to the puzzle. Only when you have accepted your share of responsibility will you be free to apply the recuperative formula that has put Clarence back on track.

Boiled down to its essentials, the formula has three parts: First, you must distinguish between what is your fault and thus within your ability to change, and what is the fault of the illness and so beyond your powers. In the case of the former, this may involve disciplining your ego and forbidding it to gear up and ride blindfolded into battle. As for the latter, practice your arts of persuasion and turn your efforts to encouraging treatment if none has been sought, insisting that medication be taken as prescribed, or finding a better doctor if the present one has failed to accomplish much of anything.

Second, recognize that you cannot take responsibility for someone else's life, no matter how much you love the person and want to help. Everyone, including depressives and manic depressives, must engage in their own survival unless they are physically or emotionally incapacitated. Lina was neither; she was badly handicapped by her illness, but instead of helping herself by taking her medications, she left them in the bathroom cabinet and complained of side effects, all the while asking God, and Clarence, to deal with what ailed her. But God had more important things to do, and Clarence's efforts to fill the vacancy were slated for failure. Both he and Lina were misguided.

Finally, you, the depression fallout sufferer, must look to your own needs and wants. Thrashing about in emotional turmoil never solves a problem. When we lose our objectivity, we lose our ability to disengage and to analyze the situation, and we push solutions beyond our reach. We can only react, and react again, burrowing ever deeper into our den of messy despair.

Clarence recognized early on that an "it" had entered his life along with Lina, but he had seen the two as inseparable. Learning to reduce his chief antagonist to an impersonal pronoun has enabled him to distinguish the Lina he loves from the Lina governed by her illness. Better informed about manic depression, he now puts his faith in medicine rather than in his own ego, or in his love for her, to control the "it." To this end he has established a good rapport with Lina's doctor, keeps abreast of her medications, and does what he can to encourage Lina to stick with her treatment. He has mobilized her large family of aunts, uncles, and siblings to help him look after the children and to give Lina support when she needs it. Sharing the burden has reduced the strain on Clarence. His concentration has returned, his marks at school are up, and he's seeing old friends again.

Perhaps most important of all, Clarence knows he must not put his survival in the hands of someone who is unable to handle it. So long as the "it" inhabits Lina, her own survival is more than she can manage. Deeply in love as he still is with the "good" Lina, he knows he must attend to his own well-being. He no longer allows himself to be turned on and off like a faucet, no longer waits for someone to come and rescue him. Doing so in any relationship is misguided; if that relationship involves someone with a depressive illness, it is akin to suicide. When I checked back in with the new Clarence, he had an up-to-date example to offer.

"Not long ago we were watching television late at night, some stupid call-in show with a psychic, and Lina went and called the on-screen phone number. The psychic actually took her call, which was all about that same old thing of me and other women and drinking. And the psychic said yes, it was all true and she could see me with a lady with a pear-shaped bottom and long legs, and I was pouring drinks for us both. Lina threw a terrible scene. I got up and went home to my place because I knew it was her mania making her do that, and I wasn't going to sit around listening to a lot of illness-speaking garbage. Instead of trying to sweet-talk me back, she admitted she hadn't taken her pills for three days. I gave her hell for that, and she respected me for it. You could say I forgave her, but not her illness." As I listened, I wished I had a bottle of champagne to pop, or at least a blue ribbon to offer. Clarence and Lina may or may not survive as a couple, but Clarence now knows that he will survive as an individual.

Depression and Faith

Clarence attributes his survival not only to his recognition of the need to disassociate Lina and her illness and his understanding that he must sometimes love her from a distance, but also to his faith. While faith has done much to help both of them deal with the effects of Lina's manic depression, Clarence sees very clearly now that faith in God, Allah, or Buddha cannot cure a serious depressive illness. God is neither psychiatrist nor psychopharmacologist. Be that as it may, many people turn to their priest or pastor for help when someone they love falls prey to depression. If they go looking for support, they usually find it; but if they are seeking reliable information on the treatment of depressive illness, they probably won't get it. Given that fewer than half of all doctors consulted about depressive symptomology fail to recognize what they are seeing, and given also that many psychotherapists are strongly anti-pills, one can hardly blame the ministry for being imperfectly informed. Because the church holds so much authority for believers, if it lends itself to the dissemination of inaccurate or misleading information, the results can be extremely detrimental. Such was the case when a highly respected church sponsored a discussion of depression and faith.

The meeting in the parish house drew some seventy New Yorkers from their homes despite subzero weather and snow-clogged streets.

There was a scramble to find enough chairs, as attendance greatly exceeded the church's expectations. After a few words from the vice-rector, the program was turned over to the evening's leader, a man whom I'll call Dr. Jones, introduced as an expert in the field of depression.

Dr. Jones opened the proceedings by asking if anyone cared to volunteer his or her reason for being present. An eighty-two-year-old woman said that her husband had been extremely down for a year, and that she hoped to learn how to deal better with his depression. Because her daughter was a friend of mine, I knew the husband had been driving her to distraction and that she hoped to gain some insight into her own emotional disarray. A middle-aged mother described her daughter as clinically depressed and implacably negative, argumentative, and angry, and went on to say that she herself now often became angry with her daughter and was ashamed of her reaction. A young man added his voice, saying that he was very depressed because he had cystic fibrosis. We all waited for the expert's comments, but instead he passed out paper and pencils in preparation for a written exercise.

Dr. Jones asked us to write down something that depressed us, and then add a benefit we derived from our depression, or from the problems another's depression was causing us. Remembering my own depression, and failing to see that any benefit had come of it, I left my paper blank. All the others chewed their pencils and jotted something down. The young man with cystic fibrosis was the first to volunteer his example: "I cough a great deal, and it embarrasses me, so I use that as an excuse to stay home instead of having to go out and be with people." Many present laughed nervously; inexplicably, Dr. Jones joined in. This was apparently the sort of example he was looking for, because when he stopped chuckling he nodded in knowing agreement and encouraged others to speak. A woman who had not previously spoken told us her depression had brought her closer to God, to whom she had turned for strength and solace.

I thought perhaps Dr. Jones was going to infer that depression was sent to us as a means of testing our faith, but instead he described it as a "red flag" that might signal other problems we have chosen to ignore. Explaining himself more fully, he added that often we prefer to remain depressed, terming this as "a secondary gain." Some people, he said, cling so tightly to their depression that they feel they are losing a friend when they start to get better. To me, this had the ring of psychotherapy jumbled up with the healing aspects of faith.

The two were at the heart of the second exercise he set for us, which he introduced by warning that depression might be a sign or a messenger from God. Asking us all to close our eyes and visualize depression, he invited us to tell him what we saw. After a few moments of silence, one man raised his hand to say he saw in his mind's eye—indeed, could almost feel it, as though his hand were upon it—a cold, metallic object rising out of a bleak landscape, and that it filled him with dread. Suppressing my immediate urge to offer some words of comfort to a person in such pain, I waited impatiently while Dr. Jones went on turning from face to face, listening to people's sadness and hurts until I could no longer contain myself. "What is your opinion," I asked him, "of antidepressants as a treatment for depression?" He rolled his eyes, spreading his hands in deprecatory recognition of my ignorance. He replied that although there might be very extreme cases in which medication was called for, it was a highly controversial subject. Surprised, I asked in what way and under what circumstances he would condone medication. He blew a low "ohhh" in and out of his mouth, replying that that was a highly complex subject, and never again acknowledged my oft-raised hand.

No one else disputed or questioned him. He was, after all, the expert their church and pastor had provided for them. My rebuffed intervention remained the sole mention of treatment of the illness until, at the end of the session, Dr. Jones passed out another sheet of paper. On it we were invited to write our names and addresses so that we might receive more information on the topic. I added my name to the list, and received, some weeks later, a newsletter published by what proved to be Dr. Jones's clinic, billed in it as "New York's foremost provider of quality mental health services." These services are psychotherapeutic, not medical, and, as the newsletter stated, the clinic's primary way of helping is to select their very best therapist for each of its clients.

This church has a long history of good service to its parishioners and to the community, but the misinformation provided there that evening did a great disservice to the attendees. The so-called expert on depression, perhaps himself a parishioner, presented a stereotypical view of depression as nothing more than a distressed psychological state that can be eliminated by talking. Because this faulty vie was colored with religious overtones, it ensured that the devout would pay close heed to what was said and recommended. Even the basic symptoms of depression, sketchily and inaccurately referred to at the opening of the meeting, reinforced this depression-as-mindset concept. There was emphasis on the old psychoanalytic chestnut of depression as anger turned against oneself, but no clear and accurate description of the illness was offered. Although Dr. Jones once referred to something he called an "agitated" depression characterized by "frenetic activity," he never used the words manic depression. The adjectives he chose during his presentation were not those used by doctors, but until I noted, in the ensuing literature, that Dr. Jones was a Ph.D. rather than an M.D., I had failed to comprehend his non-medical approach to the illness. I am still troubled by the image of a cold, metallic object endured by a man so obviously depressed, and though I hope he has retained his faith, I also hope he has added to it the antidepressant he needs to treat his illness.

Although medication does its job, some people still need additional help in coping with their negative feelings. Faith in God is an indispensable support to them in this respect, but never expect it to eradicate the symptoms of this illness. Clarence came to understand this. The following chapter may help you to do the same.

6

YOUR ROLE IN THE
DEPRESSIVE'S TREATMENT

CLARENCE EVENTUALLY LEARNED THAT IF he was going to get any love back from Lina, let alone any calm and order in his life, he had to involve himself in her treatment. You may have to do the same. Indeed, your first task may be to help your depressive see that he or she isn't just temporarily down in the dumps, and that medical treatment is in order. There are two big reasons why depressives need a boost here: either they don't realize there's anything the matter with them, or they suspect what the problem is and don't like the idea so won't admit it. I fell into the first category.

When depression began to descend upon me, I was engaged in launching the then-fledgling National Foundation for Depressive Illness (NAFDI), now a thriving educational organization that alerts the public to the prevalence and treatability of depressive illness. For months I worked away, writing brochures and press releases, organizing meetings, and generally feeling myself quite the expert on a then relatively undiscussed subject. As the shade of depression came down, I had more and more trouble getting myself to the office each morning. In the evenings, if a friend called to suggest dinner, I lied brightly that it was a shame they hadn't rung thirty minutes before, as I had just made another date. Hanging up, I sank back into bed, reached for the wine and potato chips, and studied the cracks in the ceiling.

It is remarkable to me now that the truth was so long in dawning.

My co-worker, himself a less-than-perfectly medicated depressive, began casting hints in my direction, all of which fell on deaf ears. I easily saw that he had the problem, and would sometimes give him little pep talks when I arrived on winter mornings to find him huddled at his desk, aimlessly pushing papers around with no lights turned on. But when he suggested I shared it, I insisted I didn't suffer from what I termed "real" depression; I was just feeling a bit disorganized and down. For me, the notion that I had an illness, let alone a mental one, seemed absurd. Finally my co-worker stopped hinting, told me outright that I was a textbook case, and made an appointment for me to see an expert, whose diagnosis was surprising to no one but myself. My immediate reaction was one of tremendous relief. Having castigated myself for feeling terrible yet unable to do anything about it, I eagerly leaped to transfer blame to the illness instead. While waiting for the medication to work, I repeated over and over again to myself, with grim satisfaction, "It's not my fault." And indeed it wasn't.

In addition to unknowing depressives, most of whom will seek treatment when led to it, there are reluctant depressives. Getting these horses to water presents a far greater challenge. A 1993 survey conducted in England asked two thousand people if they considered depression to be a physical illness; 79 percent answered yes, but 53 percent went on to say they were afraid their family doctor would think them "unbalanced or neurotic" if they complained of being depressed. I suspect many Americans would agree with their English cousins, using *unbalanced* and *neurotic* as euphemisms for *crazy* and *lazy.*

Those who believe they can beat their feelings of depression by clenching their teeth and smiling through are in one sense correct, since, for many, depression is an episodic condition rather than a chronic one. Eventually, especially for first-time sufferers, it will cycle itself out of existence, as previously explained. But the six to nine months or so while it is in residence are going to be very unpleasant ones; sometimes no amount of teeth-clenching can persuade a boss that a lethargic and inattentive employee is on the ball, and a lot of husbands and wives can testify to getting plenty upset with someone who sits around and criticizes them for that long. Treatment is a better alternative, although suggesting this bluntly may not be the best approach to your job of persuasion.

The Art of Persuasion

There is no perfect way to introduce the topic to your depressive; everyone is different. For most, the best way to begin is to ask some probing questions based on all the information about symptoms you have absorbed from chapter 3. If your depressive isn't interested in doing much of anything, doesn't get any joy or satisfaction from work, and doesn't want to talk or play with the kids, ask if he or she has noticed a lack of oomph and energy lately, and if everything seems to be a big effort. This is a better opener than asking if they're aware of how disagreeable they've been to you and everyone else, which may make them defensive and unresponsive to your initiative. Try to sound sympathetic, not as though you're complaining. Your depressive probably has close to zero self-esteem, and you don't want to make him or her feel even worse by bashing it further. Tell your depressive you have read an article lately about the prevalence of the illness, and suggest that perhaps that's what the problem is. Similarly, keep checking the television listings for programs about depression. All the networks have run stories on the subject. A call to your local affiliate may help you locate tapes you can buy and play on your own VCR. Ask your local library how to find magazine articles on the illness. Leave a book or two lying around the house; some titles are suggested in the bibliography.

If you know someone your depressive likes and respects, arrange for them to chat. A peer who has emerged from hopeless gloom and now feels great can be a powerful persuader. The two can compare notes; your depressive will likely find it easier to admit to feelings he or she might want to hide from you, and at the same time will be encouraged to seek treatment by the "thank God it's behind me" outlook of the friend.

You can talk with them about how many famous people and high achievers are or have been depressives or manic-depressives. Since your own is feeling incompetent and unimaginative, he or she may respond positively to being compared with some extraordinarily talented people. The list is astounding: Abraham Lincoln, Winston Churchill, Ernest Hemingway, Emily Dickinson, Mike Wallace, Virginia Woolf, Rod Steiger, Michelangelo, Irving Berlin, William Faulkner, Lord Byron, and Robert Schumann, to name only a very few. At least one expert who has looked into it is inclined to the view that depressive illness is far more prevalent among the great artists and doers than among the population as a whole.

Dr. Arnold M. Ludwig, a professor of psychiatry at the University of Kentucky Medical School, spent ten years looking at a representative sample of one thousand deceased twentieth-century figures who were prominent in the arts, the sciences, public life, business, the military, and social activism, compiling information on their lives and paying special attention to such symptoms as depression, anxiety, mania, psychotic episodes, suicide attempts, and drug and alcohol abuse. Next he developed an achievement scale that correlated with the number of lines allotted to the famous in the *Encyclopedia Americana* and the *Encyclopedia Britannica*. Of these one thousand greats, he found creative artists to be by far the most likely to suffer from mental disturbance, averaging a rate of 72 percent, while in the social, business, and investigative professions it ranged from 39 percent to 49 percent. Overall, achievers had a rate far higher than that of the general population's 20 percent. If your depressive is a poet it's something of an achievement to have escaped the illness, with fiction writers and musicians following close behind. Of the creators, only architects and designers were relatively depression-free. Among the nonartistic, only the military, scientists, and politicians showed "excellent mental health," according to Ludwig's results. Even a depressive will be able to understand that this is not just an affliction of deadbeats.

Constantly emphasize the treatability of depression. Many depressives still harbor the fear that their version of the illness is the exception to the rule, and that they will never recover. Admitting that they are depressed may feel like condemning themselves to a lifetime of despair. The way to reassure your depressive is to cite the facts: The treatability rate is 80 percent, usually within six weeks; it's closer to 90 percent when the doctor keeps at it, replacing medications that don't work with others he thinks might do the trick. Be aware that your depressive's notion of time probably differs markedly from your own. To him or her, six weeks may sound like an eternity, given that the depression has probably already affected their lives for months or even years.

Stress also that antidepressants are not habit-forming or addictive; and that they are not "happy" pills, but ones that return the brain's operations to normal. An actor friend of mine, not a depressive, told me scornfully that some of his peers popped a pill before auditions. While this example may explain in part why some blind clinical trials have demonstrated a placebo effect for antidepressants—that is, some people who believe they are taking antidepressants feel better even when they've only popped a sugar pill—it is certainly not evidence that the pills are "uppers." If they were, there would be a flourishing illegal street trade in them.

If the possibility of feeling better doesn't seem to be sufficient motivation to seek treatment, you might turn up the heat a bit. One woman I know persuaded her husband to get himself to the doctor by pointing out that his co-workers were far more likely to guess what the matter was if he did nothing about his depression than if he discreetly took it to a doctor. In the first instance, they might well begin gossiping and speculating about his irritability, forgetfulness, and under-par performance; in the latter, they would be relieved he was back to normal and swiftly forget about it.

A similar tack can be taken in the context of a more personal relationship. In the case of spouses, parents, or children, tell them how much you miss the "real person" they are, that you are lonely without them, that you long for the intimacy and good times the illness has stolen from both of you. Never suggest that you no longer love them because of their depression-driven behavior, but that you miss them. Although love and sympathy won't cure the problem, withholding either one will damage your case and cause the depressive great pain. If a long and untreated depression has in fact undermined your love by subjecting it to unpleasant behavior, try not to give any hint of your real feelings. They will resolve along with the other's depression.

If possible, involve other family members in the persuasion game, but don't count upon their help. The experience of one depressive's wife who attends the support group is typical here. Although her husband worked in his family's business and saw his parents every day, they were engaged in a denial of their own—"Our son, mentally ill? Never!"—and even went so far as to blame his wife for his problems. Family members who are not primary targets for the depressive's behavior may see only the sanitized public mask, and so find it hard or even impossible to believe what you say. Stigma plays a part here, too. Families do not willingly embrace the idea of mental illness in their midst. Steven, whose story of his manic-depressive wife is told in chapter 2, tried to communicate to his mother why his marriage was failing by reminding her of a cousin who had experienced a relatively minor mental illness. His mother's reaction was to deny all recollection of the problem and to launch a not-in-my-family tirade. If you have encountered a similar reaction, try to overcome it as you need all the help you can get.

The tone you adopt in your campaign of persuasion is important. Be practical and matter-of-fact, avoiding a doomsday or you're-so-sick attitude. Do not nag and harass the depressive, or you will eventually be perceived as part of the problem. Do not shame your depressive; this only reinforces whatever humiliation and embarrassment he or she is already feeling. If necessary, and if it helps, cajole and manipulate, but do not attack, threaten, or criticize. Revisit the topic a number of times, but briefly and succinctly. There is not much to be gained by arguing with depressives; it only generates resistance. Choose occasions when they may be more receptive, not when they are particularly irritable, anxious, or angry. Reinforce what you say by giving them relevant articles, or by marking passages in books, but don't give them too much at one time, as their concentration is probably impaired.

Persuading a Manic-Depressive

Most people in a depression will eventually do something about it because they don't enjoy feeling as they do. For someone in a manic state, the issue of persuasion is far more problematic. Indeed, persuading manics that anything is wrong presents a major challenge for two reasons. First, they have the giddy assurance that everything they do is going to turn out okay. Thus, whatever they're doing seems to them just great and certainly nothing to "cure." Second, in contrast to depressives, manics *like* the way they feel. In fact, until the higher, psychotic or delusional phase hits them, they feel wonderful—better, smarter, and more powerful than other people. While it is difficult to argue with a depressive, arguing with a manic is truly pointless. Often they will make you feel that something is the matter with you, something that renders you unable to understand or be persuaded by what they have to say instead of the other way around. Why this is so, and why depressives are just the opposite, is covered more fully in chapter 9. In the meantime, rest assured that you are not stupid or lacking in insight. Your manic is way off track.

Involving other family members in your effort to get your manic-depressive to a doctor will help greatly, but you will probably meet with resistance there, too. Your best bet is to do everything you can to educate the other family members about the deadly seriousness of manic depression. Untreated, this version of the illness almost always leads to disaster. Most manics will spend any money they can get their hands on, yours and relatives' included, and that means credit cards as well as checks and cash. They take astonishing risks because they don't perceive the consequences of risky behavior, including gambling, pronounced sexual promiscuity (with the possibility of contracting sexually transmitted diseases), and physical endangerment. They destroy personal and professional relationships with lies, outrageous actions, and duplicity. Let reluctant family members know that they will, like you and the manic-depressive, share in the catastrophes to come, either personally or monetarily. Enlist as a persuader any family member or friend who has a strong relationship with the manic-depressive; in this respect, a sibling is often a better bet than a parent.

Your best hope of persuading your manic-depressive out of denial and into treatment is to catch him or her in a down phase. The downs of bipolar sufferers are similar to those of unipolar depressives, with the singular exception that they will feel even worse if they have just crashed from a high in which they did outrageous things. Then, genuine remorse and shame at what they have wrought will make them contrite and far more likely to listen to you and to seek help. There isn't much point in telling someone in a manic state about all those brilliant achievers who were manic-depressives. When they are up, they already see themselves as stars.

You know the character and personality of your depressive or manic-depressive better than others do, and so you will know which are the most persuasive arguments to use. The main point is to use them. A year ago I ran into a friend I hadn't seen for ages, and in the course of our catch-up conversation I mentioned this book to her. "Oh boy, have I got a story for you," she said. The story was a typical one: a depressed husband, a troubled relationship, an unhappy wife. Ten minutes later she left, determined to buy a recommended book about depression and armed with specific advice on how to persuade her husband to see a doctor and get treatment. Six months later I saw her again. Nothing had changed except that she now exhibited a marked disinclination to discuss this situation, about which she had done nothing. Don't be like this woman.

How to Find Good Treatment

Let's assume that both you and your depressive now believe or strongly suspect what's wrong. The precursor to treatment is professional confirmation of your joint suspicions, so you need to find the best person to do that. Judging from the long list of where to go and whom to see cited in the brochures and pamphlets, finding good judgment and sound treatment sounds easy. Like so much that is written about depressive illness, this is not necessarily so. One typical list is provided by the National Institute of Mental Health's D/ART Program (Depression/Awareness, Recognition and Treatment Program) and includes physicians, physician assistants, nurse practitioners, psychiatrists, psychologists, talk therapists, social workers, and psychiatric nurses. Of these, only the physicians and psychiatrists, both of whom have medical degrees, can write a prescription for medication. Missing from the list are psychopharmacologists, who are psychiatrists specializing in the treatment of depressive illness with medication. All the others must refer their patients to one of these three if a prescription is to be written.

Most people start off by seeing a family doctor. In the perfect world of diagnosis and treatment, this is what then happens: The doctor agrees that you, the person closest to the depressive, are welcome at the first visit. He listens carefully to both the patient's subjective description of how he or she feels and your objective corroboration or qualifications; at the same time he makes his own assessment of the patient's demeanor, mood, and speech pattern. Next comes a complete physical exam to be sure there are no medical complications such as hepatitis, thyroid problems, mononucleosis, or other physical illnesses that may look like or contribute to depression. Having eliminated such possibilities, the doctor then takes a medical history to determine if there are other mental illnesses in the picture, such as obsessive-compulsive disorder or schizophrenia, or if there is any family background of depressive illness.

On the basis of all these diagnostic tools, the doctor decides that depression is the root cause of the problem, and prescribes an antidepressant. Your depressive takes the medication as directed, and tolerates the side effects because they seem minimal compared to feeling hopeless and despairing. In four to six weeks the medication significantly improves the depression, and he or she feels that life is worth living. If your depressive has been down and out long enough to settle into a gloomy, negative mode of thinking, he or she takes the doctor's suggestion of a course of short-term talk therapy specifically designed to help break negative habits and thought patterns into which the depressive has fallen during a long period of gloom.

When the illness seems to be under complete control—let's say five or six months later—the doctor suggests that it would be prudent to continue the medication for an additional six to twelve months before stopping. However, about a year after discontinuing the pills, your family member or friend feels he or she is slipping downward again, and reports this immediately to the doctor, who starts the medication again, perhaps this time on a permanent basis. The patient says, "That's fine with me," and lives happily ever after.

Unfortunately, it doesn't always happen that way. There are many pitfalls along the way, the first being that there are many fine family doctors who don't have the information and training to play this role. Sometimes they prescribe antidepressants, but restrict the dosage to a level that may be too low for the specific case; many people need a higher-than-average dose. Instead of responding well, the patient feels only minimally better and becomes discouraged. He or she is probably also coping with constipation, dry mouth, and some of the other side effects, and the feel-good payoff doesn't seem to warrant the discomfort these symptoms cause. The doctor doesn't try upping the dosage, doesn't switch to another drug, doesn't try a mix of drugs.

Or perhaps the doctor does prescribe an antidepressant, and the patient, after as little as two or three weeks, complains of feeling just as poorly as before. So the doctor switches to another pill, and then to yet another a month later. The patient still feels terrible, and no wonder—the physician allowed the medications insufficient time to do their work. In both of these instances, the patient jettisons treatment, thinking his or her case is hopeless. Life worsens for all concerned.

When prescribed correctly, the first antidepressant usually proves wholly effective. In some instances, however, it may be necessary to try another, as not everyone responds to the same drug. Finding the right one is an exercise in expertise and patience for both doctor and patient. Each drug must be given a fair trial of six weeks before being abandoned as inappropriate for the patient in question. Unless or until the patient is in the hands of a skilled practitioner, this is not going to happen, with the result that some will end up in the "untreatable" category when such a diagnosis is wholly unwarranted. For even those with an exceedingly stubborn depressive illness (half of whom will respond well to electroconvulsive therapy), there is hope. New medications are coming into use all the time. The specialist will be conversant with the most recent developments; inevitably, many others will not be so well informed. The patient will then suffer, and so will you.

It is hard to say which is worse: a health provider who is a poor diagnostician and medicator, one who fails to recognize the illness, or one who recognizes it but does not treat with medications at all. Unfortunately, there are plenty of all three, as testified to by members of the friends and family group. The topic of failure to diagnose and/or failure to treat with drugs is a standard one in the group.

The quality of the treatment provider is always important. In cases of manic depression—which is usually more difficult to treat than unipolar depression—it can tip the balance. Here, too, you have a major role to play. Use your information about the illness to full advantage. Whatever money is available for treatment should be put into paying the best psychopharmacologist or psychiatrist specializing in manic depression that you can find, especially if the illness has been around for a long time.

As in any profession, there are good practitioners and bad ones. Usually "bad" means insufficiently knowledgeable about depressive illness and its treatment. "Very bad" is someone who fails to follow up with a phone call if a patient suddenly stops coming or misses an appointment.

Some practitioners are cautious, while others are perfectionists. "Cautious" may mean a doctor who is satisfied with some improvement—that is, one who rests on his laurels when a severely depressed patient can get back to work but still feels half-empty. Or one who is relieved if his manic-depressive patient is no longer giving money away on street corners or trying to jump out of a window, but who still expects to start writing a best-selling book next week. A perfectionist, by contrast, is one who insists that patients feel as close to fine as their illness permits; who will carefully and patiently tinker with medications until the right one, or the right mix, is found; who treats each patient as though he or she were the only patient; who receives and makes telephone calls in times of crisis or missed appointments; and who will urge patients to let you, the family member or friend, in on the treatment and its progression.

Perfection in every realm is elusive. Many top practitioners are fully booked, although they will often recommend others they believe adhere to the same high standards. Ask around, persevere, never feel trapped or obligated by misplaced loyalty or awe of professionals as a group. Although poor, incomplete, or lazy treatment is a recurrent complaint in my friends and family support group, good outcomes often result from a switch to a better doctor.

Your depressive should start by sounding out the family doctor. If he says something like "Oh, you're probably just overtired or stressed out," or "Try to get away for a few days and you'll feel just fine," your depressive should push harder and be more specific in describing how he or she feels. If the doctor says to wait another month or two to see what happens, he's probably either anti-medication or a poor diagnostician. If this is the case, do some research of your own. You can consult such reference books as *Best Doctors in America, Best Doctors in the New York Area,* and others of this kind; they are usually pretty reliable.

Patients who regularly attend support groups for bipolar and unipolar depressives are often knowledgeable about whom to see and where to go for treatment; so are friends and family who attend support groups, where they exist. If none of these resources is available to you, write the national organizations dealing with depression and related illnesses listed in the Appendix to this book, and ask if they can recommend practitioners in your area, or a clinic or hospital with a good reputation for treating depressive illness.

For those with an uncomplicated depression, the search for a good doctor may be simple. An excellent general practitioner who is informed and up-to-date may be all that is needed. In other cases, more effort and investment may be required. Psychopharmacologists don't usually come cheap, but their fees are good investments. A first diagnostic interview, which may last up to one and a half hours, can cost $350 or more, with monthly or semimonthly follow-up visits running at least one hundred dollars. Fees vary up and down the scale depending on where one lives. Always remember that bipolar illness demands expertise; no matter how expensive, it will pay for itself many times over.

Price is not an absolute predictor of treatment quality. If you can't afford such fees, take heart; there are a lot of highly competent doctors in the public assistance arena, as members of the support group can attest. Steven's manic-depressive wife, Camilla, spent years in and out of expensive private clinics and hospitals, and during the same period saw three high-fee psychotherapists on a continuing basis. Despite several suicide attempts, only at the end of six years did she finally receive a correct diagnosis. But Clarence's Lina, a very problematic manic-depressive, had and continues to have excellent treatment at the public hospital in charge of her care. Lina has a talk therapist and a medication specialist, both of whom she is happy with, and, by Clarence's reports, rightly so. Approximately half the group's members live with people receiving publicly financed treatment. Their experience mirrors that of the full-paying half. Both halves are better off than most people simply because they have access to a knowledgeable source of information, the group itself.

Switching Doctors or Getting a Second Opinion

The group's members offer an important piece of advice: never blindly accept doctors and other health professionals as all-knowing super-persons. Once treatment is under way, if you and the person with the illness have reason to believe you have not yet found the best possible treatment provider, look for another one. Time spent with the wrong provider is time lost, and money lost as well.

Money was not a problem for Susanne, whose boyfriend Don and sister Jennifer attended the support group for several months. Like many newcomers, on their first evening they told a long, hesitant, and confused story of a year without any improvement for Susanne. Some of their confusion stemmed from lack of knowledge about her treatment. "I think she's been on the same medication all that time, but maybe not, because at one time she felt badly nauseated," said

Don. Jennifer wasn't sure, either. The group gathered itself up, waiting for the right moment to tell them that knowledge and clarity about treatment are essential for those close to the depressive.

Their hesitancy, we soon realized, was borne of their reluctance to fault the doctor, bolstered by Susanne's misplaced sense of loyalty. "She'd like to change," said Jennifer, "but she doesn't want to hurt his feelings. He's very nice to her. He always returns her calls, and she really appreciates that." At that, four group members leaped into the breach with the same advice. The noisiest of them made the group's primary point: it's not about loyalty to the doctor; it's about getting well. And then came instructions on how to check up on or change doctors.

There are two ways to deal with dissatisfaction about a treatment provider. Before making any move at all, be sure that the first doctor has had a fair shot at improving the state of affairs presented to him. Sufferers are usually easily discouraged, and so sometimes push for changing doctors too readily. As one expert put it, if a patient fails an adequate trial of a treatment—that is, if there is no improvement in six weeks, or if there is partial improvement but things aren't entirely better—then that treatment is probably never going to work, no matter how long it's continued. If the doctor doesn't suggest trying something new, he isn't working effectively on the patient's behalf. At that point, you and your depressive should act.

If you have reason to be unhappy with the results of current treatment, you can check it out by calling another professional and asking him for a consultation. When you're looking for a second doctor, pick one who works in a different orbit from the first one, someone who is neither affiliated with the same hospital nor shares a practice with him. Select one whose reputation carries weight in the field of depressive illness. When you call for an appointment, tell him that you want a consultation. He won't demand that you provide him with the name of the first doctor, and you are under no obligation to offer it. You should go armed with a history of treatment to date, and reactions to it. Be as precise as you possibly can be in terms of how long which medication has been taken, what the dosage was, and what the reactions and side effects have been. You can either take the second opinion back to doctor number one and discuss it with him, or keep it to yourself and look for a permanent second choice.

One of the leading psychopharmacologists in the country gave me a provocative perspective on consultations: "When somebody calls me up for one, I suggest they tell their current doctor that they are seeking a second opinion." That will tell you a lot about him, said my expert, because coming clean gives you a chance to evaluate the doctor. "If he comes through in a courteous, knowledgeable, and helpful fashion, then probably the patient has been lucky and is in good hands. If he is grandiose, nasty, and dismissive of the patient, you've found out something important." It's also better, he points out, because the consulting doctor receives a lot of information about the patient's recent course and response to treatment from the person who knows the most about the illness and how it's been treated thus far. Depressives—and their families, too—are often confused about what has been done and what is going on medically.

Jennifer's sister Susanne found herself unable to tell her psychiatrist, whom she liked as a person, that she wanted a second opinion, so she made a date for a consultation with another expert on the sly. On arrival, Susanne asked if her sister could sit in; the doctor was enthusiastically in favor of this. He took a detailed history of Susanne's journey into depression, which Jennifer was occasionally able to amplify with details forgotten by Susanne. When he had finished, the doctor described the treatment changes he would recommend. Then, with both women in the room, he called the first doctor, informed him that he had had a consultation visit from Susanne, and had presented his conclusions and outlined the new treatment he was suggesting—all of this without indicating that Jennifer and Susanne were listening to the conversation. Since the consulting doctor had a stellar reputation as one of the best and the brightest in the field, the first doctor listened attentively, agreed with the recommendations, and put them into effect on Susanne's next appointment with him. When, three weeks later, side effects from the new drugs were creating problems, the first doctor did not hesitate to suggest a follow-up consultation by telephone. Again, the consulting doctor had a few suggestions to make, which proved helpful. Everyone benefited from the initial decision to seek out the opinion and advice of the consulting expert.

If you and your depressive are already persuaded that a change is necessary, skip the consultation and make an appointment to see another doctor, telling him the name of the first doctor and describing all treatment he has rendered to date. In this case, before making recommendations, the second doctor will call the first doctor and discuss the case with him. This is his way of ensuring that he does his new job right. If he doesn't check in with the first physician, he may unwittingly backtrack over old treatment territory, or prescribe medication to which the patient has had a bad reaction. This is not only a waste of time and money; it's also very hard on the depressive, who will have to put up with two poor results instead of one.

Patients never have to confront their first doctor, either before or after switching to another. There is no need to explain or justify to him the decision to change doctors. The best doctor is the doctor who effectively treats their illness. This is everyone's goal; guilt or fear of hurting someone's feelings have no place in achieving it.

Your role in this business of choices, consultations, and switches is to be both supportive and helpful, taking care neither to nag nor to bully. Remember that depression often brings with it helplessness, hopelessness, and lethargy, so you may have to gather information about other doctors, rather than expecting your depressive to do so. Remember also that what may seem to you a practical and obvious step, to the depressive may feel like letting go of one lifeline before finding another. Offer to make the appointment yourself if that appears helpful. Go with your depressive to the consultation or first session with the new doctor, and periodically thereafter. Your recollections and observations will be helpful, and the rapport you establish with the doctor will enable you to stay on top of the situation and to report future problems, should they arise at home. If neither you nor the patient tells the doctor of these problems, he has no way of knowing about them. In short, you may well be an essential chronicler of progress or lack of it.

Treatment Options

If you are to be an effective partner, you need some basic information about the current state of treatment for depressive illness. Fortunately, we have traveled light-years since the days when the mentally ill were piled into boats and set adrift by the Phoenicians, burned at the stake in the Middle Ages and later, or confined to an insane asylum or the attic by the Victorians.

In this country, a nineteenth-century Philadelphia physician named S. Weir Mitchell instituted confinement as treatment, especially for women, because he believed the brain of a woman to be a soft and fragile thing, in need of male dominance and guidance. His usual remedy for the conditions in which he specialized—depression, hysteria, and anxiety—was to put the sufferer to bed for six weeks or longer, all curtains drawn, all books, pens, and paper removed, all visitors with the exception of the spouse (who, in Dr. Mitchell's book, inevitably turned out to be the husband) denied entrance. Dr. Mitchell also recommended a strong dose of "moral medication." Self-control, he wrote, was the secret of effective treatment, and he made all his patients promise to "fight every desire to cry, or twitch, or grow excited."

Charlotte Perkins Gilman, an early and prescient historian of women's rights and their subservience to the male economy, received this straight-to-bed treatment. Gilman produced only one piece of fiction, drawn from her own experience. Written in 1892, "The Yellow Wallpaper" tells the story of a woman who receives this prescription from her loving physician-husband and eventually goes mad. Gilman wrote it in retaliation for her own incarceration by her spouse, on the advice of Dr. Mitchell, whom she had consulted for postpartum depression. When she found herself going quietly but inexorably insane, she managed to escape from her warden-husband, went to California, remarried, and became well known for her nonfiction writing.

Treatment is certainly very different now, and developing at a brisk pace. As of this writing, there are some sixty different medications used to treat depression and mania, either singly or in combination. Three broad categories of drugs are prescribed for depression. Of these, the longest in use are the *tricyclics,* which include the brand names Tofranil, Elavil, Aventyl, Vivactyl, Norpramin, and Pamelor.

Tricyclics, like all antidepressants, have side effects that include dry mouth, constipation, blurred vision, difficulty in urinating, drowsiness or trouble sleeping, weight gain, and rather worrisome sexual problems (the latter are discussed more fully in chapter 10). For most people, side effects diminish or disappear over time, but they tend to be more pronounced and more enduring with tricyclics. My first medication was a tricyclic; I found that a mouth sometimes so dry that it interrupted me in full conversational flow and a dizziness so pronounced that it caused me to move like an ancient snail were still far preferable to my premedicated state. Not everyone takes the same view, and for this reason, although tricyclics are extremely effective, many doctors now prescribe SSRIs in their stead. Another reason for the doctors' switch is that an overdose of tricyclics can prove fatal; obviously, no physician wishes to give a suicidal depressive a convenient means of doing away with him- or herself.

The second, and most recent, category of antidepressants is the SSRIs (selective serotonin reuptake inhibitors), which have had a great deal of press since their appearance in the mid-1980s. With the brand names Prozac, Zoloft, and Paxil, they are effective, cause fewer side effects than their predecessors, and are not fatal if an overdose is taken. Like the tricyclics, they take, on average, four to six weeks to work. But bear in mind here that the same drug, even if it is in the same category, will not work for everyone, nor will it produce the same side effects. Prozac, for example, causes drowsiness in some, agitation in others; while one patient may feel great on Paxil, another will respond to Zoloft.

The MAOIs (monoamine oxidase inhibitors), with the brand names of Nardil and Parnate, are used to treat atypical depression, and for this group they are more effective than other medications. The problem here is that MAOIs demand a restrictive diet. Certain foods and drinks, including processed meats, overripe bananas, red wine, caviar, most cheese, and a lot of other good things cannot be eaten or drunk while one is taking an MAOI, because they provoke a potentially dangerous upsurge in blood pressure, as do certain over-the-counter and prescription drugs. For this reason, some doctors shy away from prescribing them.

This is bad news for atypicals, especially since there is a side-effect-free version called a RIMA (reversible monoamine oxidase inhibitor) that is widely sold in Europe, Canada, and elsewhere. Unfortunately, one pharmaceutical company that wanted to market their RIMA in this country chose, for market-share reasons, to test it not as an atypical antidepressant but as one for a related disorder, for which it proved wholly ineffective in its trials. Drug trials take time and are extremely costly; were the company to start from scratch, its patent would be too close to expiring to allow it to recoup its very sizable investment. This drug is, however, entirely safe; had its trials been on the basis of effectiveness for atypical depression, it would surely have passed them. Some doctors can help their patients order the drug from Canada, but there is a risk that delivery will be delayed; U.S. Customs sometimes intercepts pharmacy packages to be sure nothing is being brought into this country for resale.

There are a few other drugs on the market that differ structurally from all three of these categories, among them Serzone, Wellbutrin, Effexor, Remeron, and Deseryl. The latter, when prescribed in doses high enough to be effective as an antidepressant, causes a thoroughly nasty side effect called priapism in about 1 of every 8,000 men. This is a prolonged and painful erection, which if not treated immediately can result in impotence. Although not many doctors consider Deseryl a very effective antidepressant, a low dose is fairly often pre-scribed for women as a useful adjunct to be taken at night to over-come the stimulative effects of other antidepressants.

Drugs to control mania are far fewer, with three now most com-monly used. The one that has been longest in use is lithium, known to the early Greeks, who noted that when troubled people went bathing in springs that contained a lot of it, they emerged much hap-pier. Lithium works, but it, too, can be toxic; for this reason, blood levels must be constantly monitored to be sure the brain is getting the precise dose it requires. The two drugs introduced more recently to treat manic depression—both of which had already been used for epilepsy—are called Tegretol and Depakote, and have proved to be excellent mood stabilizers.

Quite often, manic-depressives take several medications because both their ups and downs must be controlled. Occasionally, antide-pressants can throw a patient into mania, one of the complicating factors in treating this illness. Because the medications that control mania take time to work, manic-depressives in a dangerous high are often simultaneously given very fast-acting antipsychotic drugs such as Haldol, as well. All of these drugs have unpleasant side effects, including hand tremors, muscle weakness, weight gain, and skin rash, which often, like the side effects of antidepressants, lessen or vanish over time. In the meantime, they are an added trial for your manic-depressive to bear.

Of the patients who fail to respond to drug treatment, approxi-mately half will respond to electroconvulsive therapy (ECT). ECT can work wonders for many stubborn depressions and for manic depression, too. The current practice is to give ECT three times weekly; usually nine to twelve treatments are necessary, but some patients need only six. Unfortunately, the novel *One Flew Over the Cuckoo's Nest* and the 1975 film made from it have left an almost indelible mark on the general public's consciousness, with the result that ECT is still surrounded by an aura of fear. The treatment has been around for more than fifty years and, as currently administered, often on an outpatient basis, is quick and painless. Memory loss, which used to be common, is now minimal and usually short-term. The good effects of ECT are not lasting for all patients; some will need "refresher" ECT sessions, just as a permanent course of drug therapy is necessary to maintain a manic-depressive, and many depressives as well, on an even keel. I have spoken with several people who have received the treatment, including Howard, the leader of the friends and family group; they all have given good reports about its effectiveness, the lack of pain (the procedure is done under a short-acting barbiturate and another drug acts to control muscle contractions), and minimal and usually recuperative memory loss.

Hospitalization is sometimes called for, most particularly in the case of a major depression, when suicide is a possibility, or when a patient is suffering from psychotic or delusional mania. The suicide rate among those with depressive illness is far higher than in the general population. Like many other people, I had in my amateur diagnostician's head the idea that if someone actually talked about committing suicide, he or she would never actually do so. This is not true. Turning over the possibility in the mind means that the possibility exists. This is a first-class reason for putting severely depressed patients into a hospital where they can wait for the antidepressant to do its work in a protected environment.

Putting Your Knowledge to Use

The purpose of all this information is to help you help your depressive or manic-depressive. Neither of you should try to second-guess the expert, but if he doesn't know as much as you now do, you've got the wrong doctor. If, after a reasonable time, a treatment doesn't seem to be working, both of you now know when to ask if there are alternatives, and whether or not the doctor is considering them. The manic-depressive son of Leah—whose story is in Chapter 2—was put on Haldol by his doctor, and the drug nauseated him badly. Leah knew enough to ask the doctor if he could switch him to another antipsychotic in the hope that it would not have the same disagreeable side effect. Had the doctor not made a change, but simply suggested that the effect was transient when it wasn't, she would have persisted. In a related situation, you can now do the same. Anyone who has dealt with doctors and other health professionals knows that the more knowledgeable your questions, the more complete will be their answers to them. You need to know enough to engage their attention, but don't try to be a diagnostician. If you do, they'll dismiss you as a time-waster.

Good teamwork is invaluable. Obviously you and the person with the illness must work as a team. Failing to do so will add vastly to the troubles your relationship and your nerves already suffer, not to mention those of your depressive or manic-depressive. The best team of all is a threesome or foursome: the two of you and the doctor, or the two of you, the doctor, and the talk therapist, if there is one. Good medicators and good therapists should communicate closely with each other. If in your depressive's case this is not so, you might consider making changes. Good doctors will welcome input from you as well as from the patient. Patients are not always the best of self-observers, because their viewpoint is skewed. You should also know that when your depressive or manic-depressive comes home from a visit to the doctor and reports on what the doctor said, you may not always be hearing the truth. Poor memory and confusion play a part here, but so do plain old lies. Manics are particularly prone to telling less or other than the truth; this is in part a function of the illness. If you have not established good rapport with your depressive's physician, you may be listening to false and ultimately obstructive information. Talk therapists, to whom the next chapter is devoted, will not share with you much of anything specific, because of the constraints of doctor/patient confidentiality.

Always be on the watch for a recurrence of either depression or mania. A friend of mine whose husband loops in and out of depression despite both medication and therapy tells me she can "smell depression coming" in her husband, even when he is unaware of any change. "It's like an aura. It has a presence, a place in the air surrounding him. I know what's going to happen long before he does." Mania has a similar way of sneaking up on its sufferers. Carol, whose husband is a manic-depressive, on several occasions over the past eight months told the group about a sudden return of excessive volubility on his part. "He'll suddenly start talking endlessly about anything and everything, whether it's politics or food. My heart just sinks because I know why. He seems unaware of it." In instances such as these, you should consider yourself an early warning system. If you are a solid partner in the depressive's treatment, you will speak up to him or her, and to the doctor as well. Such matters are covered more fully in the chapter on setting boundaries.

It should by now be compellingly evident that you must be an active partner and a player, not just a passive observer, in every aspect of the illness. You have a major stake in seeing that the person you love does the right thing, not by nagging or criticizing him or her, but by being informed, alert, and persistent in your goal. You will need to be patient, supportive, sympathetic, understanding, loving, and also clever, cagey, and—if necessary—manipulative. If and when you feel frustrated, discouraged, annoyed, impatient, resentful, or angry, try to hide those feelings from the person with the illness, but don't feel guilty about having them. The entire history of our world has produced only a handful of saints, and there is little point in flagellating yourself because you are not among them.

7

WILL PSYCHOTHERAPY HELP YOUR DEPRESSIVE OR MANIC-DEPRESSIVE?

IN 1987 A STRANGE AND entirely novel lawsuit launched five years previously was settled out of court for an undisclosed sum before the case came to trial. The plaintiff, a former patient by the name of Osheroff, sued a prestigious mental hospital in Maryland called Chestnut Lodge, alleging negligence because the hospital had for many months treated the man's depression with intensive, four-times-a-week Freudian-based psychotherapy instead of with medication, which was never offered him as an option. When his family extracted him from Chestnut Lodge and put him in the care of a psychiatrist who treated him with antidepressants, Osheroff's depression lifted within weeks.

Despite the voicing of many heated opinions by professionals on one side or the other, plus several attempts by researchers in the field to measure scientifically the relative effects of medication and talk therapy or a combination of the two, there is still little easily accessible evidence on which the prospective consumer can base a choice. Many on both sides would hotly dispute this statement. The case of *Osheroff v. Chestnut Lodge* helped bring into public awareness the intense and often angry debate among professionals over the respective effectiveness of antidepressant medications and psychotherapy as the best treatment for depressive illness.

That debate is still in progress, and will be for the foreseeable future. Because it has important ramifications for your depressive or manic-depressive, and by implication for you as well, a look at what started it and how it is progressing is in order here. Ultimately the decision whether to choose pills, therapy, or both depends on what kind of depressive illness is in question, what kind of therapy is used for what purpose and with what expectations, and how much trouble the person with the illness is experiencing or causing at home, in school, or at work. What works in one situation will not work in all; what may be useful in one case may be a waste of time and money in another, or in some instances downright dangerous. It is entirely possible that your depressive may embark on the wrong course simply because the professional from whom he or she seeks advice—whether psychiatrist, psychopharmacologist, family doctor, or psychologist or other talk-therapy practitioner—holds a bias of some sort that precludes a balanced and case-by-case analysis of the relative merits of varying treatments. As is so often necessary in deciding on the best way to deal with this illness, you and your depressive need to understand the debate if you are to make an informed choice.

In speaking of bias on the part of professionals, I don't mean to imply that it is always bad. Bias is an attachment to a particular point of view that, more often than not, grows out of years of clinical experience and thus can be and often is an important positive factor. But bias can also imply an attachment to a considerable investment in training, building a reputation, and achieving stature among one's professional peers, and so may not always yield to evidence that others with a different clinical experience have to offer.

The Ongoing Debate: Psychotherapy Versus Medication

Until the advent of antidepressants and clinical evidence of their efficacy began to accumulate in the 1960s, Freud and his peers had maintained a stranglehold on the treatment of all mental illness. If you thought you had a psychological problem (depression, manic depression, and schizophrenia were all seen as that), you talked your problem out in the context of your infancy and childhood, looking for the cause of your unhappiness or dissatisfaction in terms of mother and father, repressed anger, and sexuality. Those who had the time and the financial resources to undergo Freudian-type psychoanalysis—a veritable restructuring of the personality—did so by lying down on the analyst's couch four or five times a week. The patient talked and the analyst listened, very occasionally offering a comment or giving a little prod here or there. The investment of both time and money was staggering. Those patients with a large purse and a strong ego often believed they got what they paid for over a period of four to eight years. Depressives and manic-depressives did not. Nor did they greatly benefit from those psychotherapists who began to devise less rigorous and less expensive therapies that reduced the time spent, now sitting upright in a chair, to two or sometimes one session a week. The reason they did not was, and still is, that much of what the patient expressed as a "problem" had its origin in those pesky malfunctioning neurotransmitters, not in the unconscious mind. He or she felt sad, pessimistic, anxious, and irritable because of bad luck with their brain chemistry, and no amount of talking was going to change that chemistry for the better.

Dr. Ronald Fieve is a pioneering psychiatrist who first trained and practiced as a psychoanalyst. In his excellent book *Moodswing* (Bantam Books, 1989), he describes what happened when, in 1960, he completed his training in general psychiatry and embarked on a five-year training program in psychoanalysis. As he began treating patients, many of whom were depressives or manic-depressives, he applied his essentially Freudian approach of "making the unconscious conscious." At that time, says Dr. Fieve, he believed the patient was depressed because of repressed anger, or because he had experienced an early but long-forgotten loss in life.

> Although many patients who were in psychoanalytically oriented therapy tended to improve, I was never sure whether the improvement was due to true insights from treatment or whether it was due to the simple passage of time and spontaneous remission. At times I attributed it to a subtle kind of persuasion that took place. This happened, I thought, when a helpless patient came to seek change with an authority who he believed had the answer. The improvement seemed independent of the actual psychotherapeutic technique I was employing.

Unlike most of his peers trained in Freudian psychotherapeutic techniques, Dr. Fieve began, reluctantly at first, to employ the new drug therapies that were emerging in the 1960s—he was reluctant because "a key principle of most psychotherapists is that pills are no cure to problems in living." But although he agrees that in many instances this is true, he adds that "when interpersonal conflicts are secondary to (i.e., stemming from) a primary chemical depression, so that the person can't cope, the conflicts are not cured by a psychotherapeutic approach until the primary depression is first treated with antidepressants. I spent months with patients who were dreaming, gaining insights, or expressing anger they had never expressed, and who were still depressed." Once Dr. Fieve recognized that both his and the patient's efforts to "cure" the depression with the current mainstream approach had failed, he turned to the recently available medications. "The effect of these medications was tremendously gratifying, since quick relief of symptoms with or without insight was more important for patients seeking treatment." At that point, Dr. Fieve became a trailblazer, using lithium and antidepressants first, and then adding psychotherapy as an adjunct after medication had done its job. Not everyone in his profession followed his lead. Indeed, many psychotherapists dug themselves foxholes and from there launched noisy and passionate attacks upon all the medicators, whether or not they favored talk therapy as an accompaniment.

The noisiest and most passionate of all is Dr. Peter Breggin, the founder and director of the Center for the Study of Psychiatry in Bethesda, Maryland, the pad from which he and his co-worker wife, Ginger Breggin, launch their missiles at the entire field of medically oriented psychiatry. Dr. Breggin, like Dr. Fieve, also trained as a psychiatrist and as a psychotherapist, but his work experience has led him to very different conclusions. In the opening paragraphs of his book *Toxic Psychiatry* (St. Martin's Press, 1991), he makes clear his distaste and indeed revulsion for all medical treatments of the illness with no fewer than thirty-eight pejorative references to drugs (as in "many millions of elderly people" being "drugged and shocked into oblivion" in nursing homes), "lobotomy," "psychosurgery," "brain mutilation," "electroshock," "forced hospitalization," "being subdued in mental hospitals," and "permanent brain damage."

What Dr. Breggin advocates in the place of medical treatment for an illness he maintains is not biological but exclusively psychological in origin, is loving, caring support from a psychotherapist, and time. Time is indeed a "cure" in about 50 percent of depressions; as previously explained, about that percentage remit spontaneously in six to nine months on average. This is what Dr. Fieve observed when he noted that some depressive illness sufferers engaged in a course of psychotherapy tended to improve even though no psychotherapeutic insights had occurred. Dr. Breggin, however, describes what others assign to the sometimes episodic rhythms of the illness as the ability of "the vast majority of people [to] overcome depression without recourse to any mental health services. They do so by virtue of their own inner strength, through reading and contemplation, friendship and love, work and play, religion, art, travel, beloved pets, and the passage of time—all of the infinite ways that people have to refresh their spirits and transcend their losses."

Lest anyone remain unclear as to his position, Dr. Breggin goes on to state that "since the antidepressants frequently make people feel worse, since they interfere with both psychotherapy and spontaneous improvement by blunting the emotions and confusing the mind, since most are easy tools for suicide, since many have adverse side effects, since they can be difficult to withdraw from, and since there's little evidence for their effectiveness—it makes sense never to use them." He argues in the same vein against the use of lithium (and presumably also of Depakote and Tegretol, the two other principal drugs used in treating manic depression), thus eliminating medication for even the most debilitating and dangerous form of the illness.

The vast majority of mental health specialists would disagree with most of his views and his terminology. His inferences that lobotomy and other unspecified forms of psychosurgery are often used to treat the illness are grossly exaggerated; psychosurgery is used only in a tiny number of otherwise completely disabling and refractory depressions. Electroshock therapy is usually reserved for those instances (ten percent or fewer) when all other forms of treatment have failed; for them, electroshock often provides relief from unbearable despondency and, as practiced today, with little or no discomfort to the patient and minimal side effects. Although lithium and some of the earliest antidepressants can be toxic when taken in overdoses, only a small number of suicides, perhaps surprisingly, have been the result of misused medication; the newer SSRI antidepressants do not carry this risk.

Much of Dr. Breggin's rhetoric is not only misleading but dangerously off base, and his arguments in favor of psychotherapy are not part of the mainstream. "Many good psychotherapists," says Dr. Breggin, "would agree that they acquired little that was helpful in their training and that, if anything, they had to *recover* [Breggin's italics] from the process of being schooled." He plays with the idea of outlawing psychotherapy as a profession, preferring instead to rely on those individuals who are by nature caring and supportive, and who can utilize these values to assist their patients in dealing with their illness. He sums up his comments on psychotherapy at the tail end of his book with this advice to its users: "Approach [it] with skepticism and yet with a measure of hope and enthusiasm." This is excellent advice.

Although they are less improvident in expressing their point of view than Dr. Breggin, some psychiatrists and psychopharmacologists promote pills and eschew all psychotherapeutic interventions, which they pooh-pooh as a waste of time, effort, and money; a majority, however, embrace Dr. Fieve's position of medication first and therapy second, but not always. Psychotherapists, by contrast, lean heavily toward therapy first and medication second but not always, although a growing number of them do refer their patients to medical doctors for a prescription. This middle ground is the territory you and your depressive need to explore in making a decision for or against therapy. My own experience of both medication and talk therapy for the depressive illness from which I suffer is relevant here.

When my depression gradually gathered force and descended, without my awareness, upon my body and spirit, I lost the ability, touted by Dr. Breggin, to mobilize my own inner strength. When I called upon it, nothing answered. With the loss of concentration went also the loss of my ability to enjoy the pleasures of reading and contemplation, which have always stimulated and intrigued me. I lost the ability to love, and so felt my sustaining relationships and friendships slipping away from me, despite my crying need for them. Neither work nor play held pleasure, challenge, or reward. Religious faith seemed ephemeral. I felt locked out of the beliefs to which I had formerly subscribed, as though I had been blackballed from membership in my club. I had neither the energy nor the interest to get to a museum, although "lacking in energy" hardly seems to describe adequately the voracious, draining force that inhabited and inhibited me. Certainly I had no energy for travel, and with whom would I travel, since I believed no one valued my company, and where would I go, since curiosity and anticipation were lacking? I had no pets. And the passage of time was excruciatingly painful, since it was proceeding without my participation. Before I came to understand that all of this was transpiring because I had fallen into a biological depression, I went to a therapist for solace and to seek answers to why I had lost all of those bastions of my being.

For one and a half years I engaged in therapy with an eclectic therapist who described herself as being of the "quick and dirty" variety, by which she meant that she would address my contemporary issues and problems. And so she did, but within the context of that psychotherapeutic framework which has its origins, as most psychotherapy still does, in Freudian analysis. As Dr. Fieve writes, "Compared to the emphasis on the past in classical analysis, there is a greater focus in psychotherapy on the here and now, although the therapist usually employs the same principles and is most of the time a passive participant, saying very little."

Actually, my therapist was a talkative participant in my therapy. When I cited ongoing problems in work or in social or sexual relationships, she tirelessly encouraged me to find the source of my troubles and pain in my father's desertion of my mother when I was an infant, and, more pertinently, to recognize the obstacles that my own psychologically damaged self was creating. I dutifully learned to assign to every male figure in every dream the face of my father. Early on I resisted such encouragement, but my quick-and-dirty therapist insisted and I gave in because she was the authority and I was the seeker of her wisdom and advice. I learned a lot about myself, but my depression deepened. We went on with the dreams and the father thing until there didn't seem to be much more to say and I was pronounced officially free of the need for therapy.

Two years later I was in another city, where I began lying on my bed whenever I didn't have to be in the office, systematically severing all of my ties to the rest of the world. I contemplated the cracks in the ceiling and equated their quirks and turns as a message to give up. Suicide became an attractive and sometimes compelling alternative to grinding out the process of living without meaning or purpose, until I went to see a psychiatrist who prescribed an antidepressant. In a few weeks I felt better, but was told by him that better wasn't good enough. So he, holding my hand in a figurative but not a psychotherapeutic fashion, tinkered with my medications and gradually led me back to pleasure, to anticipation, and to a productive life.

I, too, am passionate and noisy about the approach that worked for me, but I recognize that although I am to some extent typical, my "case" may not present the solution for everyone. My psychiatrist's interest in my well-being, and his devotion to finding a way through medication to restore me to myself, was what I needed and received. In fairness to my therapist, I freely grant that she revealed to me several destructive thinking habits, some of which she did me the service of breaking, but my energy and my enthusiasm for life is conditional upon my pills. That fact doesn't disturb me in the least, except occasionally when I wonder what would happen to me in a nuclear disaster, my pills and my doctor both blown to smithereens. I have on two occasions reduced the dose or stopped taking them for a bit, only to return to ground zero. If the bomb didn't kill me, I might very well do it myself. In that respect I am not alone among sufferers of serious recurrent depression.

Two others who share my situation are a soap-opera star and a highly paid lawyer. When the latter's psychiatrist pronounced him "one of the most successful seriously depressed patients" he had ever seen, Peter Baird replied that even at depression he was an overachiever. Baird, a driven perfectionist who twice argued and won cases in front of the Supreme Court before he was thirty years old, did daily hand-to-hand combat with crippling depression for more than a decade before a psychiatrist prescribed Prozac and then therapy to get "some no-nonsense and practical solutions to the problems that come up every day in your lawyering, parenting, husbanding, and just plain living." Writing in *Men's Health* magazine, Baird sums up the change these dual therapies brought to his life: "Maybe I inherited some lousy genes. Maybe my parents did an imperfect job. Maybe my pain has been entirely self-generated. At this point the cause of the depression is no longer important. What matters now is that I take time to listen for the birds and watch for the clouds. I can make jokes. As long as I can do those things I'm okay." But before the right solution was found, Baird had tried psychotherapy, both transactional and Freudian analysis, self-help books, megavitamins, jogging, and meditation, none of which brought him any relief from despair. The road to successful treatment is not always direct, nor is it well signposted.

Joanna Johnson was for a number of years familiar to millions as Caroline Spencer Forrester on television's *The Bold and the Beautiful,* or *B&B,* as it is known to its fans. She had been mildly depressed since childhood, but in 1986, when her mother died, the depression deepened and she began to try talk therapy to counter her feelings of hopelessness and negativism. During that time, starting in 1987, she went to work on *B&B* as Caroline. "I think my depression came across in Caroline. It worked for the character—they gave her so much misery. I'd play this horrible stuff and I'd go home and feel horrible." Joanna often felt she was too upset to perform. "I just couldn't deal with the cruelty in the world. Just going to the grocery store would debilitate me," she writes in an article in *Soap Opera Digest.* She left the program because she felt herself unable to continue performing. "I went to a lot of different doctors. We'd do 'talk' therapy, and I'd inevitably convince them to agree with whatever my current justification was: that work, or the person I was dating, was the problem. I was never diagnosed properly." Finally, one talk therapist sent her to a top psychiatrist, who pronounced her clinically depressed and prescribed an antidepressant. She hasn't, she writes, had a bout of depression since.

My own experience, plus both of those recounted above, supports Dr. Fieve's views that medication first and perhaps then talk therapy is the best way to tackle most depressions. Fieve makes an exception for what he calls "reactive" depression, the sort that comes when someone loses a job or has overwhelming marital or financial troubles, or, most typically of all, experiences a death in the family. He believes that only in this latter category of depression may talk therapy alone prove the best choice, but not all psychiatrists agree. Such events may act as triggers for a depression that has been waiting in the wings for a signal to come onstage. The clue to whether the post-traumatic reaction is normal grief or real depression lies in its ability to impair functioning. Most people get through the grieving process without the aid of a therapist. If they can't, they may need medication.

If your depressive is down because of a life event, therapy may be a helpful adjunct. But if your depressive or manic-depressive is suffering from an endogenous gloom—that is, arising from within—or a super-elation unrelated to life events, get him or her to a medical doctor who will prescribe antidepressant and/or antimania medications; worry about tackling what the experts call the psychosocial aspects of the illness after medication has mitigated the highs and/or lows. *Psychosocial* here means the views, feelings, and behavior of the person with the illness as manifested in problems within the circle of family and friends, at school and in the workplace, such as feeling worthless and unable to connect with others. Allow the medication between four and six weeks to effect a change. When the gloom has lifted or the mania subsided, then consider thinking about psychotherapy as a mediator of the outlook the depressive or manic may have adopted as a result of the unmedicated illness, especially if it has been around for an extended period. But remember that therapy should be designed to break acquired bad habits and enable patients to think for themselves. Some talk therapists act instead as long-term validators, so that their patients remain dependent upon their approval before implementing decisions.

A psychotherapist who attempts more than sympathetic handholding and verbal, friendly bolstering of the ego with very down, recently medicated, or unmedicated patients is wasting everyone's time and the patient's money. Mania is impervious to talk therapy; therapists who seek to control the ups that are symptomatic of mania are severely misguided and should be avoided. The essential role of the therapist with a manic patient is to encourage him or her to seek and continue to use medication. In that role a trusted and supportive therapist can often accomplish what families cannot.

Classic psychoanalysis has no rational and informed advocates as the treatment of choice for either recurrent unipolar depression or bipolar illness. Further, Dr. Fieve and many others have observed that attempts to treat psychotic (i.e., delusional) manic-depressives with psychoanalytically oriented therapy before stabilization with medication may deepen the psychosis and so put the therapy recipient in even greater danger. Quite aside from the lack of benefits, the time, money, and effort devoted to psychoanalysis are wasted not only with bipolar depressives but with all but a few, if any, unipolar patients as well.

If your depressive wants to try therapy, he or she is certainly not alone in doing so. In 1987 the U.S. Department of Health and Human Services took a look at how many people had visited a professional for psychotherapy that year by surveying 40,000 people in 16,000 households. A study of the statistics collected by HHS concluded that 3 percent of the general population accounted for a total of 80 million visits that year: 32 percent of them to psychologists, 24 percent to psychiatrists, and 25 percent to "others," with the balance divided between general medical doctors and providers the study could not identify. If one assumes that each visit cost a low average of one hundred dollars, that adds up to about $5 billion in 1987 dollars spent just talking about problems stemming from depression, anxiety, nervousness, insomnia, and what the study terms "adjustment problems."

More recently, *Consumer Reports* magazine surveyed its subscribers on the topic of psychotherapy, four thousand of whom responded they had sought help from a mental health provider or a family doctor for psychological problems, or had joined a self-help group. The majority said they had "made strides toward resolving the problems that led to treatment, and almost all said life had become more manageable," even those who felt the worst at the beginning. This sounds like a solid endorsement of the good effects of psychotherapy, but before you send your depressive to the telephone, both of you should take into consideration what you now know from Dr. Fieve and others, that many depressions cycle out in six to twelve months, with or without therapy. Ascribing their disappearance to therapy may be an inaccurate conclusion, although it may indeed have made the depression more bearable while it lasted. It's tempting also to wonder if any responses came from people who might have spent thousands of dollars and several years with not a great deal to show for it. Probably not.

Neither of these surveys can tell your depressive, the consumer, which therapy might help him or her, but the following information provides some guidelines on which to base a decision.

"Supportive" Versus "Expressive" Therapy

All therapy lies on a spectrum extending from "expressive" to "supportive." The extreme example of expressive therapy is the sort in which the client is the big talker and the therapist assumes the role of a listener. Here the burden of proof, so to speak, lies with the patient. At the other end of the spectrum is "supportive" therapy, in which the therapist plays a more active role. Dr. Herbert Fox, a well-known New York City–based practicing psychiatrist who is in charge of Lenox Hill Hospital's annual Depression Screening Day (during which anyone who suspects he or she suffers from depression is free to turn up at the hospital for an initial screening and diagnosis), says that what the therapist looks to give depressive patients is support.

The therapist, says Dr. Fox, should be comforting, helping, "on your side" (i.e., the depressive's side), and "rooting for you." He points out that in his opinion there are few if any medical doctors who quarrel with the origin of depression as a biological illness, but that there are plenty of talk therapists around who don't know or do not recognize this. "As far as therapy is concerned," says Dr. Fox, "you should not apply insight talk therapy (that's expressive therapy) when depressive illness is present.

"Every psychotherapy is a continuum," he explains. "When necessary, the therapist drops insight approaches and turns to supportive therapy. Those with depressive illness do poorly with insight therapy, although some may successfully return to it when they are ready." By "ready," Dr. Fox means medicated to a more rational and insightful point of view, and thus able and willing to seek further understanding of what makes them tick. I personally, for instance, might have taken better advantage of my quick-and-dirty therapy, albeit Freudian-based, had I entered into it after rather than before I turned to medication.

I raised with Dr. Fox the example of the psychologist Kay Redfield Jamison, a leading expert on manic-depressive illness, whose moving and illuminating book, *An Unquiet Mind* (Knopf, 1996), recounts and addresses her own manic depression, previously concealed from all except her closest personal and professional companions, and of course her psychotherapist. Dr. Jamison, who would probably not be at the top of her profession as a tenured professor of psychiatry at Johns Hopkins University without the benefit of medication, speaks in her book about her psychiatrist of many years: "He kept me alive a thousand times over. He saw me through madness, despair, wonderful and terrible love affairs, disillusionments and triumphs, recurrences of illness, an almost fatal suicide attempt, the death of a man I greatly loved, and the enormous pleasures and aggravations of my professional life—in short, he saw me through the beginnings and endings of virtually every aspect of my psychological and emotional life. He was very tough, as well as very kind. He treated me with respect, a decisive professionalism, wit, and an unshakable belief in my ability to get well, compete, and make a difference." Dr. Fox, in answer to my query about his opinion of the value of psychotherapy for Dr. Jamison, replied that she had needed and found a trusted and professional friend, a knowledgeable adviser, and a supportive hand-holding counselor in her therapist. Medication had made her continuing impressive work achievements possible; psychotherapy had made her illness bearable.

The evidence comes overwhelmingly down on the side of supportive rather than expressive therapy as the most useful adjunct to medication, but there are lots of therapists who are persuaded that talk therapy is either the only answer or a large part of the answer to dealing with the illness, and with the behavior and feelings it provokes. Your depressive, with your help, has to figure out whom to see for what reasons and with what expectations. Unlike the issue of medication, the issue of therapy lies principally with your depressive and not with you. Furthermore, whereas you can and should insist on being a participating partner in medication therapy, sitting in on the initial session with the medicating psychiatrist or psychopharmacologist as well as periodically therafter, you have no similar rights with the therapist. A rare few will invite a close family member to share an occasional session if they believe this will help them to help their clients, but you can't count on it. Who would bare his inner thoughts and feelings to a therapist if the therapist reported it all back to you, the close relative or intimate friend who is on the receiving end of the depressive or manic-depressive's behavior and attitudes? The answer is nobody.

This explains in part why so many psychotherapists resist even minimal inputs on the part of family members, but it doesn't really excuse it. If you believe you have useful information to offer—not complaints—mention that you are willing to answer any questions the therapist may have that bear upon the patient's moods and functioning, and to volunteer information you think may be of consequence to the therapist. Make it totally clear that you seek nothing in return, that you understand and respect the need for patient/therapist confidentiality, and that you are making no demands of the therapist. You may just get yourself a hearing.

The stay-out-of-my-backyard attitude of many therapists complicates the issues of therapy as far as you, the depression fallout sufferer, are concerned. You will be not a recipient of the therapy, but a recipient of the results of someone else's therapy. Your interest, therefore, is usually confined to helping the depressive find the most effective therapy for him or her, to knowing what kind of therapy has been selected, and what purpose and goals it presumes to achieve. What follows is a run-down on therapy options.

Short-term Talk Therapy Options

The psychotherapists have been slow in emerging from their expressive mode, the classic training given to all who enter the field. This is a problem acknowledged by even the most rigid anti-medication theorists, including Dr. Breggin. The emphasis remains on expressive rather than supportive therapy, but this is changing, and excellent alternatives are now available. Two effective options are cognitive and/or behavioral therapy (they are often now combined and called CBT for short), and interpersonal therapy. The former was developed by psychiatrist Dr. Aaron T. Beck, at the Beck Center for Cognitive Therapy in Philadelphia.

The theory behind cognitive/behavioral therapy (CBT) is that people with depression develop errors in thinking and unrealistic attitudes about themselves and the world. In their clear and easy-to-read book, *Understanding Depression* (Oxford University Press, 1993), Dr. Donald F. Klein, of Columbia University and the New York State Psychiatric Institute, and Dr. Paul Wender, of the University of Utah School of Medicine, write that there are three major kinds of thinking errors: underrating oneself as inadequate and of little value; having a negative view of one's current experience, as in believing oneself incapable of achieving goals or experiencing pleasure; and pessimism, holding an inherent belief that things are not going to change for the better. The job of the cognitive therapist is to convince the patient that there is no evidence for these beliefs, with the goal of changing the patient's distorted attitudes and helping to alleviate the depression. In therapy the person is taught not to overgeneralize from one negative experience while ignoring the positive ones.

The second technique, interpersonal therapy, comes out of the work of the late Dr. Gerald Klerman, who had a long and rich career including a stint as President Jimmy Carter's director of the Alcohol, Drug Abuse and Mental Health Administration of the Department of Health and Human Services. This type of therapy, called IPT for short, addresses patients' key relationships, such as recent conflicts with significant others, co-workers, and those people with whom they deal on a regular basis. The goal is to help them understand how their attitudes and behavior affect others, and to mend their ways through better understanding of the dynamics of their interpersonal relations. IPT has the advantage of having been developed specifically as a response to depression. The therapist first addresses with the patient the need for medication based on severity, history, response to treatment, and patient preference, and then educates him or her about depression by explicitly discussing the diagnosis (including symptoms) and what might be expected from therapy. Together they consider options to current interpersonal disputes; if these fail, they may conclude that the relationship has reached an impasse and consider ways to replace it with better alternatives. Both of these therapies are short-term, usually taking about four months from start to finish.

There is a distinct difference between the positive or negative personal experiences of therapy by those who have tried it and unequivocal proof that one or another therapy works for depression. As Dr. Steven J. Kingsbury of the University of Texas Southwestern Medical School recently observed in the *Harvard Mental Health Newsletter,* there are about four hundred varieties of psychotherapy out there which have not been adequately tested, and therapists don't always follow the manual. Still, his view is that "in the treatment of major depression without psychotic features, behavioral, cognitive-behavioral, and interpersonal psychotherapies are as effective as antidepressant drugs. Psychodynamically oriented therapies are less useful, but better than a placebo. No psychotherapy has been found to be effective in bipolar (manic-depressive) disorder." You have by now, of course, noted that not by a long shot does everyone believe that CBT and IPT are "as effective as antidepressant drugs."

In 1989 the National Institute of Mental Health published the results of a study of 250 patients who suffered from depression; none were currently hospitalized and none were manic-depressives. Some were treated with imipramine, one of the earlier antidepressants, which, though effective, has troublesome side effects, and received no formal therapy. Others received either ITP or CBT, but no medication. Still others received only a placebo. Both imipramine and placebo recipients benefited from "case management," which means that once a week they met with their doctors, who answered questions, kept tabs on how they felt, discussed any side effects, and adjusted dosage accordingly. Nobody, including the doctors, knew who was getting a true antidepressant and who was receiving a placebo.

The results, widely reported in the general press, indicated that for those with only mild to moderate depression, the antidepressant had no edge over therapy, and that neither was better than the placebo. For those who were more impaired or had more pronounced depressive symptomology, however, the medication was clearly the best and fastest (and cheapest) treatment. Far from settling the debate, the study heated it up. Psychiatrists who gained access to some of the raw data reanalyzed it and sharply criticized the study's coordinator, psychologist Irene Elkin of NIMH, for downplaying the importance of severity and impairment.

Mild to moderate depression means that the depressive is able to function well and get on with life despite feeling sad and negative. A depressive whose functioning is impaired, causing problems at home and in the office, has a serious depression. By blurring the distinction, the study's report left the general public with the impression that it really didn't much matter which treatment was chosen. The reanalysis failed to make the same headlines as the claims for drug and therapy equivalence.

Subsequent studies took a longer view, following patients for three years instead of the four-month period covered by the NIMH study. In 1995, two psychologists wrote up their interpretation of these studies in a paper reported in the general press. One of the authors, Dr. David Antonucci of the University of Nevada School of Medicine, wrote that "the data suggest that there is no stronger medicine than psychotherapy in the treatment of depression, even when it is severe." Dr. David Kupfer, a psychiatrist at the University of Pittsburgh Medical School and director of one of the studies Antonucci comments on, described himself as "mildly incensed" by the article, saying, "It's a selective review of the data to make a point, and may be misleading for patients and their families." Dr. Kupfer, as one of his colleagues commented, does not incense easily.

The ongoing debate is described by outsiders as a "turf war," but it is not an arcane dialogue between academics, which either depressives or their families can dismiss as unimportant in the real world. Two pieces of information will help you and your depressive chart your way through the dispute over pills versus therapy versus both. The first of these is that the American Psychological Association is actively seeking, on behalf of its members, the medication privileges currently denied them because they lack a medical degree. One has to assume, therefore, that a majority of APA members favor a medical as well as a psychotherapeutic approach to depressive illness, no matter how loudly they inveigh against the "pill-pushing" psychiatrists. It seems that they would prefer to keep all treatment in-house than refer their patients to a practitioner with a medical degree.

The second piece of information regards the investment of time and money needed to achieve relief of depressive symptoms. Medications usually take from four to six weeks to work. Costs of medication therapy will depend on whether the diagnosis and subsequent prescription are provided by a general medical practitioner or by a psychiatric specialist, whose fee is usually much higher. Psychotherapy takes longer and costs more, but the costs of CBT and IPT are lower because they are short-term, goal-oriented therapies typically applied over a four-month period. By contrast, open-ended therapy like my own, conducted on a once-a-week basis for eighteen months at an hourly fee of one hundred dollars (far more would be charged today by most psychotherapists), would cost a total of $7,800. Small wonder that the cost-cutting managed-care businesses opt for pills over therapy, although some plans do cover short-term therapy. Check before you make a decision to embark.

Before going on to look at how family members and close friends of depressives in therapy view the therapeutic process, here is a brief list of what to consider when deciding for or against therapy:

1. About half of all depressions disappear in six to twelve months without medication or therapy, so if living with depression is tolerable, just waiting it out is an option. The guiding principle should be whether or not the illness is sufficiently impairing to cause problems at home or at work, bearing in mind that such negative consequences can't be helped by an after-the-fact pill.

2. If the depression has obviously come about as the result of a specific life event, therapy may prove beneficial to the healing process, but "reactive" depressions often gather force and become clinical depressions. If this happens, medication is needed. Again, the cue lies in the degree of impaired functioning.

3. Recurrent depression and manic depression should always be treated with medication. Talk therapy is a matter of choice, and is helpful if the illness has been around long enough to give rise to negative, harmful attitudes that need rethinking and correcting. It's a good idea to wait until medication takes hold before trying therapy, because some of these attitudes may remit.

4. Supportive and short-term therapy, as opposed to expressive and long-term therapy is a better choice for all depressive illness, although client and the therapist may decide to move on to gaining insight through expressive therapy. While insight may prove enlightening, it cannot cure depressive illness.

5. Time, money, goals, and one's health insurance are all factors to be considered.

When Your Depressive Comes Home from the Therapist's Office

Although you can make suggestions about your depressive's or manic-depressive's choice of therapy, once therapy gets going, you will not be privy to the process unless the depressive chooses to discuss it. Most do not. Therapy is a two-way street, but it is a private one reserved for the therapist and the client, not the client's family or partner. So what's in store for you when your depressive comes home after a stroll down that street with his or her therapist? Plenty of family members find themselves greeting a kinder, gentler person, but not all. Many come to see the therapist as an advocate for the depressive against the family, forming a sort of unholy alliance. An alliance has indeed been formed, but it is a natural and desirable one, according to the psychotherapists. As Dr. Fox points out, the therapist's responsibility as a supportive professional is always to help the patient, not the spouse, parent, child, or lover of the patient. Supportive therapy is about the here and now, not about what happened in the recesses of childhood. Therapist and client address current problems, and the information the therapist has at his disposal comes from the depressive client, not from those who live with him or her.

The first and most important thing you need to understand is that your depressive's view of the world, and of you, is not the same as your own. You are not depressed or manic. You are not seeking help to cope with what's going on; the depressive is. It is the depressive, not you, who has hired the therapist. The therapist works with the information provided by his patient, and adds to that his own clinical experience and point of view. His concern is for the patient, not for you. Usually the therapist doesn't want your input, even though you believe it to be important in order for the therapist to have a balanced view. But shouldn't the therapist want to hear that Dick or Jane is lying in bed all day, leaving it only to visit the therapist? Yes, but most won't allow you an opportunity to contribute such useful information. More's the pity, because reality counts and would indeed be helpful to the therapist. This is one source of the advocacy problem. Often family members feel that the therapist is not addressing with his client the behavioral issues that are causing stress within the family or the relationship; they want a say in the matter. They want to point out to the therapist that the depressive did this and said that, because they're convinced that when the therapist understands what's *really* going on, he will shape up and confront his patient with all this "bad stuff." Then everything will be okay and life can go back to normal. But it doesn't happen that way.

Going back to normal is not what therapy is designed to accomplish. It's designed to bring about change. So why, you may be asking yourself, can't the person just change back to what he or she was before the depression? As a depressive myself, I can testify that the experience of depression creates its own barrier to the past. Anyone who has been in those black, depressive holes passionately wishes to avoid revisiting them. While one may wish to return to one's normal self, that self has already been transformed in various ways. One may be back to normal, but normal now includes the memory of the depression and what it did to one's sense of self. The traces always remain. This is why many who live through prolonged depressive illness may eventually emerge from it with negative views that stick around long after the illness has been brought under control. Even without the accumulation of negative thinking habits, the depressive experience becomes part of life's experience, and life can never again be what it was before that experience.

Another point to understand is that many patients in therapy erroneously report what their therapist has said to them. Many who suffer from the illness could hire themselves out to the CIA as disinformation specialists. Some simply have poor memories and concentration and thus are confused; others dissimulate because it is human nature to present oneself in a good light, and so may pass on to those at home misleading reports of "what my therapist said." Never assume that your depressive is being absolutely straight with you about what the therapist has said, particularly when it relates to your being "wrong." "If the patient comes home and reports 'It's all your fault I'm feeling this way,'" says Dr. Fox, "then the patient is into some gross misreporting. And yes, of course, some do misreport and misrepresent the therapist's comments or advice."

Usually your only recourse is to hunker down and see how it all turns out, with two important exceptions. The first is that among the most outrageous liars are those manic-depressives in a high-flying up, who often announce that their therapist has advised them to stop taking their medication because they don't need it anymore. You should never accept this as truth, and a call to the doctor is in order here. The other pertains to those depressives who fail to communicate to the therapist their thoughts of suicide. In both of these cases your responsibility is to make the problem clear to the therapist. If the therapist doesn't want to talk to you about the patient, leave a forceful message stating that the medication is still in the pill bottle, not in the patient, or that he or she has been talking about suicide. Even more important, tell the medicating psychiatrist, who will be very interested in this information. Whenever the illness is serious, there is usually both a therapist and a medicating doctor involved. The two professionals should have a cooperative relationship, sharing information and opinions. Ask the psychiatrist to intervene on your behalf and communicate to the therapist your worries about medication and/or suicide. Such a situation transcends the usual hands-off policy when it comes to insinuating yourself between your depressive and the therapist.

Switching therapists is tricky, because the decision lies with the patient, not with you. You can state your case for doing so, but if your depressive is attached to the therapist, you won't have much luck and may rock a boat best left untroubled by your partisanship. Don't argue with your depressive about what the therapist has said, or what he or she claims was said. Since you weren't present you can't know, and your dissatisfaction or criticism of the therapist will place you firmly in the enemy camp. If you indicate that you lack confidence in the therapist, your depressive will make the contrast between the therapist, who is on his or her side, and you, now on the other. That position will complicate your relationship with the depressive, and it will also make you frustrated, angry, and even more miserable than previously.

This is what happened to Willy, whose depressive wife, Consuela, spends a large part of her life in an unrelieved down. Consuela's therapist is not a medical doctor; she is a psychologist who referred Consuela elsewhere for medication, but still sees her once a week for talk therapy. Willy, in our conversation about his life as a depressive's husband, plays two distinctly different roles, flipping back and forth from one to the other with overlaps. The first is that of the loving husband of twenty years, the last four of them colored by his wife's illness. About a year ago, says Willy, "Consuela did something about her mood swings. She went to a shrink. It was as if the shrink had discovered the newest disease, and so why not decide that my wife has it? Like it was a way to keep Consuela as her patient. It seems to me the shrink is catering to her illness. Consuela doesn't like me to talk about it as an illness, any more than she likes my referring to her pills as a 'cocktail.' There are a whole lot of things she doesn't like me to say now, but I understand that. Anyway, the shrink gave her the label 'depression,' and now she has the illness. Twenty-four hours a day. I've accepted that."

Sticking determinedly to his caring-husband role, he explains further: "She needs stroking and she needs structure, and she also needs support. I'm not a particularly romantic person, but I go to the movies, I understand the need for touching. For structure we have a big calendar where each of us writes in where we'll be every day, like Fridays I'm at the support group. If she says she wants to be alone, that's okay with me. I have a million things to keep me busy." Willy works hard at being a good husband; he calls Consuela several times a day, to remind her to watch a television program she enjoys or just to check in. Once a week they have a family meeting at which they try to settle any problems that have come up between them. But, he adds, sliding toward role number two, "recently I've become really put off in her presence. Cabin fever, you might call it. The weekends seem very long. We begin barking at each other. I can't imagine what it would be like not to be able to go to the office. There's a really uncomfortable climate at home. I've got to get my own life. Consuela agrees with me; she's really sympathetic to my point of view."

Then the facade slips further, fully revealing his alternate persona, that of the resentful and frustrated spouse facing an unholy alliance. "Consuela's shrink is a woman; she specializes in depression. I've had three sessions together with her and my wife. In all three sessions I've said to the shrink, 'What have you done to my wife? You've created this depression. You gave it to her. You put it in her mind.' The shrink says to me, 'Trust us; you'll know later what this is all about.' I mean, I'm not privy to what's going on. It's almost like my wife has run away with another woman, and the shrink keeps saying, 'Trust us.' It might be temporary, or it might be forever. How can I tell, if I don't even know what's going on?"

This is a classic example of a spouse in pain because the other has gone into therapy for his or her depression. Because the therapy is open-ended, no one other than Consuela and her psychotherapist will ever know whether goals were set and met, or whether insights were part of the goals. Indications are that some of the therapy is expressive in nature, but perhaps that is what Consuela needs. The point is, Willy doesn't know and he feels locked out and alienated.

This feeling of being locked out, of "them" (therapist and patient) against "me" (family member or close friend), causes a great deal of frustration and unhappiness among the latter. Some express it less overtly than Willy, preferring instead to remark ominously, "Oh, I know all about *that* problem." Others, however, are even more out-spoken, among them the son of a clinically depressed mother who underwent numerous hospitalizations over a twelve-year period, during which time she saw a long line of psychiatrists who treated her with both medication and psychotherapy.

> Every one of them was always pitting my mother against the family by telling her, "You have needs, too; you have to stand up to them," even though the family had been thrown into turmoil for twelve years by my mother's behavior. She lost her second husband this way, and she came very close to losing all her children, too. It's taken five years to reestablish any kind of rapport with her. I totally attribute all these problems to the psychiatrists. For them everything was black and white, with no middle ground at all, even though clearly that

was not the healthiest route to take. All this Freudian stuff was stupid and useless. I'm talking about more than one psychiatrist here. I had no good experiences with any of them. Each family member went in to see each new guy alone. All the shrinks ever said to me on my visits was, "Gee, Max, do you ever worry you'll get this illness, too, given that your mother and others in the family have it? We think you might." It was as though they were dealing with case studies. There was never an ounce of compassion. I can't speak strongly enough.

Practitioners do vary widely in personal style, point of view, and experience. There are many who are neither cuddly nor even sympathetic. Psychiatry and psychotherapy are like every other profession in that they produce some stars, some duds, and quite a lot of competent performers in between. But the duds, and among them I include those who present themselves as cold and remote, are potentially more dangerous than they would be if their chosen profession were, say, particle physics or writing novels. In the first place, they are tinkering with our heads, either biologically or psychologically. Second, neither profession is a science with exact rules and formulas. Psychiatrists and psychopharmacologists learn more every day about the brain's mechanism—how it can go wrong and what can be done to put it back on track—but doing so is still part experience and part guesswork, as much an art as a science. Psychotherapy, for all the years it has been in use, and for all the confidence many place in it, does not lend itself to precise measurement and prediction. Psychotherapeutic approaches to helping people have undergone changes, with attitudes and techniques once accepted as sound now abandoned as errors. New ones are sure to emerge.

Added to these problems is another: both use terms and jargon that are beyond the layperson's vocabulary, yet both speak with great authority. We are reluctant to challenge them, or even to question them, because they are the experts, yet we have granted them the right to meddle with our most precious commodity, our brain, with all its wondrous, mysterious powers to grant us joy and despair. When we encounter the duds who lead us in the wrong direction or who treat us like fodder for case studies, we simply don't know what to do, and we are at our most vulnerable. This vulnerability extends beyond the patient to the patient's spouse or lover, parent or child. In this respect we are all at risk together. So what are the answers, what are we to do? In the case of medicators, look for the very best, as described in the preceding chapter. Among psychotherapists, find one who is a good fit, someone who is supportive of the patient and who also understands that families feel locked out. The solution, once again, is to help your depressive collect information, to use that information to pose savvy questions and to press for answers, and to make choices and changes when necessary. Your own solution is to have patience and understand that neither the depressive nor the manic-depressive has asked for this illness. It has just descended upon them, and they want it to go away as much as you do.

How Two Psychotherapists See Their Job

Among psychotherapists from whom I sought more specific answers, two in particular had some jargon-free and interesting observations for family members. The first of these is Andrew Hearn, a psychiatric social worker who trained for two years in "object therapy," one of those four hundred varieties referred to by Dr. Kingsbury. Hearn is himself the offspring of a depressive mother whose long-term illness helped to create a dysfunctional family of two parents and eight siblings. He is also the product of nine years of unsuccessful insight-oriented therapy to deal with his homosexuality, followed by a supportive therapist whom he trusted and liked. When he and his wife eventually divorced, it was in part the result of having found that second therapist, who helped him understand that he was trying to be someone he wasn't and encouraged him to allow himself to be the person he was, not the person his parents, siblings, and wife preferred. His own experience adds a lot of heft to his observations about the advocacy issue, and he knows about depression as well from both his mother and his own once-suicidal downs.

Hearn works with about fifty patients, most of whom have some form or degree of depression, and only three of whom he has referred to psychiatrists for medication in addition to his therapy. "Therapy," says Hearn, "is good for them because in their rational moments they feel terribly isolated; my office is a safe place for them to talk. They are dealing with what they were like before they went down, and what their life is now. I measure my effectiveness according to the degree of understanding about themselves which I can lead them to, the realization that yes, there is somebody inside that illness, a person. I try to help them stop focusing just on the illness and start focusing on themselves. The therapist is like a good father." When asked about the advocacy issue, he replied that whenever one member of a couple is in therapy, for whatever reason, it causes dislocations in the partnership. The point of therapy, he believes, is change, and it is the therapist's responsibility to bring that about. He offered the example of a wife whose depression is the result of a persistently overbearing husband; she always feels ineffectual, trapped beneath his feet. "I would strongly encourage that woman to get a life of her own, to make of herself an individual. Maybe this is what had happened when your interviewee Willy felt the therapist was trying to take his wife away from him."

Hearn believes that when a patient is mildly depressed, the therapist can usually come up with a cause, as in the case of the downtrodden wife. He gave two other examples: First is the empty-nest syndrome, when children fly off to college or jobs and leave parents without the glue that may have been holding them together for years. Second is the birth of a first child, following which the mother may suffer from the "baby blues," and the father may feel alienated because he is no longer the sole center of his wife's attentions; she is now busy bonding with the baby instead of with him. "Any change in the pattern that people have set up to explain themselves to themselves can be disturbing," Hearn says. "Change is always a problem for someone, even when the change may be for the patient's betterment."

I asked Hearn why depressives are so often difficult, demanding, and fault-finding. Depressives," he explained, "externalize stuff. If they owned that stuff themselves, it might be overwhelming, too painful, so they lay it on another. They can't be self-reflective because it hurts too much, so they cut that circuit short and blame someone else." When I had posed the same query to Dr. Fox, he answered as the psychiatrist he is: "When we feel lousy and cranky and negative, all things the depressive is, we also feel nasty. You could say that misery loves company, so they are demanding and critical. Why? That's like asking why someone with a cold sneezes; he sneezes because he has a cold." Fox described a group of research psychiatrists who were probing the brains of anesthetized cats with tiny electrodes. "Sometimes they missed their target by a fraction of a millimeter and by mistake hit the amygdala, where irritability and aggression are controlled in the brain. They always knew when this had happened because the next morning when they opened the cages, the cats would leap out at them, snarling." These two differing views explain why psychiatrists and psychotherapists don't always think fondly of each other. They operate on different wavelengths.

Dr. Nyere Baxter, a practicing psychologist based in New York City, had to cut our interview short for an emergency patient before I could engage her on the nastiness issue, but she cast further light on advocacy, which, she says, is a "tricky problem for all concerned, including the psychotherapist." The therapist does indeed try to bond with the patient and to establish an alliance; if the therapist is unable to do that, she believes, not much of anything will be accomplished. But it may seem to the family as though the patient were pulling away, and as though there were a secret from which they have been excluded. "There is always a secret," says Dr. Baxter, "and the therapist needs to create a place where secrets are kept. Sometimes that secret is anger, and the depressive needs to express it, but first to the therapist and afterwards, perhaps, directly to the family." This interpretation of anger as a source of depression is common among psychotherapists and is one of the defining distinctions between them and psychiatrists.

When family members feel that the depressive is misrepresenting their viewpoint, or that the therapist is not adequately addressing problems caused by the depressive at home, they often want to be in on the process and have a joint session or sessions. Prefacing her remarks by noting that each therapist's approach is highly individualized, she explained that about two decades ago, the family approach to therapy was very much in vogue, but in her view it no longer is: "We've moved away from that because it is better to make patients their own advocate and to reach the family through them. This is a much more powerful position." There remains, however, a difference of opinion whether or not family should have some opportunity to express their views: "Some practitioners absolutely refuse to let the family make an input because they regard the therapeutic relationship as so valuable. Even though the family's input may be extremely important, you can't have the latter without messing up the former. Those therapists will often advocate that the family member and the depressive go together to see another therapist on the side, a family counselor, for instance." Dr. Baxter says she has used both approaches; the important thing is not to mix them up, because if you're going to give the depressive a place to say things unsaid elsewhere, you need to defend him or her. "You really need to make that clear," says Baxter, "in the sense that, for instance, a daughter doesn't feel her mother can come wandering into my office whenever she wants." It has to be carefully orchestrated and controlled.

Some depressives absolutely do not want their families involved; others start off the process by saying they do. Dr. Baxter, though not all therapists, sees this as a possible advantage and a clue to the relationship between the depressive and the family member. "You have to understand," she says, "that we therapists don't get to deal in persuasion. All we are allowed to do is offer and recommend. I have plenty of people who say, 'Please tell my manic-depressive husband to stop doing whatever he's doing to upset me,' but I can't do that." Families, she observes, can be very beseeching, "but we psychotherapists have parameters within which we have to work."

It is hard to disagree with the need for parameters. What your depressive must do, and you as well, if you are allowed some early input, is to establish what those parameters are before embarking on therapy. Here are some questions it would be wise to pose before making a choice of therapist:

- Do you practice expressive or supportive therapy? In other words, are you hoping to encourage insights into what sort of a person I am and why, or are you going to address my current issues and help me through this difficult period?

- Do you subscribe to, and are you trained in, a particular psychotherapeutic technique? What was your training, and where did you get it? Are you affiliated with any school of therapy, and if so, what is it? How does that therapy work, and what are its goals? How long have you been in practice?

- Do you practice short-term therapy, such as cognitive behavioral therapy or interpersonal therapy? If so, which do you think would be most helpful for me, and why? Why might one suit me better than the other? How long will my therapy take? Please make a guess, even if you cannot be exact.

- Have you had experience in treating depressives and manic-depressives? [This is an important question, since some therapists really prefer to deal with what you and I would call just plain neurotics.]

• What is your attitude toward the participation of family members? Are you entirely opposed, or do you allow their participation? If so, to what degree, under what circumstances?

• [If your depressive already has a psychiatrist:] Would you be willing to talk to my psychiatrist or psychopharmacologist, so that you'll both know everything you need to know about my depression?

• [If your depressive is not on medication, but suspects that might be a good idea, either now or eventually:] What is your attitude toward medication for depression/manic-depression? Are you in favor of it sometimes, always, or never? Why? Have you a medical doctor to whom you refer patients you believe would benefit from antidepressants? What hospital is he affiliated with?

• What are your fees, and what portion are reimbursed by Medicare or Medicaid? What health plans, if any, are you associated with?

The information in this chapter, and the comments and opinions offered by the experts, are provided to help you come to a conclusion. In the end, whatever conclusion you reach will be a matter of personal choice, but now that choice will be an informed one, rather than a haphazard shot in the dark.

8

NEGATIVES AND POSITIVES:
LOSING AND REGAINING
SELF-ESTEEM

THE MORE STORIES I HEAR about depression fallout, the more I am struck by their similarities. This is arresting because I'm receiving my information and anecdotes from a remarkably diverse group of people who are living with an equally diverse group of human beings. They have in common only their bond of intimacy with a depressive or a manic-depressive. Although the first people I spoke with included members of the friends and family group, my long-term acquaintances, and people I met at cocktail and dinner parties and all manner of gatherings, the web has expanded to include a population which reaches far beyond my own immediate milieu. Some conversations have been the result of casual encounters—two, for instance, took place at restaurants, and one with a handyman who came to unstop my sink. One was the result of a casual telephone conversation: When I said I was writing a book and couldn't deal with interruptions, a fund-raiser who phoned me from PBS revealed that his father was a depressive and caused his mother much misery. But, despite all their differences, their complaints about the depressive or manic other fit neatly into pigeonholes. When a storyteller leaves one of these pigeonholes empty, a pointed question from me first provokes a surprised, "How did you know?" Then comes the answer.

When I first began my research, I had a complicated filing system to organize the various aspects of depressive or manic behavior as seen through the eyes of depression fallout sufferers. As I filed away, I noted that a lot of little behaviors were pieces of larger patterns. The clue to the existence of these patterns was that when different people in different situations talked about how they felt, they all prefaced or concluded their remarks with the same phrases. The three that echoed through everyone's story were "Nothing I do is right"; "Nothing I do is enough"; and "Everything is always my fault." These pigeonholes were soon stuffed to overflowing. Other patterns also emerged, including the one peculiar to spouses and lovers, of threats of divorce or separation (discussed in chapter 10). But the three that burst their pigeonholes are the ones that produce feelings of exhaustion, frustration, resentment, and futility in all my storytellers as they reiterate their plaintive themes. These are the feelings responsible for stages three and four of depression fallout—demoralization, resentment, and anger.

I found myself wondering, Where do these patterns originate? Other questions followed: What's going on in the brain of the person with the illness to produce identical responses from all the onlookers? Why does everyone with the illness see everyone else's efforts as inadequate and faulty? Why can't depressives take a look at themselves and mend their ways of dealing with others? Why can't they be depressed without making us feel lousy, too?

The most comprehensive and understandable answer I have received to these questions comes from Dr. Donald F. Klein of Columbia University and the New York State Psychiatric Institute. The outstanding thing about disease, says Klein, is that it simplifies you. You can't be the same person with the remarkable range of flexible adaptations, emotional reactions, and intelligent perceptions when you are hit on the head by a major disability, especially a major disability that affects your ability to see, think, and react. It is the predictability of diseases, says Klein, that convinces us that they actually exist. We knew about measles long before we knew about viruses because there is a predictable set of symptoms and a course to the illness. The same goes for depression and manic depression. The negative patterns explored in this chapter manifest themselves in the hefty majority of those with depressive illness because they are symptomatic of mood disorders, and mood disorders simplify the feelings and resultant behavior of those who have them.

Negatives: When the Pleasure Feedback Loop Shuts Down

These days, just about everyone who reads or watches television has been exposed to the idea that depression is not just a bad attitude, or laziness, or self-indulgence. Most of us accept it as a biological illness that selects its victims, not the reverse. Such terms as *malfunctioning neurotransmitters* and words like *serotonin* are working their way into our daily vocabulary. We receive all the correct information about depression, but when it appears in our own backyard, we give that information no more than lip service. The facts convince our intellect, but may not work their way into our emotions. When your depressive criticizes you, you are not going to stop and explain to yourself that his or her neurotransmitters are in trouble. If your manic-depressive is in a high state of mania, maxing out credit cards and coming up with wild schemes, you most likely don't stop to tell yourself that this is inappropriate elation brought on by bad brain chemistry, or inappropriate irritability.

To me, Klein's way of looking at what is going on is far more relevant and useful, because it maps the depressive mind on an emotional level—the level on which we operate every day. Instead of thinking *brain chemistry*, he suggests, think *pleasure response*. Our pleasure response is what motivates our passage through life. It gets us out of bed in the morning, propels us through the day, sends us in pursuit of food, pushes us into sex and marriage, and into bed when the day is done, full of the anticipation of a restorative night of sound sleep. In the most basic sense, he says, our pleasure response causes us to survive and reproduce. All depressive illness involves alterations in the pleasure response. Unfortunately, these alterations are for the worse, not the better.

Klein separates our pleasure response into two parts, the *appetitive* pleasures and the *consummatory* pleasures, and uses two of the human race's most basic survival activities—food and sex—as metaphors to explain his thesis. Appetitive pleasures are the pleasures of the hunt for food and of sexual foreplay. The appetitive part of the pleasure system makes us feel good about both the anticipation and the pursuit of consummatory pleasures, which are those of the feast that follows the hunt and the orgasm that follows the foreplay.

But the former are much more than a prelude to the latter. Appetitive pleasures can be their own reward, enjoyable in and of themselves. A good example is sports: we engage in them not just to win, but for the sheer pleasure we experience in a game of tennis or soccer, or when we go jogging or walking through a gorgeous patch of countryside. Although we may think to ourselves, "Do this because a wonderful thing will happen as a result of our effort," our pleasure system runs more on feelings than on thoughts.

When both parts of the system are functioning well, they form a healthy feedback loop, interrupted only by an interlude of what Klein defines as *satiation*. Satiation is the post-consummation pause, the feeling of being deliciously full, happily satisfied. Klein sums this up by saying, "So, first comes anticipation of consummatory pleasure, which is immediately accompanied by appetitive pleasure, which is followed by zestful pursuit, which leads to consummatory actions with their associated intense pleasures, resulting in satiated relaxation." We do not "think" our way through this process; we experience it, using our feelings as antennae. When the sequence is completed, we loop back and start it up all over again, because satiation is a temporary phenomenon. It is as though we have been stoking the furnace and have taken a rest. When the furnace runs out, it's time to get more fuel, so we start the cycle all over again. This is the normal pleasure process, unless or until depression arrives to switch off all or part of the mechanism.

Typical depressives lose both kinds of pleasure; their entire system shuts down. As an undepressed person, you wake up in the morning and begin to think about all the activities in the coming day. You have a meeting scheduled, clients to see, a report to write, a dentist's appointment, perhaps some errands to run or a child's school play to attend, a television program you want to see, phone calls to make, friends coming to dinner, bills to pay, and so forth. Some of your commitments you look forward to with enthusiasm. Others, such as paying bills and having your teeth filled, are less appealing, but you know in advance how glad you will be to have them behind you, filed away in the *Done* box. You can anticipate the satisfaction of accomplishment. Your eye is on the payoff.

Not so the depressive. He or she wakes up and contemplates the same schedule, but it all looms as one unending, costly, and painful session at the dentist's.

Nothing but Negatives: Depressives

Depressives behave as though they anticipate bad outcomes. They do indeed anticipate bad outcomes, but that is because when they try to anticipate good ones, they don't feel anything at all. Put a juicy steak in front of a depressive, and he will dutifully chomp away because he knows juicy steaks are supposed to be tasty, but when he takes a bite, it tastes like cardboard. He tried; nothing happened. Unable to expect good to come from their efforts, depressives grimly gird themselves up to grinding their way through the day. They have lost the ability to assume in advance that their efforts will be productive and appreciated; they experience them as wasted, unsuccessful, misinterpreted, and ignored. Everything is the same old pointless stuff, and so they don't want to engage in it. They have no interest in working toward achievement, because they cannot feel the pleasure of anticipating achievement.

Depressives experience life as set up to disappoint them, and so it does, time and time again. You are part of the depressive's life. No matter how diligently you try to disabuse depressives of their negative convictions, you will fail because their minds have been made up for them by their depression. They really cannot feel good, so nothing you do is right. Nothing you do is enough. Thus the fault is yours, not theirs. A depressive spouse does not go through the appetitive business of preparing dinner because she has lost interest in consuming food and cannot anticipate that you will be grateful for her effort. She may "think" you will be pleased, but she cannot "feel" you will be. A depressed child doesn't want to play in a baseball game because she can't imagine winning, or even having fun trying to win. A depressed friend declines an invitation because he "knows" he isn't going to have a good time and that you are only asking him because you are sorry for him. He cannot imagine you really want to see him. Nothing matters, nothing has value, nothing provokes appetitive pleasure, so why go after the consummatory ones? Not only does steak taste like cardboard; sex is an unsatisfactory spasm. For depressives, there's never a good payoff in sight, only another boring, meaningless, or discouraging effort. One dreary step follows another, whatever path they take, so they stop trying. Pleasure is no longer a part of their lives. This explains why "lack of pleasure in previously enjoyed activities" is a preponderant symptom of depression.

The other principal symptom of depression usually cited is "persistent feelings of sadness," but this is really a bit of inaccurate shorthand. Everyone has felt sad at times, so using the word *sadness* makes sense to a non-depressive, while "being in a feelingless void" may not. Non-depressed people cry for a reason; depressives, as personified by Constance in her depressive's diary (see chapter 4), have no idea why they are crying. If you ask them why, they cannot explain. The most deeply depressed can't cry at all; coming out of their depression, they are often relieved to recover their ability to do so.

Negative Appetite, Positive Consummation: Atypical Depressives

Atypical depressives, who make up about 40 percent of all depressives, get to keep half of the loaf, the consummatory half. While they have lost their ability to look ahead and see good things coming down the pike (no appetitive pleasures), if and when a good thing falls into their lap, they enjoy (consume) it as thoroughly as an undepressed person. If you manage to entice, cajole, or shove an atypical depressive into a pleasurable situation, whether it be sex, a good meal, a game, or a movie, once in place to consume, he or she will have a good time. When the consummation activity comes to a close, they cannot imagine it might happen again. While there may be a memory for the pleasure, it has become a useless memory. They can verbalize it, but now once again they feel terrible, and so have no desire for a repeat performance. The next time you will have to cajole all over again, because they are back in that pleasureless void, the same void inhabited all the time by typical depressives.

If your depressive enjoys the payoff but can never see it coming, you should tell the diagnosing and prescribing physician. Given that something close to 50 percent of doctors fail to recognize depression even when it is present, it is not surprising that even fewer can discern the difference between typical and atypical depressions. The distinction is a critical one, because atypicals do not respond to the same antidepressants as typicals do. Insufficiently knowledgeable practitioners will prescribe for them the same antidepressant they give to everyone, probably Elavil (a tricyclic antidepressant) or one of the newer drugs such as Prozac, Zoloft, or Paxil (all SSRIs, or selective serotonin reuptake inhibitors). Neither will work nearly as well as an MAOI (monoanime oxidase inhibitor) antidepressant. If the doctor makes this error, the depressive will go on being depressed and your life will continue to be a misery, too, no matter how many months on medication go by. If the physician fails to ask the right questions of your depressive, you need to discuss the matter with him or her yourself to ascertain whether they hold on to the consummatory part of the pleasure system even though the hunting pleasures are gone. If the answer seems to be yes, then you both need to present your evidence for a change in antidepressant medicine to the doctor. If the depressive tries to do this without your help, he or she may never get around to it, discouraged by the very thought of trying.

When Positives Lead to Negatives: Manic-Depressives

Manic-depressives, when they are down, have the same dead-on-arrival pleasure system as any typical depressive, but when they are in an up phase, that system works overtime. "The manic," explains Dr. Klein, "is extraordinarily energetic, expansive, searching, and hunting. Everything looks terrific to him, everything is going to work well. He's going to go and do it and it's going to be wonderful." The manic pursues everything, and in everything sees a bang-up payoff coming. Judgment goes out the window because manics don't reason; they have no insight into the consequences of their behavior. They are a law unto themselves.

"Manics," says Klein, "don't feel any anticipation of loss or danger, so the feeling premises which influence our thinking, yours and mine, are absent. When we anticipate danger, for instance, we feel badly in an anxious way, and our thoughts revolve around how to escape from or overcome the danger. Since the manics don't feel it, there's no reason for their thoughts to circle in that fashion." They won't change strategies when a plan doesn't pan out, because next time the plan will work. If what they are doing fails, it's certainly not their fault—they are always right—so, QED, the fault lies with something or someone else, usually you.

For manics there is no such thing as satiation. Nothing is ever enough. Like cocaine users, a significant number of whom are mild or severe manics, they just go on and on until there is nothing left— no relationship, no money, no job, no anything. Their out-of-control pleasure system follows an upward curve, with no satiated pause. There is nothing to let them know that enough is enough. This is one reason why manics are so prone to alcohol and drugs; their brakes are gone.

The runaway pleasure system of manics makes them feel great, powerful, and invincible, so how can they possibly believe that you are right and they are wrong? Hold on to your courage, and wait for the changeover into depression. At that point a good doctor and a little luck will bring your manic back to reality. If, on the other hand, your manic has already visited the upper reaches at least once, there are ways you can apply the brakes when another episode is in the offing, as you will read in chapter 9.

How Their Negatives and Your Negatives Lead to Depression Fallout

Your depressive's broken pleasure system directly affects how he or she treats you, and thus influences your own emotional state. The following chart illustrates this chain of events.

Your Depressive's Symptom:	*Your Intervention:*	*Your Depressive's Response:*
Sad, anxious, and empty	What's the matter? Have I done something to upset you?	Nothing you could fix. Can't you see I'm thinking? I wish you'd leave me alone.
Experiences no pleasure	It's a beautiful day. Why don't we go for a walk and take a picnic? Let's ask the Browns to have dinner. That will cheer you up.	What makes you think I'd want to do that? You know I can't stand the Browns. Why can't you get anything right?

Your Depressive's Symptom:	Your Intervention:	Your Depressive's Response:
Has no energy and feels slowed down	You really should get some fresh air and exercise. Why don't we go skiing next weekend?	I spend all day trying to pay the mortgage. Isn't that enough exercise for you? Anyway, it won't snow and it's too expensive and you'll pick the wrong hotel, as usual.
Has sleeping and eating problems	I bought/made the veal you love. Let's have an early dinner and finish our wine in bed.	The last time you bought/made it, the stew was dry. There's a program on TV I'd rather see. Just give me the bottle now. I'll come up when I feel like it.
Lacks concentration and memory; can't make decisions	Did you fill out those insurance forms I gave you? They're due in two days, and you have to make some decisions before I can turn them in.	You never told me about any forms. Why do you leave everything for the last minute? Why do I always have to make all the decisions? I'll get to it when I have time.
Feels hopeless and worthless and guilty about it	I know you're depressed and I'm trying to help, but all you do is bark at me and criticize.	I just can't cope with your nagging. You make everything worse. I suppose now it's *my* fault you're unhappy. Why are you blaming *me*? What am *I* supposed to do?

Acts irritable and prone to weepiness and crying	Now what's the matter?	All of the above, plus now you've made me cry. I just can't stand it any-more.

While one part of the depressive's brain is producing all these negative responses, another part is trying to apply the brakes and say what he or she really feels: I am so lost, I feel so awful, please help me. But the brake rarely works, and so you get run over. No wonder depression fallout sufferers are always asking themselves, Why is nothing I do right? Why is nothing I do enough? Why is everything always my fault?

Since the depressive is imbued with pessimism, one might expect the manic's uncontrolled optimism to produce a different set of responses in you, but it doesn't. The depressive sees nothing but obstacles, and refuses to be encouraged by anything you say or do; the manic sees no obstacles at all, yet finds your efforts to question or discourage him equally baffling, tedious, unimaginative, or enraging. Both view you and your reactions as illogical and pointless, so they end up attacking you with the same accusations: Why do you always say or do the same old thing? Why do you never listen to anything I say? Why can't you understand me?

The Pleasure Response in Depression Fallout

Klein's pleasure response theory clarifies not only the depressive's or manic's feelings and reactions, but yours as well. Their faulty system short-circuits yours. This is exactly what occurred between me and my mother. My story of depression fallout began with my realization that nothing I ever did was good enough to please my mother—not my grades, not my accomplishments, not the boys I went out with, nothing. It wasn't that any single criticism of a good school grade ("Why didn't you do better?"), the results of my dieting efforts ("That dress looks too tight on you"), my invitation to her to have dinner ("Why do you always ask me at the last minute?"), a new boyfriend ("He's not as attractive as the last one"), or a job promotion ("It sounds like what you've been doing all along"), was in itself a fatal blow to my sense of self; it was the relentlessness of my mother's negative stance that eventually did me in. I never entirely gave up trying, but I stopped trying for her. When I reached adulthood, I cut her out of the loop. Instead of trying to please her, I tried to please myself, with spotty success. I found myself endlessly lacking and was always suspicious of my achievements.

Your depressive may be short-circuiting your pleasure system in the same way. You set off on the hunt, full of the anticipation that you're going to please or help them, to jolly or reason them out of the negative mood. When you're not successful, you pull back, regroup, and try to achieve the same goal with a different tactic. That doesn't work, either, so you start all over again until you give up in frustrated irritation. You love them and you want to help and to please them, but everything backfires. They don't even appear to welcome or appreciate your efforts.

Klein suggests an explanation. Everyone's pleasure system, he says, has a central comparator, a sort of internal judgment-maker who evaluates the success of the appetitive part of the system that gets us in place for consummation of our goal. When your judgment-maker signals you that things are going well, then you have a positive feedback loop with a crescendo of good feeling, activity, and expansiveness as you get close to your goal. Conversely, if you're in a failing situation, your pursuit activity isn't working. This, too, gets evaluated and inhibits your appetitive pleasure center. The result is feelings of demoralization, fatigue, boredom, and hopelessness, causing you to hunker down and wait for better times. In other words, your pleasure system puts itself on hold when the loop fails to work properly.

This is why depression fallout is so akin to depression, producing many of the same feelings of hopelessness, helplessness, and irritability. But similar is not "the same as"; there is nothing wrong with your brain chemistry, nor is there anything intrinsically wrong with your pleasure mechanism; it's just behaving like a smart appliance plugged into the inappropriate current source. You keep changing the fuse, but the fuse keeps blowing. Every time you set yourself up to win, you come up against the other's gloom, belittlement, and angry face. Eventually your pleasure loop decides to stop working.

You decide that there's no point in trying because there's never a satisfactory payoff. Eventually you lose hope and become totally demoralized. Although you feel bad, you feel that way for a good reason, not because you have a depressive illness. Your internal judgment-maker is serving you well. It wants you to conserve your efforts for something that's going to work, that has a nice payoff, and will let you rest on your laurels for a bit and enjoy yourself. Your judge is giving you good advice.

How a Broken Pleasure Response Acts in Real Life

Most depression fallout stories lack drama; rather, they approximate melodrama of the soap-opera variety, full of I-said-he-said/I-did-she-did details that don't seem to add up to much of anything, which is why nobody but you and the friends and family group is interested in listening to them. Yet cumulatively all that trivia has a weighty impact. It's that impact which may tell you to stop running after your depressive's or manic-depressive's approbation and appreciation, that there's no point to it, no payoff, an assessment they share. And it's the impact that eventually may cause your pleasure system to shut down.

My own experience with my mother, matched by that of many other depression fallout sufferers, has led me to the conviction that it is almost impossible to please or satisfy anyone who has a depressive illness. We will practically always disappoint them, and they will recurrently disappoint us until they get well. We will always see this as their fault; they will always see it as ours. Just as we cannot apply the brakes to the manic's pleasure system, we cannot activate the depressive's by urging him or her on to anticipate and enjoy. A short story from the friends and family group illustrates this point.

Jeff is a sportswear buyer for a department store chain and spends his days in a hectic round of showings and buyers' conferences, coping with delivery problems and a shopping public that prefers sale merchandise. Although free time is for him a rare luxury, he acceded to his seventy-year-old father's request that he arrange for and supervise needed repairs to the father's apartment. Jeff made countless phone calls to workmen, solicited and evaluated bids, put everything in motion, checked in at his father's every morning on his way to work, and usually did the same on his way home. He kept on top of everything, and everything proceeded as expected, but his father never stopped complaining about the plumber's rudeness, the electrician's lateness, and his son's supervisory skills. At the end of five weeks, when the work was approaching completion, the father began telling Jeff that what had been done was not what he had expected or wanted.

Jeff's report to the group droned on for almost fifteen minutes and was heavily loaded with he-said-I-said/he-did-I-did dialogue. We were probably the only audience in the world willing to sit through his whole dispiriting recounting of events. "I said that I had arranged to have everything done that he wanted done. We went over everything in detail before it began. I should have had a tape recorder going. I could have played it back and shown him he was totally wrong. He said I hadn't listened to him, that I never listened to him. I said I had listened very carefully and that he had just changed his mind. I couldn't believe it. He made no sense at all. He never thanked me, not once. He absolutely never realized what all that did to my schedule." And so forth. Winding down at last, he reached into the three big pigeonholes. "No matter what I do for him, it's never right, never enough. Something is always wrong, and whatever it is, it's my fault. I don't know why I bother."

Jeff will continue to bother because he loves his father and wants to do what he can to demonstrate this to his recalcitrant depressed parent. But since that initial tedious tale, there have been others, all dead ringers for the first. Recently Jeff took his father to a movie his dad had said he wanted to see. "Oh, how nice," said a first-timer to the group that evening. "Did he enjoy himself?" Before Jeff could elaborate, an old hand interrupted him. "Of course not. We all know he didn't like it, and we all know he said you should have realized in advance he wouldn't. It was your fault he didn't like it, right?" Almost anybody in the room who had been coming to the group for more than a month or so could have uttered the same comment.

At this point the group took over and told Jeff that he had two alternatives. The first was to not make an effort on his father's behalf, and to feel mean and guilty. The second was to make the effort, even knowing in advance that it might not succeed in pleasing his father, because not making an effort would only produce alternative negatives ("If you cared about me, you'd spend more time with me").

Doing something positive would at least make Jeff feel he had sent the right signal to his father, the equivalent of saying "I'm here, I want to help, I love you," and at the same time provide some appetitive pleasure for himself.

The ultimate solution, the one that will really make a difference in both Jeff's and his father's life, is to persuade his father to take his prescribed antidepressant despite the temporary side effects that have in previous attempts caused him sufficient discomfort to toss out the pills. In the meantime, suggested the group, Jeff should continue to demonstrate his affection for his father in ways that would cause him less frustration, such as through small presents—a book, perhaps, or his father's favorite cookies, or an unexpected bunch of flowers—reminiscences of times spent having fun together in the past (without drawing comparisons), and more frequent phone calls to show his father he was thinking about him. Even if none of the above results in straightforward pleasure on the part of his father, Jeff will feel better and less guilty, and his father, in his own fashion, will appreciate and be reassured by the efforts of his son.

Depressives, and manic-depressives too, when they hit a down, are terrified of being abandoned by those they love and rely on—a topic covered more fully in chapter 9. For the moment, keep this fact in mind when you feel like giving up on your depressive. Yes, it's true that for now they may view you as incapable of doing anything right, and as responsible for their inability to enjoy themselves. You will never persuade them, by reason or by demonstration, that the fault is theirs, not yours, because their broken feedback loop won't allow them to. Only antidepressants, sometimes with the assistance of a good therapist, will.

Sticky-Flypaper Depressives

Most depression fallout sufferers who step forward with complaints live with the it's-your-fault brand of depressive, because those are the ones who make life exceedingly tedious and difficult for everyone within range. But there is another brand: the sticky-flypaper depressive. These leap to place themselves at the bottom of every totem pole and every pecking order. Neither aggressive nor mean, they gather unto themselves responsibility for everything that has ever gone wrong, including, as one psychiatrist noted, the bad Broadway season of 1947. While the it's-your-faults are self-righteous and enraging, the sticky-flypapers are self-critical and at times absurdly self-reproachful, and their constant crushed assertions of guilt can be maddening. While you cannot assuage their gloom, doom, and guilt, which are built in by the depression, you can and must constantly reassure them that you love them, that you are on and by their side, and that you will remain there.

The difficulty is that you would like to take them by the shoulders, shake them, and shout, "Shape up, for heaven's sake! Be a person, stop saying you're sorry!" Should this urge come upon you, resist it. Extravagant self-blame is corrosive. What starts as "Excuse me, it was all my fault" can sometimes cycle down into "Excuse me for living." Depressives who see themselves as abject failures and as burdens to others, even when they have achieved demonstrable success in their personal and professional lives, lose hope. Loss of hope in oneself and one's future can lead to suicide.

If you tell a flypaper, or indeed any depressive, that he or she is wrong, and that they have everything to live for, your words will be heard not as encouragement but as yet another put-down. The internal din of their depression drowns out your arguments and refutations, and they are left with only their own dismal sense of immutable failure and inability to cope. Such phrases as "Life is not worth living," "You'd be better off without me, I'm just a burden to everyone," and "There's no point, no purpose to living" can all be accurate reflections of a depressed person's state of mind, one on which they may decide to act.

The tack to take here is to tell your depressive you are sorry things look so black, that their feelings stem from their illness, and that better times are coming. This approach affords the depressive some hope of eventual relief, and hope is what your depressive needs. Hope does not spring eternal in the breast of people suffering from depression. Your patience and steady reassurance that hope will spring again is, together with antidepressants, their best medicine.

But how are you to follow all this sound advice when you are cross, resentful, and feeling fragile? Indeed, how are you to do anything positive when your depressive or manic-depressive keeps telling you that you're always wrong, that you never do anything right, that everything is your fault? In this state, demoralization threatens to drown your self-esteem. When it does, you lose all possibility of positive change either in your own life or the depressive's. Rescuing your self-esteem is an indispensable prelude to a positive outcome, and the best way to repair your broken pleasure loop. Self-esteem is the critical connection between the negatives and the positives. There are, fortunately, ways to restore it to health, but first you have to learn how and why you lost it.

Positives

Loss of self-esteem is a prevailing problem for every traveler along the depression fallout continuum. My dictionary defines self-esteem as "an objective respect for or favorable impression of oneself," but I would quarrel with that definition. Objectivity is exactly what's lacking in assessing our self-worth, and never more so than when we live with someone who is depressed. Far from considering the situation rationally from a distance, we approach it, often in the middle of the night, from an entirely subjective viewpoint. If you are among those who have never added up their pluses and minuses at two in the morning, and failed to find the pluses, skip to the next chapter. Otherwise, welcome to the club, and read on.

Low self-esteem is as much a symptom of depression fallout as of the illness itself, but although the net result is identical, the source is entirely different. The depressive's self-esteem is stolen by the illness; that of the depression fallout sufferer dwindles because of interactions with the other's depression. The depressive's will return when the illness is competently treated by a professional; the future of yours lies in your own hands.

Loss of self-esteem among depression fallout sufferers is virtually inevitable, and is not a sign of personal weakness. Its cause does not lie with you, but with the depressive and how he or she has behaved toward you. Once you have correctly assigned the blame for your loss of self-esteem, you've taken an important first step toward rebuilding it.

As you now know, interactions with depressives range from difficult to unbearable. When you offer love and affection, they are not returned. When you offer sympathy, you are told you don't understand what is wrong. When you offer support, you receive complaints that it is not enough, or not the right kind. Those who remind us of the depressive's need for sympathy, support, and love are correct, but they leave out the other half of the equation: it is hard to give all those things when you're not receiving them.

In any adult relationship we come to expect some balance in our dealings with the other, of giving and receiving in more or less equal measure. Living close to someone else's depression throws the balance out of whack and causes us distress. Trying hard to keep up our end of the implicit bargain, we grow increasingly aware that our partner is no longer doing business with us. Soon we feel not only bad, but bad about ourselves. All human beings require positive reinforcement. A psychic diet lacking in affection and kindness, in little compliments and favors, in all the normal exchanges of intimate coexistence, will result in an undernourished ego. The depressive already possesses such an ego. One depleted ego in any relationship is already one too many; two is a recipe for pain and trouble.

What makes proximity to someone else's depressive illness so perilous to your self-esteem is that at first you can't see why your ego should be affected by the other's problem. It's the depressive who is the insecure pessimist, not you. Since you don't see your own psyche as an issue, you do nothing to shelter it from the coming storm. By the time you realize you need an umbrella, your self-esteem is drenched and consumptive. Hearing the story of someone else's rained-upon ego may allow you to view the process objectively and thus to understand better what may be happening to yours.

How One Depression Fallout Sufferer Lost Her Self-esteem

Diana and Roger, both in their early thirties, fell in love as soon as they met. Marriage was a topic from the start, with Roger pushing for it, Diana holding back. "We had so much in common, so much fun together, so many things to talk about, but I was always aware of some little connection between us that wasn't being made. I figured it would come eventually." Like most in the throes of powerful attraction and growing love, however, Diana focused on the positive aspects of their relationship, not on the one small nagging doubt in the back of her mind.

Diana and I were talking because the week before she had turned up at the group and sat mute and miserable until the final minutes when Howard, the group facilitator, had asked her what was going on in her life. She had started off bravely enough, telling us her boyfriend was a depressive, that they had recently separated after more than two years together, and that she was there to try to understand what had been the matter. Twenty sympathetic faces were her undoing. From behind a wad of Kleenex, she skipped the details and muttered something indistinct about it always being her fault. "Oh, we know all about that," chorused the parents of a manic-depressive daughter. Everyone else nodded in confirmation. Diana produced a small smile and looked relieved, but the hour was late and she chose silence as an alternative to tearful talk. As we were leaving, I asked if she would come and talk with me about her relationship with Roger, offering both Kleenex and a glass of wine. Without hesitation she accepted, and added "Please," as though I were doing her a favor.

Some who have depression fallout stories to tell launch into the heart of the matter the first time around, but a far larger number, Diana among them, unpeel their tales like an onion, gradually revealing more and more about the source of their distress. Loyalty to someone much loved puts a brake on the tongue. Diana began with the statement, "I'm as much in love with Roger now as I always was. I walked out six months ago and nothing's gotten better since then." I believed her, but I still didn't know much about why she had left. She had spent a lot of time telling me about Roger's intelligence, his wonderful job, how much they had in common, and how much she missed him. Although she had provided a few examples of "what Roger always does," they seemed minor annoyances compared to the strength of her leftover love.

One such incident turned upon an evening she had spent with another woman, a friend of long standing. "Roger told me to have a good time, that he'd miss me. He asked me to call him when I got home, said all the usual nice things. But when I phoned him at eleven to tell him good night, he was mean and sullen. He kept saying I didn't love him, wasn't committed to him. He said going out with another woman proved I had a singles mentality and that I didn't want to get married." Diana did what most of us would do in similarly bizarre circumstances: She told Roger how much she loved him, that she never would have gone out with her friend had she known it would upset him, and other reassuring pronouncements of affection and attachment. Thus far her rendition of her depression fallout tale was sufficiently dispassionate to dispense with the Kleenex and all but a sip of the wine. Not so the second and third times around.

The next unpeeling opened with a clarifying statement: "Roger operates behind a facade of assurance. When he's in his office and with his friends, he gives the impression he knows just what he's doing, that he has no doubts about himself. When we're alone, he's full of them. None have any basis in fact. He's writing his own internal fiction." Diana contradicted him and tried to rewrite his negative self-assessment. "I wasn't giving Roger empty compliments. He is smart, he is capable. I was telling him the truth, but I couldn't make him believe me." Forging on, Diana shifted the blame onto herself. "I was throwing all this supportive good stuff in his direction, but it wasn't sticking to him. It was as though he was Teflon-coated. I saw that as the missing connection, and thought it was my fault I couldn't reach him. I figured I was doing something wrong."

I asked Diana if she and Roger had ever talked about his depression. It seems that not long after they'd met, he had told her that toward the end of his senior year at college he had experienced something akin to a nervous breakdown. Too many final exams to take and papers to complete, too much pressure and too much fear of failure, had resulted in his delaying his graduation until the following year. "He said it got to him and he ended up in a total funk." Since that time, almost ten years ago, Roger has faithfully taken an antidepressant each day and, off and on, backed it up with talk therapy. Perhaps the dose is lower than it should be; perhaps it's not the right medication for Roger; perhaps he has ingrained thought patterns that the therapist has failed to alter; perhaps all three are true to some degree. Whatever the case, his depression is in imperfect control and still powerful enough to quench his sense of self-worth and, by proximity, Diana's as well.

By now both Kleenex and wine were in active play. This layer turned on an evening when they had dined with a friend of Roger's. During the course of the meal, Diana had been outspoken in her reaction to something the friend had said. When she worried later that she had been too blunt, Roger assured her that she had been right to speak out, that her criticism had not been unduly harsh, and that in any event it wasn't at all important. Yet some months later Roger had a serious falling-out with his friend and assigned blame for the broken friendship to Diana, although he and his friend had seen each other often in the interim. "I absolutely knew the whole thing had nothing to do with me, but still this tiny voice kept telling me that Roger was right, that I was somehow to blame. He is extremely intelligent. I think I am too, but his intelligence has this tremendous force behind it. Even when I knew he was way off base, that force pushed me toward his reality and away from mine. When you're in the habit of loving and trusting someone, you believe him."

The real issue was neither his intelligence nor hers, but Roger's "it." Having drowned Roger's sense of self-worth in a torrent of doubt, the "it" began to rain on Diana. She cataloged for me the endless daily showers. It was Diana's fault if Roger gained weight; she had cooked pasta instead of steak. But he had asked for pasta. It was her fault if Roger was short of money; she liked going out too much. But he had proposed a restaurant, not she. It was Diana's fault if a weekend away together wasn't perfect; she had not planned it well. But she had planned what he wanted. "Everything was always my fault, in little ways as well as big. Every discussion, every argument we had, eventually turned on the fact that I was the cause, that something I had said or done, or failed to do or say, was bad or wrong or inadequate. I came to believe him." Here was another major misstep. First Diana had assumed blame for Roger's doubts about himself because she could not dispel them. Then she began to accept blame for what was an increasingly troubled relationship, and tried desperately—and futilely—to make everything better.

"I was being gaslighted," she told me, and went on to explain. The reference is to the classic movie *Gaslight,* in which a turn-of-the-century husband sets about deliberately driving his wife insane. Having tinkered with the gaslights, he tells his wife who notices them flickering that she is mistaken, that the lights are steady and strong. Eventually the wife believes he is right and that she has lost her mind. Roger would claim Diana had said something she hadn't or had failed to say what indeed she had. As she says, every discussion, every argument ended with him accusing her of having done something wrong. She began to accept this as true.

Yet along with the criticism and accusations came declarations of love and flowers addressed to "The Most Beautiful Woman in the World." Despite complaints about the cost, there were always invitations from Roger to go out. Despite the imperfect weekends, others were planned. They somehow managed to go on loving each other because love, once planted, is hard to uproot. Finally, one day Diana wrote in her journal, "My self-esteem is in the toilet." Rereading this inelegant but accurate description of how she had come to feel about herself marked the beginning of her disengagement from Roger. "Self-esteem was the hardest issue for me. I had focused so much of my attention and energy on Roger. I thought it was within my capacity to look after myself as well, but it wasn't. When I saw what I had written, I realized I had only this tiny dam of self-esteem left against this huge wave of criticism. I knew I couldn't hang on to myself if I stayed, no matter how much he loved me or how much I loved him." Two months later Diana wrenched herself away, still in love, then and now, although the love is slowly fading as she realizes how manipulative Roger's behavior toward her has been.

All depressives are riddled with self-doubt, just as all depression fallout sufferers are. Roger's rarely made an appearance in public; within the context of their relationship it ran rampant. Although his poor opinion of himself caused him great private pain, he salvaged from it what he could. When he expressed it openly to Diana, this won him sympathy and praise. When he avoided blame by placing it on her, he felt less guilty. When he attacked her self-esteem, his own grew a little. There are two sides to the manipulation coin; what made Diana feel worse made Roger feel better.

Diana will recover from her painful experience—and so will Roger, if he or his therapist wakes up to his predicament, or if Roger ever decides to tell his doctor how he really feels.

Rescuing and Rebuilding Lost Self-esteem

Diana was lucky not only because she was able to turn to the group for help, but also because she left a lover, not a spouse, a parent, or a child. Most depression fallout sufferers aren't so fortunate, and so must ride out the other's illness, either hoping the dam will hold or learning to shore it up by themselves.

Friends are the first line of defense for a battered ego. The expectation is that friends will understand, will share your perspective and your interpretation of the problem, and will offer you what the depressive withholds, and in the beginning this is what they do. But friends are also human beings. Like you, they feel uncomfortable around an excess of negativity, particularly when they are powerless to act on your behalf. If, time after time, you bring negativity with you in your quest for support and companionship, friends, even though they love you, will stop offering what you seek from them. When you revisit over and over with them the same unhappy ground you cover in solitude, you are doing a fine impersonation of a broken record. All the details so important to you will merge for them into one sad and dreary drone. In an attempt to move you beyond the scratch, they will offer you advice: Get out of the house, think about yourself for a change, just stop listening to him/her. You will probably respond that they don't understand, it's not as easy as that, and so forth. You will, in fact, assume the role with your friends that your depressive plays around you. Like you, they will begin to resent it and start looking for excuses not to be around you. Unlike you, they don't have to stay put.

Diana's sister, who is also her closest friend, helped her avoid this trap by giving her a piece of insightful advice. "She sat me down and said, 'No one else can feel your pain as you do, not even me, no matter how hard I try. It's your job to make yourself well and happy.'" This is your job as well, and one in which your friends can and will participate if you view them as doors out of your world. In short, get out of your own head and start paying attention to things around you. Instead of asking them to feel your pain (this may not be what you are doing, but it's how it feels to them), ask them to see a movie, visit a museum, take in a baseball game, go on a hike or a bike ride. Ask them about their life, their job, their vacation or problems or family. Whenever the urge to return to your theme comes over you, remember how boring it was the last time you visited a friend in the hospital and he could only talk about how awful the food was, that the nurse didn't come when rung for, and how terrible he felt.

Treated unselfishly, your friends will broaden your horizon and bring you energy, but there is much you can and should do for yourself. First and foremost, you must get back in the habit of tending to your own needs and wants, not just those of the depressive.

Looking to Your Own Needs

Old-timers in the friends and family group will often interrupt a more recent member's detailed and usually repetitious tale about the illness of spouse, parent, or child to say, "Yes, yes, but what are you doing for yourself?" Newcomers appear confused and puzzled by the question, as though it had been spoken in a foreign language. Others shift uneasily in their seats, guilty at the very thought of turning their focus from the depressive to themselves. Living next to someone else's depression, or indeed any serious illness, fosters the conviction that you have no right to think of yourself. Instead of acting on your own agenda, you react to the other's, thus shrinking your horizon to one unhappy point. When nothing you do cheers up or pleases the depressive, you judge yourself inadequate and useless. Although being selfless may sound like a high-minded goal, playing the martyr will not make you feel good, and it won't do much for your depressive, either.

Those who have no support group to remind them of this down-home piece of wisdom must find it elsewhere, and these pages are a good place to learn how to consider your own wants and needs without ignoring those of the depressive. Set your own agenda. Find a new interest to anchor your life other than their illness, because as long as you give in to its forceful currents, you will be carried to the same place where they are, and at least temporarily, marooned.

The following commonsensical suggestions will help launch you on a more positive and productive course. If you implement one and nothing happens, persevere. If still no change for the better occurs, drop it and try another. In this respect, a step taken to restore self-esteem is similar to an antidepressant; if it fails to make you feel better within a reasonable time, it probably won't ever work. Something else will.

Whatever you do well, do often. This may sound like advice for a chronic underachiever, but for those whose self-esteem is where Diana's ended up, it is practical. Since your ego and your depressive both have been telling you that you are worthless and ineffective, it's not clever to put the rest of you in a position where you must agree. If you have a special talent in the arts, in sports, or in dealing with people, indulge it. If you are good at bowling, go bowling. If you are a good cook, cook. If you are good at what you do in your office or in school, spend more time there, or on the tennis court or wherever your best playing field happens to be. Avoid what you do poorly or do not enjoy, unless it is a commitment that if left unfulfilled would harm someone else or produce guilty feelings in you. Positioning yourself as a punching bag for your depressive does not fall into this latter category. Do what is rewarding.

If you have an interest, whether it is judo, Renaissance art, jazz, or belly dancing, pursue it, if that's what you have always had a sneaking desire to investigate. Take golf or tango lessons; join an amateur theatrical or singing group, or a book club; learn Japanese flower arranging; sign up for a lecture or concert series, or a writing course; experiment with baking bread or stringing beads; try your hand at watercolors or repairing furniture. Trace your genealogy, study the Civil War, surf the Internet, write a letter to the editors. Learn a language, unless you're bad at languages. Sign up for a course in computers, unless they loom in your mind as mysterious and unmanageable machines. Choose not only what interests you, but what you already have a facility for. Check out what the local Y, university, civic center, or your own internal billboard has to offer, and select something that sparks your enthusiasm. The purpose of this exercise is to engage in something completely unrelated to your problems with your depressive. The pursuit of pure, unadulterated pleasure is what counts here, whether it be through making trout flies, moving the living room furniture, or watching old movies.

Another effective way of rewarding yourself, other than acquiring new information and skills, is to share those you already possess. Volunteering is one way to do this. Take on a once-a-week responsibility: address envelopes, answer phones, raise money for a local charity or political organization. Help out in a homeless shelter; read for the blind; visit those who because of age or illness can't get out of their house; weed someone else's garden; invite a lonely friend to dinner; help a teenager write a résumé; set up your neighbor's VCR. The list of opportunities to communicate and share your abilities stretches as far as your imagination. The purpose is to give pleasure to someone in a position to receive it, which, at the moment, your depressive is unable to do, or which your manic will not notice.

The point here is to feel good. When helping someone else cheers you up, you have achieved your goal. Altruists and philanthropists are rarely blind to the kudos their generosity brings them, which is why museums and hospitals, for instance, name wings and rooms after large donors. Think of yourself as a donor, and the other's pleasure as a plaque with your name on it. Looking for a reward or a return on your investment is not selfish; it is normal and will make you feel good, or at least better, about yourself.

Remind yourself that you are a good, intelligent, giving, loving, and responsible individual. Whatever task you assume, whatever endeavor you undertake, look for a positive feedback loop. If someone doesn't want or appreciate your skills and efforts, put them where they will be wanted and needed; do not waste them. You need to be loved, appreciated, and enjoyed. Go for it. Think about yourself.

Any of the foregoing activities have the added benefit of shifting the focus from the person with the illness to yourself. Depressives and manic-depressives alike tend to be self-centered and selfish. The former are overly passive, the latter overly active, but both are adept at sopping up the limelight. Unless you get a limelight of your own, you will hang about in the shadows, thinking you do not deserve one, letting their demands absorb all your energy and time. Depressives do need your love and support, even though they have a peculiar way of seeking them. Lodged deep in all depressives is a fear of abandonment and of being left helpless to deal with the unwelcoming world out there. But there are ways of assuaging that fear other than sitting in their shadow, waiting to hold their hand whenever they feel like extending it. Being forever at the beck and call of their needs will not lessen their distress, and it certainly will not promote your own self-esteem.

Putting Structure and Order in Your Life

Depression fallout sufferers often spend so much time worrying and hovering around, waiting to help the other cope, that their days lose structure as well as focus. Planned commitments—even something as simple as meeting a friend for coffee—put the structure back and give you a time-specific reason for getting away from your depressive for a bit, a far more acceptable one to all concerned than just announcing you want to get out because you are fed up. They will also give you something to look forward to, and something to enjoy in retrospect. While it may be impossible for you to get a life of your own (advice often given by well-meaning friends who live with undepressed people), you can maintain a schedule to call your own—that is, one not set entirely by and for the depressive.

Achievement gives a great boost to self-esteem, and much of that achievement comes from our work. When we worry constantly about someone else, both the concentration and quality we apply to our jobs suffer. Telling you to stop worrying is a fatuous suggestion, but there are ways to contain your worry. If you leave home for work each morning, put feelings of guilt about abandonment of your depressive aside. If you are delighted to have an excuse to get away from him or her, do not feel guilty about that, either. Everyone who lives with another's depressive illness is glad to get away from it, so in that respect as in others you are perfectly normal. If guilt insists upon rising, remember that you have done nothing to bring on the illness, and remind yourself that staying home will not bring joy to your sad person.

Once in the office, concentrate on the work that lies before you, not on what is waiting on the other side of the front door when you return in the evening. Depressives are given to calling up during the day with rather pointless requests: Where's my red sweater? What time did you say you would be back? Bring some milk with you, and did you know the kitchen sink was leaking? They are unaware of, or unconcerned about, your work schedule, and so may not consider their calls inconvenient. You do not share the same perspective; what is important to you holds little importance for them, and vice versa.

One way to solve this problem is to set aside one or two mutually agreed upon times during the day to telephone your depressive, thus reassuring him or her of your affection and attention, and freeing you of unwelcome interruptions. If you allow the depressive unlimited access when you are trying to get a job done, your annoyance will ring in your voice, and so confirm what the depressive is all too ready to believe, that you have neither concern nor time for him or her. Cross impatience on your part will double the possibility that you will be met at the door by someone who more closely resembles Darth Vader than your spouse, lover, parent, or child. If you work at home, impose a meeting schedule there, too.

When business trips are necessary, step up the number of phone calls. If possible, arrange for a mutual friend to invite your depressive to a meal or on a walk while you are away. What depressives need is assurance that you love them, even though they are not at their best. Their broken pleasure system precludes any real pleasure on their part; reassurance will make that lack a bit easier for them to bear.

One final work-related issue is whether or not you should inform anyone at your office about what is going on in your home life. This is a judgment that only you can make, depending on how critical the illness is, how much your concern affects your performance, and how responsive and sympathetic your employer is. One group member, driven close to despair by his son's recently arrived manic depression, was unable to concentrate, arriving at his office each day red-eyed and exhausted. For months he kept his problem hidden, until one day he felt so unable to work that he broke down and told his boss. Far from disapproving, she not only offered sympathy, but ordered him to take time off when really necessary.

Given the prevalence of depressive illness, empathy as well as sympathy is possible if you choose to open up. Against this you must weigh your own sense of privacy. What you tell one person in the office, whether an assistant or someone else with whom you work closely, will probably soon be general knowledge. If this bothers you, keep your silence, unless, of course, your depressive or manic-depressive has a critical episode and lands in the hospital, or you have reason to believe that this is a possibility. In that case it is advisable to have a co-worker who knows at all times where you can be reached during the business day, should an emergency arise. If it makes you uncomfortable to label the problem as depression or manic depression, call it something else, such as mononucleosis, heart arrhythmia, Lyme disease, hepatitis B, or that old favorite, a nervous breakdown brought on by stress.

To a large extent these same guidelines apply to less intimate friends and to acquaintances. In such cases the what-to-tell-the-world problem turns not on your ability to perform, but on the depressive's. They will frequently psych themselves up to do something, and then back out at the last minute. You are then left holding two tickets to the theater or expected as a couple at dinner, and your partner is nowhere in sight. This is inconvenient and also embarrassing, and once again your decision on how to handle this must be a personal one. If you think your depressive might, at five in the afternoon, inform you that he has no intention of meeting your friends at the restaurant at seven, warn the friends that this might happen. If you choose not to cite the illness, allude to a pending business or personal conflict that might preclude his or her presence, and ask whether it would be a problem if you turned up on your own. If you have tickets to an event, ask someone ahead of time if they'd consider filling in at the last moment if necessary, giving the same reason. Don't stay home with your depressive, wishing you were elsewhere, but warn those concerned that you might be a single rather than a couple. It's not a good idea to turn up alone without previously stating that possibility.

If you're aggravated by the depressive's refusal to make his or her own excuses, speak your piece, but don't expect that your displeasure will push them into doing their own tidying. Just as every depression has its own fingerprints, so does every depression fallout. You can choose whether to hide, fudge, or come clean. Your aim is to avoid a situation that places your self-esteem in jeopardy, and if that takes a little white lie or two, don't hesitate to tell one. While you cannot restore the depressive's self-esteem, you can protect your own any way you please.

The Importance of Health

All such problems and issues, whether in your professional or social life, create stress, anxiety, and frustration. Finding ways to diminish their impact is imperative. The more stressed, anxious, and frustrated you become, the less able you will be to cope with the other's illness until the ultimate solution—good treatment—is achieved. Trying to remain calm and stable in the eye of a sustained hurricane upsets one's body as well as one's spirit. Most of us in such a pickle gravitate toward the solace of junk food, alcohol, cigarettes, bed, and other sources of temporary pleasure, most of which in the end make us feel even worse. At the risk of offering advice more often found in books on how to lower cholesterol or avoid heart attacks, I strongly recommend you look after your health. Putting on an additional ten pounds or waking up with a hangover will vastly add to the stress you already endure. If you have long toyed with the idea of getting yourself into shape, this is a good time to do so. Not only will you feel better, but you will be pleased and proud of yourself.

Aerobic exercise, yoga, and t'ai chi increase the flow of blood to the brain, producing feelings of well-being and alertness. They also make us feel we are in control of ourselves and our lives. So does a weather eye to one's diet. You may have watched your depressive lining up a store of processed snacks and ice cream to eat in front of the television or while reading a mindless book, all the while looking gloomy and lethargic. They will have the same effect on you. Gloom and lethargy are ruinous to self-esteem. This is not an exhortation to lose twenty pounds, become an exercise freak, or give up alcohol forever. Setting unattainable goals is precisely what you should avoid. Instead, decide not to gain weight and not to drink or smoke more than previously. Instead of trying to run four miles a day, make up your mind to walk two. Instead of shorting out your own pleasure center, set goals you anticipate with pleasure and can enjoy working to achieve.

It's important to maintain reasonable expectations not only toward the way you eat, drink, and exercise, but toward everything you approach as a depression fallout sufferer, including the other's illness. Do not cast yourself as a Mother Teresa or an Albert Schweitzer, neither of whom, although saintly and selfless, knew much about depressive illness. See yourself for what you are: a good person trying to do your best for someone you love and for yourself as well. Time and good treatment bring all but a tiny handful of depressives and manic-depressives back to their previous norm. However, should you allow your self-esteem to plunge, you will find, as Diana has, that restoring it is a long-range task that will extend well beyond your depressive's recovery. There are no medications for failed self-esteem, so it is best to shelter and nurture it as you go along.

All the advice offered here starts with the premise that since you live with a depressive or manic-depressive, your ego is already in need of protection. The illness is like a black hole in space, pulling into itself everything and everyone within range of its powerful force. You don't need Einstein's wisdom to resist it; you need advice from those who have done so, or, like Diana, have failed. You also need objectivity, as well as a short list of protective and restorative remedies. If you feel unable to do everything suggested, choose one thing. With your first success you will find it easier to go on to the second, and to the third. Each one will represent an addition to the plus column when next you contemplate yourself at two in the morning.

A Checklist of Remedies for Self-esteem

- Know that you feel as you do because of the other's illness, not because you are at fault or lacking.

- Understand that friends cannot feel your pain; see them as doors to a more active and positive world rather than as recording devices for your negative one.

- Cater to your own needs and wants, not just to the depressive's.

- Whatever you do well, do often.

- Do what rewards you.

- Learn a new skill you can count on mastering, or one in which less than perfection is neither inhibiting nor discouraging.

- Volunteer your skills to those who lack them and need them.

- Do whatever reminds you that you are a good, intelligent, generous, responsible, and loving person despite all evidence to the contrary offered by the depressive.

- Turn the limelight upon yourself rather than wait about in the wings.

- Make your own schedule of commitments and activities; don't allow your depressive to do this for you.

- Concentrate on your professional life, and don't permit your worry or the depressive's interruptions to destroy your concentration or impair your achievement.

- If your performance is threatened, assign blame for this to the other's illness, calling it by any name you choose to select.

- Plan for your depressive's probable absence from your social life until he or she feels better.

- Protect your health.

- Set yourself reasonable goals.

Psychotherapy: A Helpful Option

Living with another's depressive illness is very difficult, especially over a long period of time. If your self-esteem has already fallen into that black hole, you may need outside help to retrieve it. Although the curative effects of psychotherapy for those with depressive illness are open to argument, a skillful psychotherapist who understands your own demoralization and what caused it may do you a world of good. One Friday evening I asked how many in the room were seeing someone for help, and a lot of hands went up. It's not easy to live with someone you love and not be able to help him or her. Knowing all the right things to do isn't hard; it's actually doing them that's the big obstacle, one which many find insuperable without a boost from a therapist. Things you try to tell yourself but don't really believe, you often believe when they come from a pro. However, if you do go looking for one, make sure you don't put yourself in the hands of an overenthusiastic Freudian. What you need is a skilled and knowledgeable hand-holder and reinterpreter of your feelings, not a year on the couch. In the meantime, there's plenty you can do on your own to control your depressive's behavior to you, which is what's causing your problem in the first place. That's the topic of the following chapter.

9

SETTING BOUNDARIES

KNOWING WHY YOUR DEPRESSIVE FEELS and behaves as he or she does doesn't automatically bring tolerance for their actions—nor does it lead to saintly patience. Depression and manic depression alike produce a constellation of disagreeable traits including verbal abuse and sometimes violence. Gilbert, a group member whose spouse ran the gamut of bad behavior, voiced a question in the minds of many in his position: "What do you do when your spouse treats you badly? Do you cry? Get pissed off? Talk to friends and try to get some support from them? Or do you go back and say, 'You can't do this to me. I'm someone you say you love'? It's not a good idea to blame everything on the illness," he said. "Use your understanding of the illness to cope, not to excuse." This wise advice is right on target; how to follow it is the subject of this chapter.

As you already know, those with the illness are experts in blaming others for the way they feel. Pointing out that the fault lies with the "it," not with you, may seem a practical strategy, but it's one that the depressive's altered responses will probably defeat. But even though faulty brain chemistry does make for irrational, nonsequential thinking on their part, it does not rob them of all sense of reality. They are often aware of how poorly they treat others. Their awareness will not, however, act as a brake, nor is their illness an excuse for unacceptable behavior. "I kept hoping someone would rescue me," Gilbert continued, "but I came to realize I had to rescue myself." So must you. Putting the brakes on such behavior by setting clear, established boundaries is how you do it.

The friends and family group had its origin in the pent-up anger carried by the intimates of depressives and manics. In the early days of the group, they came with their partners. Usually it was those with the illness who did all the talking, stressing how awful their lives were, how nobody understood them, how all their friends had deserted them. Meanwhile, the other half of the couple sat with eyes glued to the floor, knuckles white, face impassive. When encouraged by Howard to speak up, they gave rote confirmation of what had been said: "Well, her life is pretty bad," or "Things are pretty rough for him." Although the sick person often returned to participate, the family members or partners rarely did. So Howard began to take them aside after the meeting was over, and encourage them to speak more freely. Once the cork was loosened, out poured the angry fizz. Howard then realized that these people needed a place of their own to release the furious resentment that had been fermenting within them. So was born the separate friends and family group.

Suppressed anger creates needs: a safe place to vent negative emotions and ways of controlling the depressive or manic behavior that created them. Everyone who lives close to those with the illness needs to establish dividing lines between what they are prepared to tolerate and what they will not. These boundaries must take into account both the symptoms and impairments of the illness and also one's own rights as a human being and caregiver. Such boundaries have two overlapping purposes. The first of these is to ensure that you do all you can to keep your depressive on the straight and narrow path toward medical progress, and to help him or her stay out of trouble in the meantime. Trouble can be trouble with the law or trouble with life, up to and including the possibility of damage to themselves and others through suicide attempts or violence. The second is to protect your psyche from the battering ram of depressive disagreeableness and the feelings of helplessness and resentment that come from providing love and support without reward.

Both depend on recognition and acceptance of one guiding principle: the only person you can take responsibility for is yourself. You cannot cure someone else's illness. You can point them in the right direction; you can cooperate with them, you can give love, support, and advice; but you cannot live their life for them. If you try to do so you will lose your own. This does not mean taking a passive position;

passivity will lead you to more resentment and anger. Instead you must identify those aspects of the situation that are accessible to your influence, and use your own power to control or moderate them.

Most of us are leery of exercising power over others, and assign pejorative terms to doing so: domineering, bossy, self-serving, even abusive. But power and control are the tools you must use if you are to achieve your goals of wellness for the person with the illness, and self-esteem and well-being for yourself. Depressives and manic-depressives are not bad people, but they are, for as long as the illness is in the ascendant, tricky, difficult, and unrewarding. The universe of the depressive is characterized by self-doubt, an inability to anticipate or feel positive emotions, and a lack of will and purpose. That of the manic is driven by ludicrous overconfidence, irrationality, and the conviction they can do no wrong. Insisting that your depressive cheer up and be nice, or that your manic be reasonable and considerate, is like telling a cat to bark, but you can take steps to ensure that their unpleasant traits are kept under control. They are sick; you are well. Because you're the well person, you bear the responsibility for exercising control, and the vehicle for that control is your power to set boundaries.

The Quintessential Boundary: Compliance with Treatment

The ultimate responsibility for complying with treatment lies with the person who has the illness, and failure to accept that responsibility is an indication that there may not be a happy ending. Without medication the illness will persist, so refusal of medication is, in a very real sense, a refusal to maximize the chances of getting well. Noncompliance also indicates ignorance, shortsightedness, and selfishness on the part of the primary sufferer. There are, after all, two of you, and you inhabit the same world. If your self-absorbed depressive or manic refuses to recognize that their illness affects you too, they are making a statement: I am the only person who matters here. Although it is true that depressives and manics find it difficult to see much farther than their own noses, this is a giveaway that you may have to live with their illness longer, and more unhappily, than need be.

Noncompliance is always a big boundary issue, but it manifests differently in depressives and manic-depressives. Few depressives choose misery, once given the option for relief. There do arise, however, three instances in which they may resist medication. First, some find the side effects intolerable, even though most disappear over time. Carping about them is normal (who could be expected to embrace wholeheartedly medication that sometimes causes weight gain or reduces sexual drive?) and no reason for rebuke on your part. If they are seriously inhibiting, the doctor in charge should consider switching to another drug.

The second arises when the search for the right antidepressant is long and drawn out. Depressives become discouraged when they must try first one, then another, and perhaps still another medication without feeling better. A prolonged search for a solution is hard on them; they may be increasingly reluctant to try a new drug, fearing that perhaps no drug will work. As long as they keep trying, they deserve, and need, your support. A good doctor tells his patients up front that finding the right drug sometimes takes a while. If he has not done so, try to make up for it by offering consistent encouragement and hope. Remember, at least 80 percent of depressives will respond to drug therapy.

The third situation is one in which a depressive, after several months on medication, pronounces himself "cured" and opts to stop taking it. One husband laments his depressive wife's view of her illness as a once-in-a-lifetime occurrence, despite having twice in four years succumbed to it and twice been restored by medication. Eight months after the second bout, she once again decided, against her doctor's advice, that she no longer needed the help of medicine. As she slid downward, she derided her husband's warning as nagging criticism. He was right, she was wrong. Now he finds it hard to sympathize with his wife, and is entertaining thoughts of leaving her. He needs to make clear to his wife the connection between her compliance and his continued presence.

Compliance with treatment for manic depression is absolutely imperative, yet especially hard to maintain. For some, the side effects of anti-mania drugs are more unpleasant than those of antidepressants, and some demand frequent monitoring by both doctor and patient. Unfortunately, at present, the National Institute of Mental Health has no ongoing research to find ways of making treatment less discomforting and so more acceptable. A number of manic-depressives take not just one, but two, three, or even more medications to control their illness. The most difficult problem for

manics is resisting the temptation to revisit the highs that are suppressed by medication. Memories of them are a siren song luring
the manic toward noncompliance and drowning out recollections of
the appalling things they did while flying high. Manic-depressives
need a strong commitment to wellness if they are to stay on course.
Often that means you will have to set boundaries to reinforce that
commitment.

Long-suffering James, the husband of rapid-cycling Ursula,
chooses to remain married to her, but with a caveat: "Compliance is
the key. As long as Ursula continues taking the seven drugs that keep
her illness at least partially under control, I'll stick with her. I grew
up believing that marriage in and of itself is reason for not copping
out on your partner. She didn't ask for the illness, but she has it, and
now it's part of our life together."

But recently something new has entered the picture. Alcohol and
marijuana counter the effects of medications, and Ursula has been
dipping into both. They make her feel better for an hour or two, but
they certainly aren't good for her. Does that mean, I asked, that
you'll leave her? James waffled. "Well, I'll do what I've never threatened to do before. I'll send her to a rehab clinic." And if that doesn't
work out, if she goes back to them when she comes home? "I'm not
sure, we'll see," was his reply. "The only thing that sustains me is that
she's a good complier. If they aren't, then the relationship won't last
long." We in the group have learned that a switch from "she" to
"they" means James is retreating from engagement in what he knows
will be an angry, ugly scene with Ursula. We're pretty sure she'll
never see that rehab clinic, even if she merits a visit. He's backed
away from other confrontations, retreating into his mantras. The lesson here? Don't kid yourself; threaten only what you believe yourself
capable of enforcing.

Another clue to potential compliance is whether or not the
depressive accepts you as a knowledgeable partner in his or her
treatment. Depressives and especially manic-depressives are poor
reporters. What they tell their medicating doctor may not reflect
accurately the way they feel and act at home. Since visits to the pre-
scriber are usually on a monthly basis, they may report how they feel
at the time of the visit but not how they felt one, two, or three weeks
before. Manic-depressives in a high often lie outright about what the
doctor has told them, while depressives often can't concentrate well
enough to report accurately what the physician's comments or

instructions were. Both you and the physician need to know the truth, and the only way to guarantee that is joint visits. Most good compliers won't quarrel with this, because they have nothing to hide and want to get well. But some depressives and manic-depressives just don't want any company when they go to see their medicating psychiatrist. While this doesn't make much sense, (would they resist your presence if the problem were a broken arm?), there is a second-best option. This is to sit down in advance of the appointment and together make a list of what needs to be discussed with the doctor. A list is an orderly and effective way of ensuring that problems which occurred several weeks ago—and are now perhaps minimalized or forgotten by the depressive—will be addressed, and it has the added advantage of not provoking a useless scene that can become a permanent sore point.

If the doctor hasn't already suggested that your depressive keep a daily diary like Constance's in chapter 4, you can propose it. Should you suspect the entries will be sketchy or inaccurate, keep your own as a supplement. A few words each day will suffice: "very down," "never got dressed," "more agitated," "seemed more cheerful," and so forth. A diary can help confirm suspected noncompliance by calling odd fluctuations to your attention.

Compliance is closely linked to a good partnership among yourself, the person with the illness, and the doctor. A team approach covers not only the problem of inaccurate reporting, but others as well. Often family members are the early-warning system, able to identify a recurrence of the illness well before the depressive or manic-depressive is aware it has returned. One solution is for you and the person with the illness to sign a contract: if your manic starts cutting down drastically on sleep, yet never seems tired, and is talking on the phone at four in the morning, he or she must agree to see the doctor immediately, no matter how silly an idea it seems to them. If your depressive returns to a previous pattern of symptoms, do the same. Foresight and cooperation are far more effective in getting your manic or depressive back on track than nagging, and will also save both of you frustration and anger.

Support groups for those who have the illness are of tremendous help not only to sufferers, but to you as well. Their peers have the right to come down hard on noncompliers, and they'll use it. Where you may pussyfoot, they will trample and issue orders like drill sergeants. And they will keep doing it week after week, without letup.

Manics who have jettisoned their medications will be given the hardest time. Fellow manic-depressives can identify an unmedicated peer with ease and accuracy, ensuring that lapses will not go undetected. Support groups also encourage depressives to tolerate side effects. Whereas you assure them that these will diminish, fellow depressives can testify to their own experience, and will be more readily believed. Many in the group will have had to make one or more medication changes, and in this respect, too, they are in a position to offer encouragement based on personal knowledge.

The boundaries you choose to set in the matter of compliance will depend on how serious the illness is, on your relationship, and on how much medical and emotional damage is being done to all concerned, as will those you set to counter other aspects of unipolar and bipolar behavior.

Tough-Love Boundaries for Manics

"Tough love" entered the American lexicon back in the 1970s, when seeing young people on drugs was still a shocking rarity for most adults. Parents who had reasoned and pleaded with, wept, wheedled, yelled at, and bribed their addicted kids in an attempt to get them to lay off were warned that none of these would work. The alternative presented was tough love: Don't help them by providing room, board, clothing, or money unless or until they're willing to help themselves break the habit.

A tough-love boundary takes courage to impose, but sometimes it's the only alternative to the excesses of mania. While depressives usually wreak their damage on others by Chinese water torture, manic-depressives prefer to push you off a cliff. Applying a tough-love boundary to manic-depressives' compliance is a must. In *Understanding Depression,* Drs. Donald Klein and Paul Wender write that the average person whose manic depression remains untreated is incapacitated for close to one-fifth of his or her adult years, an attention-getting fact if you happen to live with one. This is never an illness to be taken lightly; medication is the only remedy. If tough love is the route to medication compliance, then it is an appropriate response.

Much of the behavior that travels under the name of mania is devastating to those who live within its path. Spouses, children, and parents of unmedicated manic-depressives are constantly placed in jeopardy: income and savings are squandered, jobs and careers are lost, and families are thrown into disarray and confusion from which they may never recover. An unmedicated manic-depressive needs to be controlled somehow, and by default the agency of control is you. Accounts like the following three stories of tough love applied to unmedicated bipolar sufferers are mercifully rare, but the lessons they exemplify can be applied in lesser crises. The essential message is that tough measures are necessary and effective means to preventing even more painful consequences.

Sara's husband, Lucas, had the first of many manic episodes when she was eight months pregnant with their first child. When, after three years of starting and stopping his medication, he went into yet another manic state, she swept up her child, climbed down the fire escape when he blocked the front door, and took refuge with her parents, where she has been living for four months. Now Lucas is behaving like a lamb, back on his meds, back at work, and proclaiming that he loves his wife and son and never again wants to risk losing them. He and Sara are in couples therapy, facing the issue of whether or not Sara will return home. "I have to give him an answer now," she told the group. "I can't leave him hanging on such a major decision." "What's the rush?" Howard asked. "Why now? Why not six months or a year from now as a deadline for your decision? This has been going on for three years already." Manic-depressives, he told her, are always absolutely sure they are on the straight and narrow forever, but then the mania creeps in and takes over, often without their awareness that it's back. They feel great, go off their meds, and bang, all the good intentions are down the drain. Howard should know; he's done that himself in the past.

Sara could have stayed put and gone on arguing and pleading with Lucas to stay on his meds, but three years of doing that hadn't worked. Leaving and taking their son with her shocked Lucas into awareness and responsibility. Waiting a full year to see if his commitment has staying power is a far wiser course than a precipitous return. It also sends Lucas a warning that should he ever again toss his meds aside, Sara will be gone for good.

Karen's daughter Stella, married and the mother of three children under the age of seven, has been traveling in and out of mania once every couple of years since her late teens. Six months ago her husband recently had to quit his job to look after the children, bringing the family to the verge of welfare. Through all this, Stella, often charming and persuasively "sane," has been in total denial about her illness, telling anyone who'll listen that there is absolutely nothing wrong with her. Stella's unmedicated mania has landed her in the hospital three times. Each time, medication is prescribed for her while there. Now her husband has given up trying to deal with his wife's illness and has moved out, so mother Karen is trying, as she has for years, to rescue her daughter, running over at all hours to look after the neglected kids, giving Stella money, and trying to persuade her to see the damage she is doing to her family.

In all this, the one thing that frightens Stella is the prospect of returning to the psychiatric ward; in this respect she is typical of most who have been in one. The tough-love boundary suggested by the group had three elements: First, the kids should be transferred to their father. Second, Karen must discontinue subsidizing Stella, who has long since lost her job and thus has no source of income other than going on welfare. Instead, she should give the money to Stella's husband. "But how can I do that?" she protested, flying off into a dead end as people in crises often do. "I think he's wonderful, but he's not family, not in the same sense my daughter is." Think of it, said the group, as money for your grandchildren.

The third and most difficult element was that Karen try to commit her daughter to a hospital and to persuade the medicating physician there to keep her longer than the usual four or five days—all this in the hope that the environment she finds so frightening will make a dent in her noncompliance pattern.

The tough-love boundaries here are multiple: No medication means no husband, no children, and no money, but only the hospital. This suggested solution might seen unduly harsh to most people, but not to anyone who has lived next to this illness. A destroyed family cannot save anyone. Only the hospital and the anti-mania drugs she must take there will render Stella capable of understanding the consequences of her actions.

Jim and Audrey have worked hard at staying sane. Their daughter, Susan, now just turned twenty, is a manic-depressive in complete denial despite the horrific consequences of going four years without medication. She has lived on the streets with a drug user, become pregnant, and had an abortion. She has managed to support herself during periods of low mania rather than in high mania through jobs held for three or four months at a time. In that state she is irresistibly attractive, good at anything she does, and fun to be with. The group has followed this story for several years now, and was excited when Jim and Audrey reported recently that they had persuaded their daughter to see a doctor and go on medication. But her resolve didn't last.

Through all this, her parents have maintained a tough-love stance by telling their daughter she was always welcome at home, but not with her lover; that goods, not money, would be forthcoming—a position they took when they realized that any cash they gave her was being converted into drugs, not food, shelter, or clothing; and that they would support her in every way, including financially, if she accepted and stayed on medication.

This story of manic depression is not as bad as it can get. Jim and Audrey could have opened the doors of their home to their daughter and her drug-abusing lover, the equivalent of inviting chaos home to roost. They could have put themselves in deep debt by giving her the money she has abusively demanded of them, only to have her spend it on drugs for her lover and eventually for herself. They could have allowed her to give birth to the baby and then brought up the child themselves, leaving their daughter on the streets and the child with no parents. They could have fought with each other over how best to handle the bottomless pit of pain and suffering their daughter has brought them, and so lost each other. They could have stopped loving their daughter. But they did none of these things, instead managing to preserve both love and sanity. They have once been able to persuade their daughter to do what she must in order to have a future, and one day they will do so again, this time for good. All they have accomplished has been the result of tough love and their own strength.

Setting Boundaries Against Anger and Insults

Depressives and manic-depressives alike are prone to expressing irrational anger and hurling verbal abuse. "He refers to me all the time as 'the enemy,'" said a bewildered father of his depressive son. "He picks fights with me, knows just which buttons to push, so when he yells at me, I yell right back. What's going on here?" What's going on is that his son is behaving like many with depressive illness. So is a depressed husband who not only snaps constantly at his wife for what he calls her stupidity, but also heaps abuse upon her two sons by a former marriage. "I won't tell you what he says about them," she reported, "because you'd think he was crazy." But he's not; he's just a nasty depressive who doesn't put on the brakes when at home with his wife.

Anger and insults may be typical, but they are not acceptable. There is rarely much to be gained from arguing, but what are your alternatives? One way to respond to mild displays is to leave the scene, not in anger but as pleasantly as you can manage. While "Oh, is that what you think? Well, I'm off to the movies" may seem an inadequate reply to someone who has just called you a stupid piece of shit, it is an effective way to curb initial manifestations of verbal abuse. People with the illness are not dense, and will sometimes get the message early on, if each time they are abusive or become irrationally angry you leave them on their own. Their testiness may be only a minor relapse on their part and not worth wasting your ammunition to shoot it down. Prolonged and constant belittlement, however, let alone rage pointed directly at you, call for a counterstrike.

One mother in the group has a mostly unmedicated twenty-eight-year-old manic-depressive daughter who has returned home to take up residence on the living room sofa. From there she lets fly a sustained stream of insults and bursts of temper. Increasingly her mother—a possessor of excellent manners and accustomed to receiving respectful treatment from her daughter in times past—takes refuge in a friend's apartment. She would do better to combine her disappearing act with articulation of a clear boundary line: "This is my apartment; you live here on my sufferance, and as long as you do, you will behave civilly to me." The mother holds the purse strings, and, as so often when dealing with seemingly impossible depressives and manic-depressives, ought also to jerk them firmly when needed.

Arguments without constructive action on your part will turn into cockfights. Putting some distance between you and your depressive will avoid a bloody conclusion. State your position clearly: "You can't do this to me. I'm someone you say you love." Once you have laid down your boundary, back it up by withdrawing yourself emotionally, physically, or both whenever the nasty depressive enters the arena. If finances and time permit, go away for a weekend or longer. Or simply leave the house for a walk or a visit with friends. Don't linger at the table when the meal is over; go read a book or phone someone to chat. In short, go about your business in order to drive home to the depressive both your unhappiness and your intention to avoid its source. This is not another version of hiding out elsewhere, of slipping off silently to avoid poor treatment; it's drawing a boundary line, and it will work because almost all depressives, no matter how unpleasant, fear abandonment by the person they love.

To trade consciously on someone's fear of abandonment isn't fun; it makes us feel mean and heartless. But the alternative is worse; if you do nothing, the treatment you are receiving will continue. You will bottle up your resentment and it will escalate into anger. Eventually you will react far more strongly, and probably regret it, since reciprocal anger will distance you further. A minor version of tough love is more practical and more effective, and much less damaging to yourself and to your relationship with the depressive. If, for instance, your depressive decides at the last minute not to keep a planned engagement, say you are sorry they don't feel up to it, and that you will go on your own unless this frightens them. The operative word is *frighten,* which is quite different from *annoy.* Some depressives genuinely fear solitude, and if this is so, they should not be left alone to brood. If, on the other hand, they are simply cross that you are going out and they don't like it, you have no reason to remain with them. If you're really annoyed with them for copping out on a previously made commitment, instead of saying "You must come with me," try a more reasonable approach: "Unless it upsets you, I will go on my own." They might even change their mind.

There are always occasional moments of calm. Take advantage of one of these to explain in more detail to your depressive what's bothering you and how you feel; should this lead to anger on anyone's part, withdraw from the battlefield. Your anger only plays into the depressive's, and you will find yourself hot-headed and sputtering when the purpose of discussion is to clarify, not complicate. Unless you can lay out your position calmly and clearly, your depressive will see you as the villain. The following vignette from a friends and family group member offers one example of how a boundary to control anger and verbal abuse can be set.

A wife whose depressive husband makes ugly scenes—not only in the privacy of their own home but also when they go visit their daughter and grandchildren—sat through a particularly bad weekend in a miserable muddle of self-blame. Over dinner Saturday night, her husband provoked arguments, spewed profanity, and slung insults at her, all in front of their daughter, their son-in-law, and three small children. After he had gone to bed, she apologized privately to her daughter and attempted to explain away his behavior by citing problems in the office, stress, and other irrelevant factors. When she later broached the topic with her husband, he flew into a temper tantrum and resumed his verbal abuse of her, calling her, among other epithets, a self-righteous bitch. At that moment she made a decision, communicated to him on the eve of their next visit to her daughter's home: he was not invited. Period. The explanation? Bad for the children, uncomfortable for everyone else. He was angry, but he didn't go. On the following visit, a number of months later, he moderated his behavior, thus complying with the boundary his wife had set for him. Her next boundary will, one hopes, pertain to his treatment of her.

Whether you use leverage or simply draw a boundary that says "You may not cross this line," what makes the act of control effective is following through. Crying wolf defeats the purpose. Like young children, depressives and manic-depressives alike test for boundaries, pushing to see how far they can go without retribution. If you constantly threaten to react and then don't, they will try again, encouraged by your vacillation. And when next you draw a line they won't believe in it, so set your boundaries with care. Choose first the issue most important to you—compliance with medication, for example. Then move to the next on your list, which for most is verbal abuse. Although there is no need to grovel in gratitude if your stratagem works, do acknowledge the cessation or suspension of disagreeable behavior. Just state the obvious: "I like it better when you're polite," "you don't call me names," "you make an effort," "you behave like your old self," "you speak to me civilly," or whatever suits your style. When forgiveness is too easy to attain, boundaries don't work very well and you may be trapped in a cycle of bad behavior followed by forgiveness, which is no improvement over all-bad behavior.

Handling Physical Violence

Some people with depressive illness move beyond abusive talk to threatening, harassing, or even violent behavior. When they do, never tolerate it, says Agnes Hatfield, a psychologist with the Maryland Department of Health and Mental Hygiene, because aggression has a tendency to feed on itself. She lays out some helpful guidelines for determining what provokes the aggression before acting to control it. Sometimes, she cautions, expressions of anger may erupt over a legitimate issue. Everybody gets angry from time to time, so it's important to pay attention to what the person is doing, as well as to what is being said. You have probably, at some point in your life, angrily yelled at someone that you'd like to hit them, but without balling your fists and moving threateningly toward them. "His behavior might be compliant while his words are hostile. In these cases," Hatfield says, "although he might irritate you, he is probably not being wantonly aggressive."

On the other hand, violence or the threat of it may be an expression of the person's condition: "Is he under the delusion that someone is out to get him and that he must attack in self-defense," Hatfield asks, "or does he hear voices urging him to do destructive things?" The latter might be the case with a manic-depressive. You need to get a firm handle on your own depressive's or manic-depressive's way of expressing what upsets him, and act accordingly. Both are often edgy, anxious, and volatile. Try to avoid situations that aggravate these feelings.

Violence directed at inanimate objects can be an expression of immense frustration. Have you ever kicked a door and come close to breaking a toe because you were swept up by an uncontrollable urge to vent your own anger or frustration? If you had instead attempted to throttle the person you were angry at, they would probably have called the police. You should do the same if your depressive or manic loses control and tries to harm you or anyone else.

On a recent Friday evening, the mother I have come to think of as Owner of the Sofa surprised us all by reporting she had done just that. Her daughter, who was in the habit of slinging bits of cheap china, bought expressly for the purpose, into a bin in their apartment building's yard, instead hurled them at her mother, and followed them with various cherished bibelots. Her mother, who had put up with every other kind of abuse for over a year, called the police, who removed her daughter to the station house and kept her in a holding cell for six hours. She emerged chastened and very surprised because her mother had for once held her to account and given her a clear indication of what she could expect from similar transgressions in the future. We in the group are still in the middle of this story, and have no way of predicting what the denouement will be. For the moment all is calm, although similar crises may well erupt before the daughter decides to adhere to treatment. Boundaries don't always take effect immediately.

By chance, that same evening another target of violence was present in the group, this one a newcomer who is three years into a second marriage. Cynthia married after a six-month courtship during which she had no suspicion that anything was wrong. Although her husband-to-be had been diagnosed as manic-depressive, she learned this not from him but from his adult daughter, who has for several years refused to have anything to do with her father. Cynthia described her husband as a "difficult pillar of the community" around whom floated bits and pieces of gossip, but whose solid business career and considerable fortune had given him authority among, and deference from, his peers. As Cynthia's tale unfolded, emotions in the group rose. We were all on the edge of our seats, eager to press advice upon this woman whose husband is abusive to a frightening degree. She told us he had locked her out of the house at night, threatened her with scissors when they were arguing, and once attempted to strangle her in bed, later explaining it was "only a game." Such actions are never "playful," a word Cynthia began to use frequently, perhaps to cover her embarrassment at having put up with such appalling behavior for almost a year without taking action.

Leave him immediately, we all urged her. See a lawyer Monday morning. Make your plans to move out as soon as possible, and in the meantime, don't share the bedroom.

Cynthia's reluctance to agree with us on the need for instant defensive action alarmed us and brought to mind the syndrome of the battered wife who knows she is in danger but cannot bring herself to leave. Although Cynthia never returned to the group, she did call Howard a month later to tell him she had moved out.

These are not the only tales of physical violence the group has heard, and I have listened to more of the same outside the group. Violence is a very real possibility. When it occurs, you need to protect yourself by taking immediate action. If the person threatening violence is a young child or an elderly parent whom you cannot immediately leave as you could a spouse or other adult, calling the police to the house remains your single option. This is a painful step for a family member to take. Indeed, we think of it as anti-family, an act of treachery, and, of course, the ultimate admission of our failure to help someone we love get well. But the danger of violence born of depressive illness is no different from the danger of violence by an intruder. It can end in tragedy for both the recipient and the instigator. Far better to take action now than allow worse to happen in the future.

A Word About Involuntary Commitment to a Hospital

Involuntary commitment is an immensely complicated issue unless the officials in charge of the commitment deem the patient psychotic or a danger to himself or others. The police and the emergency medical service can take such a patient to the hospital, where he or she will be treated and released a few days after medication has successfully controlled the mania. Even in the absence of psychosis, violence, or attempted suicide, it is possible for a doctor to commit a patient against his or her will, but under what conditions and for what reasons is a matter best discussed with the doctor in charge of your manic or depressive. Clearly he's not going to commit someone just for driving you nuts and spending all your money. Rules and regulations for involuntary commitment differ from state to state and there is wide variance in physicians' attitudes toward this issue.

Patients have rights. They cannot be held involuntarily beyond certain defined time periods, nor can they always be forced to take medication. One wife, in a short piece written for the *California Alliance for the Mentally Ill Newsletter,* first describes two decades of chaos with her usually unmedicated manic-depressive husband, and then his most recent prolonged bout of mania. She had seen it coming and urged him to visit his doctor, but without success. After listing an array of manic iniquities—among them withdrawing $10,000 from an equity loan on their house; giving keys to their house, truck, and safety deposit box to the residents of a nearby homeless mission; and flooding the house by leaving kitchen and bathroom taps open and gushing—she explains that she tried to have him committed before filing for divorce. Far from an act of vengeance, this was one of kindness, as her husband had offered abundant proof that he was a menace to himself as well as to others. This husband knew his legal rights and called for a jury trial. The jury found him "competent" and able to provide his own food and shelter. After the trial, she writes, the jury members agreed that he suffered from a mental disorder, but they felt it did not warrant putting him under such control against his wishes. Inform yourself before you act.

Manipulative Games and How to Win Them

Both depressives and manic-depressives are world-class manipulators. Sometimes, suggests psychologist Agnes Hatfield, they use threats of aggression to get their way. Intimidated family members often give in because they're afraid of what might otherwise happen. Doing so is a truly bad idea because it will only encourage return engagements. But while only relatively few with the illness use physical threats, almost all engage in more subtle manipulative games. Clarence's girlfriend Lina turned him on and off like a faucet with promises to be adorable if he would just return to her fold. She rarely kept those promises, but Clarence went on being hopeful far too long for his own good.

Depressives, says Hatfield, "have a way of looking or sounding helpless or incompetent that brings others to their rescue." As examples, she offers announcements such as "I can't find my keys" or "I'm out of toothpaste," accompanied by a helpless, expectant look. Her advice is to express sympathy over the nuisance of the missing object and then to let the person locate it rather than searching for it yourself. Far more enraging examples of manipulation have been cited by members of the friends and family group, but Hatfield's advice is pertinent to all of them. Do not get in the habit of doing for your depressive what he or she is perfectly capable of doing. Use the following short examples of manipulation to help identify your own depressive's sneaky bad habits:

• Andrew's wife always asks him to come along when she goes to see her medicating physician, and Andrew always agrees. He clears his office calendar, comes home in the middle of the day, and finds his wife dressed and ready to go. "Oh," she says faintly at the front door of their apartment, "I really don't think I feel well enough to go out." The first time this happened, Andrew was extremely solicitous and comforting. He went back to his office, called the doctor to explain and to make another appointment, and worried for the rest of the day about his poor wife. On the day of the rescheduled appointment, his wife pulled the same trick. That day Andrew returned to his office and made yet another appointment, but didn't waste much time worrying. The third time it happened, he told his wife that from then on she would have to make her own excuses to the doctor, and that he would accompany her there if he wasn't too busy. "You are in charge of making and keeping your appointments," he said firmly. From then on she did take that responsibility, because she didn't want to be depressed. She acted as she did because she wanted the attention and sense of control that her behavior was producing.

- One day Steven came home from his office to find a sizable group of women milling around the living room, looking expectant. They were there, they explained, at his wife Camilla's invitation: she had some exciting project she wanted to present to them. Steven discovered Camilla in their bedroom watching television; piteously, she asked him to make her excuses, and he did so, with much embarrassment and many lies. After that, there were often excuses to be made: to hostesses who expected two guests to turn up rather than just Steven, and to charitable groups who called to ask why Camilla hadn't come to chair her committee meeting. Steven never did learn what to do about all this, because he had no one to explain to him what was going on.

- One pair of parents arrived at the group filled with concern and sympathy for their depressive son who had quit his job because of his lethargy and inability to concentrate or make decisions. After a couple of months he stopped taking his pills because, he explained to them, they made him feel terrible. So they took over his housekeeping, lent him money, took him shopping, came over whenever he said he was lonely, and wondered what more they could do for him. Tell him to shape up and get back on his medication, said the group. "But who will look after him?" moaned the much-manipulated parents. "If he takes his medication, he'll be quite able to look after himself," was the reply. "Let him live his own life for a bit. When he realizes you aren't going to coddle him, he'll probably start taking his pills again." After a couple of months, he did.

There are a million ways to manipulate; depressives and manics seem instinctively to know all of them. When you become aware of a pattern of manipulation that is like fingernails on the blackboard for you, be specific in your demand that it cease. Don't broach the subject in a roundabout way, or become distracted by secondary issues; zero in on one thing that you really can't tolerate, and ask your depressive point-blank to stop doing whatever it is.

For instance, instead of saying "I can't stand the mess you make," request that your depressive pick up the magazines and hang up his or her coat. Instead of saying "Why don't you do the shopping for once?", write out a list and suggest what store to go to. Depressives really do lack concentration and have trouble remembering things and making decisions. Blanket requests won't help them or you. Spell out what you want, and don't pile on too much discipline all at once. When they've gotten in the habit of picking up their coat, move on to the shoes and jacket. Patience will pay off in this respect; getting endlessly cross and nagging will not.

One last piece of advice: Never be condescending, as though the person with the illness were a small child. Even though your adult depressive may on occasion sound or act like a third grader, he or she is not and shouldn't be treated like one. While they may not be able to sustain their pre-illness standard of behavior, they are often capable of returning to it for a limited period of time when they wish. Decide what you want to change and work out a strategy for achieving it. In the end you'll get your way.

The Heloise and Ann Landers of Depression Fallout

Faith and Rosemary, one the wife of a manic-depressive who swings back and forth a lot, the other married to a self-doubting, self-blaming depressive, have both discovered during long marriages how to cope on a daily basis with their respective husbands' illnesses with enviable aplomb and good humor. In both instances, medication is doing an excellent job, but the illnesses from which these two men suffer have settled in for the duration, and no medications are capable of banishing all traces of them; nor has therapy, although extremely useful, accomplished this task. Both wives will always share their husbands with an alien "it," but both have learned how to bring that "it" to submission.

Faith and Marco have been married for twenty-seven years, only the first five of which were illness-free. Marco was just embarking on his career as a lawyer; manic depression was the last thing a cub attorney and the father of an infant son needed. "We signed on as a team when we got married," says Faith. "It's true that the illness is in his body, but we have always shared the burden of it." Openness about Marco's illness within the family has significantly lightened that burden. "When our son Peter was four years old, he was always wanting his dad to play with him, and Marco was in a terrible down at the time. I explained that Daddy was sick with something called depression and that we had to work hard to make him feel better. So Peter would go into the bedroom and tell his father they were going to spend thirty minutes being depressed together, and then go outside and play baseball for thirty minutes. It worked then and it still does. We never allow Marco to lie about in a funk for longer than that."

The effectiveness of this team approach explains why it's a pleasure to be around this couple. Marco is a large, huggable Italian bear with stomach and smile of equally large dimensions. Faith, who is of Irish ancestry, is as solid as a rock but a great deal funnier. "People who have Marco's problem are singleminded and can be picky beyond belief. Sometimes he confronts me with idiotic accusations like having surreptitiously rearranged his bookshelves. So I got a Polaroid camera and photographed them. Now I have proof. When he yells at me, I show him the photos."

Humor has a prominent place in their interactions. When Marco's in a down, like many depressives he finds crawling out from under the covers the first and most difficult challenge of the day. Faith has three remedies. Normal mornings require only the cats; feeding them is Marco's responsibility. When the alarm goes off, Faith opens the bedroom door and they leap to apply their soft, pulsing paws to Marco's shoulders. This is usually sufficient to part him from his pillow, but not always. Tougher mornings call for tougher tactics. On occasion, Faith has used a water pistol to spray Marco with an icy reminder that the cats are hungry and the office is waiting. When Peter, now in his early twenties, is left in charge, he deals with recalcitrance by overturning the mattress and dumping his father on the floor. "Of course Marco gets angry when we do that," says Faith, "but I say 'Isn't it silly what we have to do to get you moving?' We end up laughing because of course it is laughable."

When Marco is down, Faith has ways of helping him. Fettucine Alfredo, she has discovered, will almost always bring him from gloom to the dining room table; chocolate cornmeal cookies cheer him up, too. So can music, turned up to house-rattling volume. "And I always open all the blinds, let in as much light and fresh air as the house can absorb." When all else fails, Faith calls Marco's best friend, John. "John can always get him started," she says, "but if he's busy I'll put something funny on the VCR, the Marx Brothers, maybe, or Monty Python. Even if Marco doesn't laugh, he feels less depressed."

When mania creeps back, Faith has antidotes for this as well. She has composed her own glossary of symptoms specific to her husband. "Marco loves books, but when he starts collecting huge piles of them by the bed, flipping through and jumping from one to another, that's a danger sign. So is cleaning out his closet, not like a normal person would, but with some crazy sense of urgency. Or when he wants to exercise all the time, as though he's in training for a decathlon."

Like all manics, Marco is a big talker; when his mania is on the rise he talks incessantly and has his own giveaway topics. "Marine biology is one," says Faith. "And so is a desire to change careers and become a dermatologist." The first antidote Faith applies? "I develop a migraine. I used to get them long ago, and I noticed that when there was something the matter with me, Marco's mania calmed down for a bit and he concentrated on helping me. So I've gone on using that tactic." But it's only a first line of defense. "I always tell Marco what I think is happening, and suggest he check in with his doctor and his therapist. If he insists he's okay and doesn't need to, that's a bad sign. Then I call his doc and therapist. One or the other will give Marco a call on the pretense that they just want to know how he's doing. That way he gets his meds and feelings checked out without my having to nag at him.

"Yes, it's true we're a great team," Faith agrees, "but it took a lot of time and effort to put it together. There were times, especially early on, when I felt very near the edge. Once I told Marco I was going away, that I needed some space. He got very angry and told me to go ahead. But a few hours later he reconsidered and asked me please not to leave him. That's when we realized we had to be a team—him, Peter, and me, and his doctor and therapist, too. That's what made it all work. It's not completely one-sided, either. I get to talk about my problems, too, whether or not they have anything to do with Marco. We all get equal time in our house."

If I think of Faith and Marco in the abstract, they seem almost like cardboard characters cut out for a how-to manifesto on handling depressive illness. But they aren't. They come every Friday evening, Faith to the friends and family group, Marco to the one for manic-depressives. While we all stand about in the sign-in area, waiting for the groups to begin, they are warm and funny and obviously very fond of each other. Sometimes Faith lets off a blast in our group; I'm sure Marco has his own complaints to vent in his. But they've found a workable solution that allows them to be a loving and very functional family.

Rosemary is a quilter as well as a fifty-year-old candidate in psychology. Every Friday evening she arrives with a quilt in progress and stitches her way through the evening, fitting her comments into the ongoing discussion as precisely as she constructs the architecture of her coverlet. Rosemary, like Faith, exudes calm, confidence, and order, qualities that enable her to cope with the lethargy and confusion that are the hallmarks of her husband's depression.

"When Harold's depression starts getting the upper hand, I don't think or say, 'Oh God, here we go again.' Instead, I tell him he's going to be just fine, that he'll get through it okay, just as he has before." This works because Rosemary believes what she's saying; this belief communicates itself to Harold and helps him keep his head above water. She tries never to blame him, or to nag and criticize; instead, she provides the order and sense of accomplishment his illness steals away.

Like Marco, Harold hates getting up in the morning. Rosemary has her own formula: First, the launching pad, counting down from ten to takeoff when Harold must put his feet on the floor, followed by a long shower. "That's usually enough to get him going, but not always," admits Rosemary. "Sometimes he just can't make it any further, and then I tell him that I'm scared and worried because he's been taking so many days off from the office. Saying that is much more effective than bullying, telling him he's going to lose his job or that he's making a mess of things. That would put too much stress on Harold and make him feel badly about himself. My being scared is something he can respond positively to."

Rosemary uses the same technique to keep her husband on the move. "If it's a weekend or a holiday, I always make a plan, not just a generalized one, like 'Let's do something fun,' but a specific one: chores, lunch, walk, museum, shopping, and so forth. And I break large items into smaller ones." When she needs help around the house, instead of asking Harold to clean the bathroom, she enumerates all the steps: take up the rug, then clean the tub, then the toilet and sink, then mop the floor and change the towels. That makes the job more manageable for him. "If he has trouble getting started, I explain I've got too much to do and really need his help to accomplish it. People like you and me do things like cleaning the bathroom on autopilot. Depressives can't operate that way. They need instructions or they'll get confused and run out of steam."

I asked Rosemary if she is really as calm and patient as she appears. Her answer was oblique but clear: "Sometimes when I'm talking with close friends I wonder why they don't seem to understand how hard Harold's illness is for me. It's as though they needed some visual sign in addition to the words I speak. Then I allow myself to cry. Then they notice I need help."

Harold, says Rosemary, is the most considerate of men. Her affection for him is palpable, but living with his entrenched depression could have undermined her feelings had she not taken steps to protect them. Fortifications haven't sprung up magically out of nowhere; she has built them, with the same attention to order, choice, and detail that she gives to her quilting. Their relationship is a carefully constructed work of art in progress, just like her coverlets. Rosemary is not an angelic model, impossible to emulate. She admits she sometimes gets discouraged and fed up with Harold. "At one point the chore of getting him out of bed got so ritualized and complex that I felt he was training me instead of the other way round. So I gave him the cold shoulder for a while. He got the message."

As Faith and Rosemary make clear, living with a depressive or a manic-depressive is not a bowl of cherries, but it doesn't have to be a can of worms. To a very large degree, what you choose to make of it will determine your own human condition. If you leave your fate in the hands of their illness, you will have a bad time of it. The more responsibility you assume for determining how your joint life proceeds, the more rewarding the results for all concerned. Think of it in terms of a recipe of your own making—some basic ingredients, embellished with your own particular flourishes. It might look something like this:

> Take equal amounts of knowledge, patience, and determination. Mix well.
>
> Fold in carefully a large dollop of strategy, using your imagination to determine quantity.
>
> Add one packet of rules and regulations in an organized manner, with careful attention to detail.
>
> Mix in whatever tolerance and compassion you have in the cupboard.
>
> Sprinkle on a sense of humor, caginess, and guile.
>
> Add any secret ingredients of your own that might leaven the batter.
>
> Bake well in a moderate oven.
>
> Will keep for six months, longer if refrigerated.

10.

PRIMARY TARGETS:

HUSBANDS, WIVES, LOVERS

THE VAST MAJORITY OF US pair up in marriage and other forms of consensual union, many of which go awry for reasons with which we are all too familiar, but an underlying cause, rarely identified or acknowledged, may actually be one partner's depression. Depressives select a primary target for their despair, someone with whom they are intimately connected, whom they trust not to betray their feelings and behavior to the outside world, someone they can count on for forgiveness. Nowhere is this targeting more evident than between husbands and wives, or lovers. If the depression is out in the open, like that of Patsy's husband Jack, described in chapter 2, it's an obvious hook on which to hang the marital problems it causes. Clarence's realization, as he describes in chapter 3, that Lina's "it" was at the heart of the intractable issues between them, enabled him to step back and achieve some breathing space. Understanding the cause didn't terminate their problems; only successful treatment of their depressives could have done that. But it did place those problems in the context of reality instead of in their imaginations. Instead of beating themselves up for all the difficulties in their respective relationships, pinning the blame on their own inadequacies, their lack of love and patience, and their inability to make things right, they placed the blame where it rightly lay: on the other's illness.

Recognizing the "it" is a major first step, but not a magic wand for

curing depression fallout. The word *depression* is so often teamed with
adjectives like *disabling, debilitating,* and *incapacitating* that we expect
its sufferers to be weak and defenseless, sapped of strength and
determination. This is indeed how they feel, but paradoxically it is
not how they act with those closest to them. Their negative cast of
mind, expressed in both words and actions, has an implacable force
that can slowly but surely overwhelm their partner, leaving him or
her unable or unwilling to provide just what the depressive most
needs: a loving and supportive relationship. In this sense depressives
are their own worst enemies.

Targeting, which typically goes on in private, is insidious. There is
no clear battle of wills, no concerted assault upon the target's persona. Variously described by spouses and lovers in the group and
elsewhere as ambush, sabotage, and endless minor skirmishes, targeting has a cumulative effect. It fuels our journey through the stages
of depression fallout, moving us from initial confusion to self-doubt
and then on to demoralization. Resentment and anger soon follow.
Depending upon their tolerance for what is going on, some will
come to see separation or divorce as a desirable option, as did Steven
in chapter 2.

Vanessa: Insecure and Feeling Stupid

However depression fallout sufferers describe their targeting experience, and whatever they decide to do about it, they are consistent in
the kind of behavior to which they are subjected. Five adjectives turn
up with frequency: *deflating, belittling, unpredictable, manipulative,* and
fault-finding. On a recent Friday when the topic arose in the group,
these words were used over and over again, punctuated by a nodding
of heads and a chorus of "Right, that's it, that's what they do."
Encouraged by this sympathetic audience, Vanessa, whose husband is
on antidepressants and also sees a talk therapist, launched into a
complaint about his latest depression-driven iniquities. "I've just
about had it with him," she wound up, providing yet another chapter in a very long tale she had already privately confided to me.

"When I was little, we had an Irish maid who used to say to me, if
I was being stubborn or contrary, 'You're as twisted as a ram's horn;
if I said black, you'd say white.' That's what Eric does with me," says

Vanessa. "It's nothing so simple as being argumentative. He's contrary and unpredictable and often downright mean. He takes the wind right out of my sails. Nothing I do or say is right so far as he's concerned."

Vanessa and Eric, both in their early sixties, have been married for seven years. It's a second marriage for both, and from the beginning it's been a good fit, providing Vanessa with everything she had wanted and hoped for from a post-children relationship: warmth, affection, companionship, and the time and wherewithal to enjoy them. Eric's job as an agent in the film business is, as Vanessa describes it, a twenty-four-hour sort of thing, but since socializing with clients is part of his work, they spend more time together than is usually the case when one spouse has a demanding career. About five years into their marriage, however, the customary ease between them began gradually to evaporate and was replaced by an edginess and a distance, "as though," says Vanessa, "the connection between us had been severed. I didn't feel loved anymore. Instead I felt shut out." It took Vanessa a year to accept that something was wrong.

In the beginning, she explained, you know how you feel but not why you feel that way. "Of course you think the fault is yours, that you are provoking in some way the bad interactions between yourself and the other person." Why is it, she wondered, that when something goes wrong we always assume it's because of something we have done, or that we're being unreasonable or stupid, even when all the evidence contradicts that assumption?

"They say that nature abhors a vacuum, and I guess people do, too. So I made up my own reason for Eric's behavior. I decided he must be having an affair, although I couldn't imagine when he found time to see anybody else. He never worked late at the office or gave any of the classic giveaway signs. But I knew something was terribly wrong, and I just couldn't think of anything else except another woman." Vanessa is not the first spouse of a depressive to latch onto the suspicion of an extramarital affair as an explanation for what looks like a change of heart. As in many similar situations, her assumption—false, as it turned out—made matters even worse. Determined not to stage any jealous-wife confrontations, she devoted herself to trying harder to please Eric. "I kept suggesting all the things we most enjoyed doing together, like going to concerts, playing tennis, and cooking fancy meals together. He never seemed to want to do anything. We stopped seeing our friends. We always used to take a walk in the park on Sundays, but he didn't even want to do that."

Every encounter became a power struggle because, she explains, those were the terms on which Eric was operating. "Even the simplest decisions ended up being one-sided, partly because I hate any kind of confrontation and partly because most of the time, as far as I was concerned, it was all about things that don't merit a fight. I'm talking about really, really petty things, like had I made a phone call when making it or not was totally unimportant. He'd turn it into some big deal, as though I was too stupid or disorganized to accomplish anything." Eric approached every interaction like a cagey commando. "We'd be talking, for instance, about having dinner with friends, and I'd be thinking that for once it was going to be okay, that he was going to say, 'Go ahead and see if they're free next Wednesday,' when suddenly he'd veer off and start to criticize them for being too fat or boring or drinking too much. All of a sudden they were *my* friends, not *our* friends. And then I'd defend the person he was attacking, and it would all deteriorate into an awful picky discussion on somebody else's character, with me being upbraided for having bad judgment or being stupid. So in the end it was always about me, and always critical. How is it possible to defend yourself in such a situation? If you say, 'No, I'm not stupid,' the discussion only gets more pointless and you *do* sound stupid. Eric was always looking for control and always in a negative way that damaged me."

People with a depressive illness can be terrific actors, playing Dr. Jekyll in public and Mr. Hyde behind closed doors. Vanessa's confusion and resentment echoes through most husband-and-wife depression fallout stories. "We'd be all ready to go out, with me dressed to kill," says Vanessa, "and then in the taxi Eric would look at me and say, 'What's the matter with your hair?' or 'Why are you wearing that dress?' Right away I'd feel graceless and ugly, and all the pleasure would go out of me. But then during dinner he'd manufacture an opportunity to say to the whole table, 'Look at my gorgeous wife, isn't she wonderful, don't you think I'm lucky?' Things like that should have made me feel wonderful. Instead, I'd have to sit there smiling and pretending that he hadn't said just the opposite in private. This all sounds so picayune, but it isn't, not when it happens all the time." What appears to the uninitiated as a niggling annoyance is, to the depression fallout sufferer, part of a barrage of attacks on his or her self-esteem. Over time, this sort of behavior feels like part of a determined campaign by the depressive to undermine, disparage, and reduce the partner to the status of nonperson.

Vanessa tried to ask Eric what was wrong between them; his response was common to many depressives. Assuming an expression of superior surprise, he insisted that nothing was wrong, and what was the matter with her that she should think so? Vanessa settled into a state of demoralization compounded by a self-imposed isolation. She is a very private person. Although by no means unsociable, she keeps her own counsel and rarely seeks to involve others in her problems, whatever they may be. Because she resisted complaining to her friends about her husband and the sad, inexplicable state of their marriage, she cut herself off from their potential support.

Vanessa carried the full burden of Eric's assault upon her ego and her sense of purpose, floating listlessly and resentfully in her own private despair for almost a year, until one day when Eric came home and announced in an offhand manner that he had started taking antidepressants. Having compared notes with a longtime depressive friend, he had made his own diagnosis and gone to see his friend's psychiatrist, who prescribed medication and a course of talk therapy. Within a month, things began to improve between them to a point where they were able to discuss openly his illness and how the behavior it had produced had ignited the negative dynamic between them.

"Everything is immensely better now," says Vanessa, a year after the start of Eric's treatment and two years after her initial confusion and pain began. "But it's not over and I've accepted it won't ever be. Even with medication and psychotherapy, Eric falls into downs, and when he does, he starts using me as a punching bag again. When that happens, the cycle of disturbance between us is reactivated. The trouble is that now it happens immediately rather than gradually. Whenever his depression returns, I'm back in my old feelings, and it's almost as though the good times since then were wiped out."

This instant throwback to the bad times is voiced by many depression fallout sufferers whose depressive or manic-depressive is receiving the proper treatment but is still subject to mood changes; even when the overall situation is vastly improved, their lives remain subject to uncertainty. "I still never know what to expect from him," says Vanessa, "so I've come to feel constantly off-balance. His perception of me and our life together changes constantly, just like his opinions on everything from politics to where we'll take our next vacation. I have no permanent center anymore. I'm living not just with my Eric but with a whole bunch of different Erics. I'm constantly making adjustments to suit whichever Eric I'm confronted with." For Vanessa and others in her situation, anticipating a return to previous bad behavior is as unpleasant as actually experiencing a recurrence.

Isolation accentuates depression fallout. All of its sufferers need a personal or professional sympathetic ear. Vanessa found both. "The year before Eric started treatment was really painful. I fell into my own pattern of behaving and reacting so I could stay afloat, and that pattern remains strong. It's taken hold. I went to a therapist six months ago, but she didn't help very much. Some of what she said made sense, but only because she drew a lot of the same conclusions I had. That did give me some confidence. But she didn't have any magic words of advice. I've found talking with two close women friends who are in almost the identical situation the most helpful. We work off a lot of steam that way. We remind each other that it's not our fault, that we aren't the ones doing something wrong, it's our depressed husbands. And we remind each other that we're not dumb. When someone keeps telling you how stupid you are, eventually you get angry. I hate the reservoir of anger I've accumulated. I've never been an angry person, or a resentful one, and now I often am."

Vanessa has recently seen another therapist, one who did have some magic words, which she has shared with the group: "Step back. Listen to yourself, not to his depression. Let the words slide off you. You know he loves you. Fix on that fact instead of his behavior. Just let the bad stuff go."

James: Closed up and in Despair

I have, stowed away in my files, hundreds of pages of notes from talks with depression fallout wives. I have trouble distinguishing one teller from another, so alike are their stories. Most find words to describe their feelings not just about depression fallout, but about many other issues that cause them pain and distress or, for that matter, happiness and joy. We women are often less guarded than men, more at home talking about our feelings. If there's a noise downstairs in the middle of the night, both the man and the woman upstairs will be equally frightened. While the wife will openly admit to terror, the husband won't because he has been acculturated to believe it would be unmanly and cowardly to admit fear. When the noise proves to be a neighbor's cat that has jumped through an open window into the kitchen, the wife will say something like, "Oh, I was so scared! I didn't know what to do, my heart almost stopped." The husband will skip all that personal stuff and content himself with saying, "Good thing it was only a cat."

Communication patterns specific to each sex may in part explain why my story files hold many more tales of women whose husbands are depressed than the reverse. Talking with the male friend with whom I first jointly explored the topic of depression fallout, we used many of the same words to describe his wife's behavior and my mother's—*fed up, resentful,* and *angry* among them. But while I went on to elaborate in far greater specificity my feelings of pain and inadequacy, he only listened to what I said, chiming in with an occasional "Me too."

In the period during which I have been attending the Friday-evening support group, only four men have come to talk about their partners' depressive illness. One is Clarence; another is Willy, who talked about his wife's psychotherapist in chapter 7. The third was a young husband who attended only a few times, volunteering little on his first appearance other than that he had lost sympathy for his long-depressed wife. On his last evening he told us he was taking a new job in California where she might or might not join him. In the interim he canceled at the last minute three appointments to talk with me, all of which he claimed to have looked forward to. The fourth is James.

If ever a depression fallout sufferer needed a skillful therapist, it's James, but his entire face wrinkles in distaste at the very idea. James has buried his anger and despair deep, but that makes them no less powerful. In the group, he adopts a forgiving and somewhat resigned attitude toward his wife's manic depression of five years' duration, but the divining rod of an interview away from other ears and eyes detected more than a hint of turbulent streams below the surface. His wife, Ursula, is a rapid cycler (as are about 10 percent of manic-depressives), defined in the books as subject to as many as four big mood swings a year. Ursula has as many as four a week despite the best efforts of an expert psychopharmacologist and a skilled psychotherapist.

James, who, at seventy-five, looks at least fifteen years younger, hails from an era when the airing of one's emotions was considered in bad taste. He learned that lesson well. His wife is more than twenty years his junior. "I told her I'd never marry her, that she was too young for me, but she said it wasn't her fault I got born so much ahead of her. Cute, right?" He smiles at me expectantly, and then launches cheerfully into a description of life with a speeded-up, rapid-cycling manic-depressive. "People with her illness march to a different drummer. It's a life of high drama. If you say something to them as simple as 'Gee, you have beautiful eyes,' they'll say, 'What's the matter with my nose?' and get paranoid and angry. They can have incredible physical strength when they're higher than high. She's broken I don't know how many telephones, and once she actually pulled the faucet out of the kitchen sink. And I've never seen so much money go flying out the window. That's typical of manic-depressives, you know, buying everything."

James goes to his office every day, which gives him a recess from Ursula's illness, but as he pointed out, he also has to return every day to a home invaded by her illness. Like Vanessa, he never knows what will be waiting for him on the other side of the front door. Often it is a verbally abusive Ursula. "Most of the time I'm the focal point, or else it's my son. You would not believe the things she says," he intones, drawing out each word and smiling broadly. When I asked him to give an example, he said, "No way. It's not for your ears. You know, another trait of manic-depressives is they can become very sexy, very promiscuous," he said, again dodging specifics. "And then there's the other side of the coin; some have no libido at all. I'd like to have a little romance in my life."

James describes life with Ursula as living under the Sword of Damocles, an existence in which the abnormal becomes the norm. Periods of calm produce as much anxiety as relief. Frequent crises stave off thoughts about the future. He estimates that one half of his time is taken up with being Ursula's "caretaker," a word that increasingly takes precedence over "caregiver" in his tale. They have little social life because it's impossible to know in advance how she will feel. "I could paper a room with the unused theater and concert tickets. My friends tell me to come to dinner alone, but that's not easy, to walk out and leave her. Sure, I can do it, but that would put me on a guilt trip." When they do venture out with friends, his wife is predictable only in her penchant for embarrassing everyone but herself. "I'm used to her insults in private; when they are directed in public at others, too, it's excruciating. I'd rather stay home and avoid that."

James is one of the group regulars. He's the resident doler-out of good-humored wisecracks and stalwart cheeriness. When he hears echoes of his own dilemma in the tales told by other members, he is quick to offer empathetic support and advice. Much of that advice stems from a series of mantras he repeats to himself: *It's not her fault she's ill. She doesn't want to be ill. I don't hold her responsible for her illness. She's not crazy, you know. She's a manic-depressive. Big difference.*

These are all good reminders for the group, helpful basics to bear in mind when things are tough, but for James they have become much more. They have become a prison for his emotions. "So I'm not angry about it," he often adds. Of course he is. James is an admirable and thoroughly likable human being, not a martyr.

"So you think I'm responsible and balanced and loving in all this?" James asked me. "I can see it now on my tombstone: 'There goes another faithful failure.' I mean, you really accomplish nothing in being a caretaker. And I feel, you know, that if you put a sick person and a well person in a room together, the sick person isn't going to get well, but the well person can get sick." And then for an instant he unlocked his feelings. "Sometimes I think I just can't go on like this. I feel as though I'm going to explode. I really don't know what the future will bring. I keep reminding myself that Ursula doesn't want to be like this, that it's not her fault. Besides, where would she go? Who would look after her?"

For a while all of us in the group urged James to take some time off, have dinner with a friend, go to a concert, spend more than his customary two or three weekends a year with his son and grandchildren. But James rebuts every suggestion, no matter how minimal, as unfeasible, impractical, or unnecessary in some way. Through the growing chinks in his carefully constructed armor shine the resentment and anger that he has devoted so much energy to denying, not only to us but to himself. Lately we have learned to stick to patting his arm when the group is over, telling him that we are worried and care about him. This is the only solace he allows us to offer. Just as his emotions have become prisoners of his mantras, his entire life has become the prisoner of his wife's illness.

The details of Vanessa's and James's tales are different, but both have traveled along through all the same stages of depression fallout. Humor and forbearance, James's weapons of choice, are helpful but not sufficient in themselves to fight back effectively against depression fallout. "You have to face that it's not just about them and their problem," says Vanessa. "It's about you, how you feel and why, and where the fault for that lies. Being selfless doesn't help anybody or anything."

Katharine Graham: The Price of Silence

Of course, not every woman is as open about her feelings as those whose stories are in my files. One such silent sufferer was Katharine Graham, publisher of *The Washington Post*, who revealed to no one how she felt during her long marriage to her intelligent, often charming, workaholic, alcoholic, and manic-depressive husband, Philip Graham. In part her silence stemmed from her generation's expectations that wives should play a subsidiary role and tolerate all kinds of behavior from their mates. It also came from loyalty to him, and, in the beginning, from not knowing what ailed him. In her recently published memoirs, *Personal History* (Knopf, 1997), she gives us a glimpse into how his illness affected her and their life together.

Some fourteen years after their marriage, the early warnings of Phil Graham's illness, which had already begun to reverberate in their personal relationship, gave way to a severe depression followed by cycles of mania and depression that led to his death six years later. During this time, in the late 1950s and early 1960s, his psychiatrist refused to give a name to his illness, believing that such labels changed how the person viewed himself and was viewed by others. "I didn't hear the term 'manic depression' until some time later," Graham writes. "Throughout this period, I viewed what was happening with confusion and very little understanding." Meanwhile, her husband was displaying classic symptoms of the illness: vitriolic anger, argumentativeness, and irritability; the ability to charm and persuade others, including his psychiatrist, that all was well; belittlement of his wife both privately and in public; excessive drinking and risk-taking; and exhaustion and despair intermixed with ebullience and brilliance. His family, colleagues, close friends, and acquaintances all attributed his negative behaviors to stress. At Phil's request, Katharine was ever at his side, consoling and supporting him, and hiding the problems from the rest of the family. "Except for [his] psychiatrist," she writes, "I spoke to no one about Phil and what was wrong. . . . [We] all excused his angry, aberrant moods as signs of exhaustion. . . . [E]ven in the midst of this darkening scene of hyperactivity, rage, and irrationality, Phil still retained much of his ability and got significant things accomplished."

In the final year of his life, Phil Graham left the woman for whom he had abandoned his wife some months earlier, and expressed a desire to return home. His wife, although still deeply in love with him, decided against it. "Having Phil back was a tremendous—and complicated—relief. For me, one of the immediate questions was whether I could go through another black depression with him. I knew all too well what it was like—not being able to leave the house except when he was at his doctor's; hours and hours of intensive talk; hearing things I wasn't sure I wanted to hear or know about. All of those years we had labored through together to get him out of the depressions had resulted in his leaving me. None of my efforts had led to a happy ending, and I felt I just couldn't assume once again the heavy burden and responsibility of being his sole support system."

Instead, he returned to the nearby private psychiatric institution he had periodically visited during his deepest depression. But Phil Graham wanted to come home; a few days later he persuaded his doctors to allow him a visit. On the very day of his return, he shot himself without leaving a note.

Kay and Phil Graham were devoted to each other, but in the end his illness brought tragedy to both. Hers is a story of both her husband's manic depression and her own depression fallout. Throughout her memoirs are many telltale comments that reveal the effects of her husband's illness upon her. "I can see now that I was having problems I didn't acknowledge to myself," she writes.

> I was growing shyer and less confident as I got older. . . . My insecurity had something to do with both my mother and Phil . . . at the same time he was building me up he was tear-

ing me down. . . . I became the butt of the family jokes. . . .
Because I had gained some weight, though not much, he
started to call me "Porky." . . . Another habit of his that
emerged in those years was that, when we were with friends
and I was talking, he would look at me in such a way that I
felt I was going on too long and boring people. . . . Yet, I felt
as though he had created me and that I was totally dependent on him. Even now I can't sort out my feelings about all
this; it's hard to separate what was a function of Phil's terrible affliction, which manifested itself only later, and what was
more basic. The truth is that I adored him and saw only the
positive side of what he was doing for me. I simply didn't connect my lack of self-confidence with his behavior toward me.

Like so many in similar situations, Kay Graham endured her
depression fallout in silence, traveling through its predictable stages
culminating, despite an enduring love, in her reluctance to have her
husband home again.

In addition to all her other problems, Graham was forced also to
endure the ignorance of her husband's doctors. From beginning to
end they failed to provide the necessary intervention—although
lithium was still in the experimental stages, used mostly in Europe,
electroshock therapy had been routinely used as a treatment for
manic depression for several decades—restricting it to countless sessions of talk therapy. The Grahams' daughter, after visiting her father
in the private institution to which he returned just before his death,
wrote to her mother that his psychiatrist "was really his only ray of
hope in the past few days, since he told Daddy that he knew he could
pull through his depressions and do it without a hospital and also
that although the words 'manic depression' might be a very adequate description of his past behavior, that did *not* necessitate a
future cycle." Phil Graham agreed wholeheartedly with his doctor
and not only resisted the label but embraced his manic highs, writing at the time to a friend, "I find it unendurable to believe that 'balance' or 'moderation' or 'middle-of-the-road' represent human
approaches to living."

Poor and irresponsible treatment of manic depression can and
not infrequently does result in tragedy, as can depression when its
sufferers become suicidal. Those who have the illness should not

always be permitted the final say on whether or how it should be treated. Not all doctors are equally competent; when they are lacking, families must intervene and find someone who knows what to do. Katharine Graham can hardly be blamed for not doing so because both she and her husband lived through his manic depression at a time when nonprofessionals knew little or nothing about it. Times have changed, but not all doctors have changed with them. Find one who has, and put him in charge. Loyalty to a sick and suffering husband is one thing; loyalty to a bad doctor is another.

What Depression Fallout Women Need to Know About Male Depression

Some depression fallout women may not recognize their husband's or lover's changed behavior as the result of a depression. Just as the sexes differ in their willingness to talk about their feelings, they may also choose different means to express those originating with their disorder. Although there wasn't any doubt about what ailed Philip Graham, depression doesn't always stand out like a sore thumb, particularly, according to Boston psychologist Terrence Real, when it happens to men. In *I Don't Want to Talk About It: Overcoming the Secret Legacy of Male Depression* (Scribner's, 1997), he advances the thesis that the traditional socialization of boys and girls results in differing reactions to their experience of depression. "Girls, and later women," he writes, "tend to internalize pain. They blame themselves and draw distress into themselves." But boys and adult men, he says, are more apt to "externalize pain; they are more likely to feel victimized by others and to discharge distress through action." The male modes of action he distinguishes as covers for depression are workaholism, alcoholism, and lashing out at others, sometimes violently enough to be termed abuse.

One of the reasons why many men who suffer from depression fail to recognize the cause of their behavior and feelings, says Real, is that "stereotypically, being a man means being strong, being 'on top of it.' The shame attached to vulnerability is one of the reasons why so many overtly depressed men [and, I would add, depression fallout men] don't want to talk about it, why they don't admit the disorder or get help that could change their lives, and why people surrounding overtly depressed men shy away from confronting them about their condition." Many men often successfully hide their depression even from themselves, resulting in a lot of what Real terms "covert depression." None of this is good news for their partners.

Depression and Marital Discord

Whether overt or covert, depression in males probably disturbs or ends as many marriages as does depression in females. When, convinced by a wealth of anecdotal evidence that this was true, I went exploring in the research literature dealing with interactions between depressed and non-depressed people and their spouses, I came upon the write-up of a mid-1980s experiment aptly titled "Depression and Marital Disagreement: The Social Construction of Despair." The researchers, Jana Kahn and James C. Coyne of the Mental Research Institute in Palo Alto, and Gayla Margolin of the University of Southern California, devised a canny test for which they assembled twenty-eight couples: seven with a depressed husband, seven with a depressed wife, and fourteen in which neither spouse was depressed. After asking all the participants to complete a questionnaire about their "marital satisfaction and typical conflict behavior," each couple was invited to talk together about a topic they considered a relevant marital issue. Afterward they were asked to rate their own and the other's coping strategies as constructive (listening attentively to what one's partner is saying), aggressive (insulting one's partner or calling him or her names), or withdrawal (sulking or pouting). The results of the experiment showed that partners of depressed spouses were just as upset in every way as their depressed husbands or wives; both were far more so than the depression-free couples.

Members of couples with a depressed person were dissatisfied with their marriages and with their spouses' overall conflict behavior, but not with their own. At the end of their discussion, both were sad and angry; both experienced each other as hostile, competitive, mistrusting, and detached, as well as less agreeable, less supportive and encouraging, and less interested in becoming and feeling close. This wasn't so among the non-depressed couples. Depressives and their partners struggle with problems in a way that produces anger and sadness but little constructive problem-solving. Many veered off from what they were supposed to be talking about, to focus on their accumulating hurt and frustration.

The researchers quote one chronically depressed wife as saying that she and her husband weren't good at communicating: "We hide and deny our feelings, and when they do come out, we don't even get to what's bothering us. The emotion [sadness, anger, or both] comes out, but not the reason for it." The failed efforts of these couples to improve their situation leave them feeling even worse, yet not making the effort would be the equivalent of resigning themselves to a helpless and hopeless situation.

The study presents evidence that both depressives and their spouses are not only hostile and often aggressive toward each other, but also that they feel equally inhibited and so withdraw. This allows the problems and resentments to multiply so that efforts to resolve them become increasingly intense and hurtful. Both parties feel they are doing their constructive and participatory best, while their partner is consistently falling short. None were critical of their own efforts, a sure formula for deadlock and hostility.

Although every relationship is sometimes subject to this sort of dynamic, it is telling that within the fourteen depression-free couples participating as controls, it was for the most part lacking. The behavior of twenty-eight couples may not be enough to permit the experts to claim discovery of an unadulterated truth, but few who love and live with a depressive would quibble with the conclusions. One psychiatrist with whom I have spoken said he had "come to believe that a lot of marital grief is due to one or the other partner's depression. Time and again, I hear someone say of their spouse that it's like living with a bottomless pit, that nothing you do can satisfy them. I think," he added, "that's often a sign of unrecognized depression." The members of the friends and family group knew that already, and a good deal more.

Sex and Divorce-Speak

There are four basic facts you need to know about this topic. First, almost everyone with a depressive illness develops a problem with sexual desire and performance, which means that you, as their partner, have one too. Second, however it manifests itself, it is not in any way of your making. Third, many depressives and manics are given to sudden, inexplicable pronouncements about divorce and to accusing their partners of sexual infidelity. This behavior also has nothing to do with anything you have said, implied, or done, so, first and foremost, absolve yourself from guilt and blame; you are an innocent bystander taking a major hit from the "it," because of course once again the illness is the culprit. Thus, to a large extent, your partner is as blameless as you, which is basic fact number four. Take all four facts to heart, because together they form a powerful defense against depression fallout.

Knowledge rarely translates into rationality when sex is at issue, but it's better than tranquilizers, anger, or the fallacious conviction that you are no longer the object of someone's desire. Depressive illness has caused many relationships to founder. Although some relationships may fail on the basis of sexual issues alone, the reasons are usually far more complex, having principally to do with the immense dislocation the illness causes in couples' lives in ways other than sexual. So, though you probably take it as a given that waning sex and divorce threats are inseparable, they are in fact two distinct problems cohabiting under depression's umbrella. Only your imagination and your emotions cobble them together, thus endowing them with a synergistic force they don't deserve.

Of the two, one is well-recognized though not widely discussed: depression usually drags with it sexual lethargy, and to make matters worse, most antidepressants cause some degree of sexual dysfunction. The second matter, which I learned about from listening carefully to husbands and wives of depressives, is their partners' "divorce-speak." This is a blanket term for various out-of-the-blue statements ranging from "You're sleeping around" to "I'm planning to divorce you." I've heard this phenomenon articulated so often in the friends and family group and in my conversations with the partners of depressives that it has gained a place on my unofficial symptoms list.

There is a natural disinclination to be formally recorded on this topic. One member of the support group remarked that his wife had declared her intention to seek the counsel of a divorce lawyer, tossing it offhandedly into his discussion of how things were going for him that week. At least three other heads in the room began nodding assertively, testifying to a similar experience of their own, but no one volunteered to contribute. I caught up with the head-nodders when the session ended. "I gather something similar has happened between you and your partners," I ventured. "Yes indeed," they each responded. "It's really bizarre," added one, "because not even in my moments of greatest frustration and anger have I ever mentioned leaving my wife. When she said *she* was leaving *me*, I was flabbergasted." Why did she do it, then? "Who knows?" contributed one. "I guess it's part of the craziness."

Once the subject had been broached, it began to make more than an occasional appearance on subsequent Friday evenings. Typically, divorce-speak comes out of bravura, and is not the product of thoughtful deliberation. These comments are tossed like gauntlets, and seem to come from nowhere. In the absence of depression, an unhappy or disaffected spouse might be expected to leave a trail of bread crumbs to mark his or her gradual progress toward the decision to separate or to divorce: signs of unhappiness, discussion, arguments, and attempts to improve or at least define the dissonance in the relationship. When depression is present, no such trail is laid; the gauntlet is simply tossed, without warning or preamble, more often than not into a mundane exchange such as about what to have for dinner or what you, the partner, have done wrong that day.

Typically the gauntlet is accompanied by insults about the partner's inadequacies, stupidity, or physical characteristics. Sometimes it takes the form of an unadorned and unelaborated declaration of intention to divorce or to separate or see a lawyer about one or the other, delivered with careless insouciance, as though to say, "Well, obviously I can't live with you; surely you must realize that?" The latter jaunty-style version is more typical of the manic than of the depressive. In both cases, expect the gauntlet to make repeated appearances. Clarence has been so often accused by his girlfriend, Lina, of sleeping around that he can laugh about it in the support group. She is persuaded, all evidence to the contrary, that not only is he getting into bed with every woman he meets, but that he has a special preference for those with large hips.

Laughing with others in the same boat about such matters is possible and brings with it welcome relief. But when one is alone, divorce-speak isn't even remotely funny. So what can you do when you have no support group? Hold fast to the four basic facts. One doesn't have to be a genius to reach the conclusion that what such utterances really mean is that depressives, in some compartment of their conscious or unconscious mind, know they are impossible to live with and choose to talk about leaving before their partner can. Feeling ugly, boring, and unlovable, they anticipate abandonment by their partner. She must want to leave me, the depressive's illogical line of reasoning goes, so I will preserve my dignity and self-esteem by announcing I will go before she has a chance to say she wants me to.

Two courses of action are open to you: softball or hardball. Your choice will depend upon the kind of person you are, the texture of the relationship (both previously and currently), and your state of mind—be it confusion, self-blame, demoralization, or anger—when the gauntlet is thrown. The softball response is to let the glove lie. Say you hope he doesn't mean it because you love him. Or tell her you hope she changes her mind because you love her. Then change the subject or find an excuse to make an exit as calmly as you can.

One version of the hardball response comes courtesy of Germaine, a wife who was nearing the end of her tether after more than a year of her husband's depression-bred nastiness. "One day Jack said he thought it would be a good idea for me to move to Vermont—it's where I lived before we got married, and I still have a house there—and that we would stay good friends and not get divorced. I told him that if I moved to Vermont we wouldn't be good friends and we would get a divorce, and that I could be ready to leave in three days. He said that we should really think about that, and I gave him a deadline of two weeks to do his thinking. The whole scene lasted about three minutes, tops. And he never mentioned it again. What was so astonishing was that he said this totally out of the blue, in a pleasant, conversational tone of voice."

An option not up for consideration in any circumstance is to engage in an argument that starts off, "What are you talking about? What on earth do you mean?" or "My God, how could you possibly say such a thing?" Arguments with depressives and manics are no-win endeavors, a piece of advice that primary targets need to repeat like a mantra. Not only won't you win, but you will certainly lose your cool and whatever peace of mind you have managed to retain so far.

Either hardball or softball approach will only work to the extent that you truly understand that such talk is born not of your depressive's loss of affection for you, but from a loss of his or her own sense of worth as a human being, and as a spouse and lover. Feeling totally inadequate, the depressive often accuses you, the primary target, of having feelings for someone else, someone who is capable of being fun and interesting and sexy—everything he or she isn't right now.

What makes all this advice hard to put into practice is the very real and documented impact that depressive illness has on sexual desire. By itself, depressive divorce-speak is relatively manageable; paired with the other's loss of interest in sex with you, it becomes powerfully threatening. You hear the words within the context of your rejection in the bedroom. If you lack the information that depression and diminished interest in things sexual go hand in hand, you suspect either infidelity or some perceived deficiency in you. But even when your logical mind understands the sex-depression connection, your emotional mind may not. In all likelihood, your depressive or manic-depressive will seize on your confused state of mind and make it worse by aiming barbs or poisoned arrows at you. One psychiatrist explained this by suggesting that most depressives feel so helpless that they take advantage of every opportunity to exert their diminished power, even if it means punching you when you're down. Whatever the motivation, it hurts. A wife whose husband is afflicted with a stubborn long-term depression spoke openly and poignantly to me about this aspect of her marriage.

Lucy is in her late fifties, a born-and-bred Southerner reared on her generation's maxim that a woman owes deference to her husband and should always acquiesce to him, even if this places her in awkward or difficult circumstances. Lucy, who earns a substantial salary as a magazine editor in her hometown, Atlanta, acknowledges that in this respect she is a prisoner of her mores and upbringing. Her husband, Ben, she says, is spoiled rotten. "I've always polished his shoes, packed his suitcases for him, turned down his bed. I've never pushed him to face up to things if he didn't want to, or to talk much about our problems—and certainly never sexual ones—because he's never been good at that. The result is he's manipulated me for years, and all that's been enormously exaggerated by his depression."

After an initial statement that there wasn't much to say about sex because there wasn't any anymore, Lucy admitted that that was only the beginning of the problem. Like so many others in her situation, she is Ben's primary target. "At one point I gained a lot of weight. I was so miserable, and eating was one of the few pleasures I could count on. I blew up like a blimp. Ben said to me one day, 'You're so fat I'm never going to sleep with you again.' I don't think I've ever felt so awful, so low and hopeless and ugly. What made it even more appalling was that he already wasn't sleeping with me, hadn't been for several years, but of course by saying that, he made me feel it was my fault. Ben never says he loves me. When I try to talk about our problems, he just walks away. Once he said to me, 'Why are you still here? Why don't you just get up and leave?' I told him it was because I loved him, to which he answered that he didn't love anyone, least of all himself."

And that, of course, was the nub of it all. Robbed of his sexual drive, robbed of his self-esteem as a husband and as a human being, Ben aimed his despair at Lucy and hit a bulls-eye. Lucy has many close women friends who, along with her job and her own strength and determination not just to survive but to survive well, are her main supports. But this aspect of Ben's depression was one she had not been able to share with them, nor did she go to a support group like mine, so she lacked the abiding comfort derived from knowing that one's private hell is shared by others. When we finished, she insisted on paying for the coffee we had had together, saying, "It's the only good therapy session I've had."

Over the years, Lucy sought the help of psychotherapy, first alone and subsequently together with Ben. "The first two therapists I went to—it was over a period of about five years—only wanted to talk about how I could help Ben, and I'm not interested in hearing that anymore. So I stopped seeing anyone for myself alone. We did go together to a marriage counselor who came highly recommended by someone I trusted. After six sessions at $140 a pop, we hadn't made the smallest progress toward anything important. By the sixth visit, I was just delivering the same litany of complaints against Ben. That was awful, I hated myself. And the therapist didn't seem very interested anyway. Like the two others I had seen, she offered me no advice at all."

Mores, and a natural reticence to discuss personal matters involving sex, may have acted as brakes on Lucy's presentation of her problem to the therapists she consulted. Perhaps, too, she filtered her story through her personal pride and her sense of dignity. But added to that is a general lack of recognition among psychotherapists of what another's depressive illness can do to their intimates. Therapists don't always listen for what they don't expect to hear. The lesson to be learned is that if you do seek counseling for your own problems with another's depression, you should shop around until you find someone who is already familiar with what you are experiencing and feeling, and why. I question the utility of going to a marriage counselor in this situation unless both partners know that depression lies at the heart of their problems and the therapist works within this area. The friends and family group members, many of whom have tried talk therapy with and without their partners, with results similar to Lucy's, endorse this suggestion.

Manic-depressives and Sex

If you're married to or living with a manic-depressive, don't bother with couples therapy or marriage counselors while he or she is in an up phase. Manics also have a problem with sex, but it certainly isn't one of low libido. On the contrary, manics often sleep with anyone they can get their hands on, and according to our group leader, Howard, they have a very high success rate in getting their chosen partner into bed. *Chosen* is perhaps the wrong word to use here because, as Howard says, anyone of the opposite sex looks great to them, and the more the merrier. Mania seems to turn every one of its sufferers into a charmer with charisma and a great sense of humor. Manics also give the appearance of listening to every word that every man or woman lets fall from their lips, a big help when you're looking to make out.

Dr. Donald F. Klein's pleasure feedback theory (see chapter 8) helps us understand the totally uninhibited manic, even if it doesn't lead us to condone their behavior. Manics, Klein says, have no concept of risk because they are assured that everything they do is going to turn out just great. But of course manics do get into trouble for sleeping around. They are indiscreet, usually perfectly willing to admit what they've done because they can't see anything wrong with it. They arrive late at their offices in the morning, utterly exhausted from making love all night. Because they rarely choose to bed their usual partners, they have probably spent a few additional hours on arriving home to deal with the man or woman in residence there. If he or she sets the ultimate boundary, threatening to walk out if the manic doesn't stop, more than likely the manic will respond by saying, "You can walk out if you want, but what's the matter with screwing around?" The only choice a partner has is to make good on the

threat or to wait for the coming depression. If the spouse or lover is
a hypomanic, that may be a very long wait indeed. Most manics also
take an antidepressant, which may have a sexual dampening effect
that their partners will welcome. The manics will not.

What to Do About Sexual Problems

Whatever therapy may do to help you, it cannot revive your partner's
sex drive if it has been blunted by depression. That job is best left to
medication, and therein lies a cruel paradox. Most antidepressants
cause some sexual dysfunction in a majority of those who take them.
For obvious reasons, this information is not trumpeted from the
rooftops. First, it could easily become a self-fulfilling prophecy. Tell
anyone, let alone a depressive, that a pill is going to reduce sexual
functioning, and sexual functioning will suffer. Second, the manufacturers can hardly be expected to advertise this hefty downside of
their products' otherwise excellent results. And, third, despite the
trillions of words devoted to sex in print, on radio and television, and
in private conversations, sexual dysfunction is still not a commonly
discussed topic. Many doctors are not helpful in this respect, neither
probing for patient responses nor offering facts and solutions that
could help. In the case of depressives, this reluctance to tell all is
exacerbated by the fact that their spouse or lover takes their disin-
terest personally, and so the problem escalates. This rubs off on the
depressive's fragile ego, and on his or her partner's, too. All relationships, and particularly those involving sex, are deeply embedded
in the ego, either in its projection or rejection, or the need to nurture it. When our ego is strong, we enjoy discussing why. When it is
fragile, we retreat into aggrieved silence or, worse, lash out like Ben.

The depressives' reluctance to discuss sex is shared by my support
group members. In the entire span of my attendance I have never
heard sex mentioned, although some members very occasionally talk
privately about it with group members who have become special
friends. Even in the more protected environment of the interview,
sex comes up in throwaway lines: "I'd like a little more romance in
my life," or "I'm not a dutiful husband anymore." These are delicate
acknowledgments designed to close rather than open doors.

The most practical approach is to know what kinds of sexual dysfunction antidepressant medications cause, and which medications

do the most or the least damage. According to Dr. Richard Brown, who practices in New York City, all antidepressants produce sexual dysfunction to a lesser or greater degree. Such dysfunction includes loss of desire in both men and women; partial or complete loss of erection or delayed ejaculation for men; loss of the ability to reach orgasm or difficulty in achieving it for women. When orgasm eventually arrives, says Brown, it may be more like a sneeze. These reactions are more than common; they are reported by a large majority of those on antidepressant medication. Less common reactions include an absence of genital sensation or a feeling of coldness, numbness, or unpleasant tingling.

These biological manifestations of the illness cause psychological problems for both partners, he says, heightened by the disinclination to discuss what is going on, either between themselves or with a physician or psychotherapist. Their reactions are deeply personal and usually unarticulated. Everyone feels inadequate: the depressive because he or she cannot perform, the partner because he or she assumes fault for the problem and views the result as rejection: "He can't make love with me because he no longer loves me," or "She doesn't want to make love with me because she is playing around on the side with someone else." Both partners invent their own reasons for the dysfunction; usually no one blames the "it," which is of course the villain here as elsewhere. Whichever partner goes to see a doctor finds it hard to elaborate, even with a specialist and professional.

The manufacturers of antidepressants do acknowledge that a problem exists, but their statistics on the degree of dysfunction are far more optimistic than Brown's. Brown, speaking specifically of the serotonin reuptake inhibitors (SSRIs), of which Prozac, Zoloft, Paxil, and Luvox are the most commonly known brand names, notes that they are all sexual inhibitors. Their manufacturers claim that the anti-desire and anti-performance symptoms are most severe in the first six weeks, and then taper off. They assign the following rates of sexual dysfunction to their respective products: Prozac in 12 percent of users; Zoloft, 7 percent; Paxil, 9 percent; Luvox, 2 percent; and Effexor, 3–5 percent. Brown's own figures, culled from his large private practice, indicate a rate of 60–90 percent for all of them, with the effects more rather than less common after three to six months of use, and most prevalent after one year on the drugs. He also has noted that in his experience the problem becomes more pronounced the longer the usage and the higher the dose.

Among the newer drugs, Wellbutrin appears to behave differently from Prozac et al., in that for many it doesn't interfere with the sex drive; its manufacturer suggests Wellbutrin actually stimulates desire. Brown has found that this is indeed initially often the case, but that the desire and performance follow a bell-shaped curve. Eventually the drug loses its stimulative effect, returning the couple to non-honeymoon status.

MAOIs (monoamine oxidase inhibitors), which affect serotonin and some other neurotransmitters as well, have varying rates of suppression: Nardil 30–50 percent; Parnate about 5 percent. MAOIs, as previously noted, are not widely prescribed due to their dietary restrictions.

Tricyclics, the class of antidepressants in longest use, have a consistently lower percentage of suppression, somewhere in the realm of 5 percent, but their side effects, although not dangerous, are so unpleasant to many that they stop taking them. Nevertheless, tricyclics are very effective antidepressants. The most commonly prescribed of these are Elavil and Tofranil. Many depressives might be happy to live with a dry mouth if in so doing they regained their interest in sex. Anafranil, a less commonly prescribed tricyclic, is estimated by its manufacturer to produce sexual problems in 50 percent of users; Brown's estimate is far higher.

The good news here is that antidepressants cause no permanent damage to the libido. Sexual performance returns to its previous level within days or weeks of discontinuing usage, with the difference in timing dependent upon which drug has been taken and the individual's reactions to it. Going off antidepressants is not the only way to deal with the problem, however. Alternative solutions include changing drugs or reducing the dosage; taking short holidays from it; supplementing the antidepressant with another drug; or switching to a new antidepressant, structurally different from the others, that has recently come on the market.

Every human being's physiology and psychology is different, and so reactions to antidepressants differ widely. For everyone whose experience contributes to the negative statistics, whether in sexual performance or in other respects, there are people who are unaffected by the same drug. Anyone can be an exception to the norm. Good doctors anticipate the possibility of wide variations in response. The larger their practice and the longer their experience, the more understanding they will have of the issue of variance. They will also know more about sexual side effects. Your depressive needs to discuss all this with his or her physician. If the doctor seems unknowledgeable, and most particularly if he sounds uninterested (stating, for instance, that the only important issue is whether or not the antidepressant is improving the depressive's mood), you and your depressed partner may want to call some other doctors and ask if they take a different view. When you find one who sounds more like a fellow human being, and who has a sound reputation, go and see him for a consultation.

This new doctor, or the original one if you are lucky, may have other suggestions. One of these may be to take a drug-free sexual holiday by stopping the antidepressant on Thursday and resuming it again on Sunday. Many physicians have found that doing this has no ill effects upon the depression, and very positive ones on sexual desire and performance. It won't work with Prozac, because that drug hangs about in the system for some time before dissipating, but it does work with Zoloft, Paxil, and others.

Some practitioners suggest taking either yohimbine or amantadine as an additive. Yohimbine, an herb, is a sexual stimulant, but it doesn't work for everyone, and its effects are pretty inconsistent. Overexpectation may prove as frustrating as the side effect yohimbine is supposed to be counteracting. If your depressive is contemplating this solution, make sure he or she discusses it thoroughly with the doctor before embarking on it. The same goes for amantadine, which, for some people, can help counter the effects of orgasmic failure.

One other alternative is proving effective for many: a new antidepressant called Serzone, which appears to lift depression without affecting sexual performance. Two studies have looked at this drug specifically from the perspective of sex. The first, conducted by Dr. Alan Feiger, medical director of the Feiger Psychmed Center in Wheat Ridge, Colorado, treated eighty men and women with Zoloft for six weeks. When they were switched to Serzone, they experienced "a robust improvement in sexual interest," according to Dr. Feiger. A second study, under the direction of Dr. James Ferguson of the Pharmacology Research Corporation in Salt Lake City, was done with seventy-five patients who had had sexual problems on Zoloft. All were taken off Zoloft and given a drug-free vacation for two weeks, during which, according to the study, sexual desire and function returned. Then they were randomly assigned to either Zoloft or Serzone for eight weeks. Although there was no difference in anti-depressant benefits, concludes the study, two and a half times more patients on Zoloft had subsequent sexual problems than occurred in those taking Serzone.

These studies and others like them are not always free from cor-porate influence. Antidepressants are big business, and a very prof-itable one. All the manufacturers are constantly vying for premier market position, and spending a lot of money to get it. When studies are carried out by independent institutions, as opposed to the Food and Drug Administration or the National Institute of Mental Health (even these have been challenged by reputable dissenters), it doesn't hurt to reach for the salt. This is yet another reason to find a doctor who's very up-to-date on what's going on in the field.

Doctors help with the medical aspects of depressive illness. You need to address the personal ones, preferably not in solitary and resentful rumination, but with your partner. Given the traits of depressives and manic-depressives, this is certainly not easy. It's hard to be with someone who's always too cross or too tired to go out, who tells you you're stupid or boring or at fault in some demeaning way, and even harder if they're bedding down every man or woman in sight. Most difficult of all is trying to be reasonable and rational with a mate who behaves as though he or she doesn't love you anymore, especially when you still love him or her. But neither depressives nor manics are monsters; they're just way off base because of their illness. Maintaining silence will only compound the problems between you.

If you do decide to try talking, remember the study, cited earlier in this chapter, called "Depression and Marital Disagreement." You have the advantage of knowing much more than the non-depressed spouses who were drawn into their depressives' irritable and argu-mentative mode. Should the conversation bog down into a point-less hassle, disengage and wait for a more propitious moment. If the moment never seems to arise, you might compose a letter to your depressive instead of trying to express your unhappiness verbally. As Ralph Waldo Emerson once wrote, "Poetry is emotion recol-lected in tranquillity." Perhaps that maxim, along with advice from other depression fallout sufferers, will bring some poetry into your relationship.

11

NO EXIT: PARENTS OF A
CHILD WITH A DEPRESSIVE
DISORDER

To MOST OF US, DEPRESSION seems as much a province of adulthood as measles is of childhood. So closely do we associate this illness with the stresses and strains of adult life that we are reluctant to believe it is capable of penetrating the protective environment we strive to create for our children. But young brains are also vulnerable to it, whether of the unipolar or bipolar variety. When a child's depression does manifest itself, parents invariably see themselves as culpable for permitting its intrusion. This makes their version of depression fallout uniquely painful. Far more than most depression fallout sufferers, they will reproach themselves for having somehow been the cause of their child's illness, and will judge themselves harshly because they cannot cure it.

A few parents do turn their backs—as Kate's did when they told her she was no longer welcome at home—but the vast majority cannot conceive of such a reaction. "It's unthinkable, impossible," said the mother of a bipolar daughter to another member of the friends and family group. "She's my own flesh and blood." "So is my mother, but I'm leaving her, I'm moving out," replied the other member, whose parent is bipolar. "That's different," rejoined the first. "I'm talking about my *child.*"

Guilt accompanies parents in every step they take, from their initial confusion about their child's behavior to the anger they will almost inevitably feel at some point. Parental love does not act as a shield against vexation and frustration, or against resentment of the responsibility that binds them so closely to their child. All the parents who attend the group have felt this way, not because they are lacking in patience and love, but because depressives and manic-depressives are very difficult to live with, children not excepted. That's a fact of life. It is senseless and counterproductive for parents to castigate themselves for sometimes being angry and irritable, for feeling that the burden is too much to bear, and for wishing themselves in some other world where their child is the perfect human being all parents hope and expect that their offspring will ultimately become.

Because parents resist believing that young people can suffer from this illness, they often chalk up evidence of a child's depression—conflicts with family members, for instance, or excessively moody or volatile behavior—as a normal part of the growing-up process. They find it particularly easy to overlook what may be a depressive illness in adolescents, because they expect erratic fluctuations in mood and a certain amount of teenage defiance from them. For a long time psychiatrists and psychologists agreed; only in 1980 did childhood depression receive a formal diagnosis. Before then, depressed children were often labeled lazy, bad, shy, difficult, or, occasionally, retarded. The up-to-date view is more accurate, and though potentially disturbing, it gives parents reason to hope that the false labels will no longer be applied, and that their children will receive the help they need earlier than in the past.

Once childhood depression was acknowledged, researchers began trying to determine its frequency. One 1982 community study discovered mild to moderate symptoms of depression in 10 percent of children in grades three to nine, while others found that 8 to 9 percent of children between the ages of ten and thirteen experienced a major depression in the course of a year. With the arrival of puberty, the rate for boys remains fairly constant, but for girls it nearly doubles, jumping to 16 percent between the ages of fourteen and sixteen. Dr. Maria Kovacs of Western Psychiatric Institute at the University of Pittsburgh Medical Center estimates that a typical episode of depression severe enough to be referred for treatment lasts about eleven months on average in children aged five to eighteen years, while its milder form, dysthymia, will last much longer, averaging about four years, and can have its first occurrence in a child as young as five years of age. Even more troubling is her finding that there is about a 75-percent recurrence rate in later life if a child has a first episode between the ages of eight and thirteen. Most distressing of all for parents, the suicide rate for boys aged fifteen to nineteen stands at about eleven per 100,000 children, and for girls at almost four per 100,000, with depression playing a significant role.

The Symptoms of Depression in Children and Adolescents

Although the bad news is that childhood depression clearly exists, the good news is that there are both psychotherapeutic and pharmacological interventions to lessen its impact. As in all cases of depressive illness at any age, catching it early is both the best offense and the best defense. The symptoms of depression in children differ from those of adult depression and, indeed, vary with the age of the child. Following are warning signs to look out for.

Infants and pre-school children have a depression incidence estimated to be about one percent. Researchers suspect that some babies who fail to thrive may be suffering from depression, but whether this is because they are born with an inherited depressive gene or because they have had the bad luck of being born to parents who neglect or reject them, no one is sure. While we can't read an infant's mind, laboratory studies of young animals separated in infancy from their mothers tell us that very young beings of every sort grow listless and apathetic when deprived of loving touch and attention.

If you are the parent of a very young child, the probability that he or she is depressed is remote. If, however, you, your spouse, or your respective families have a history of depressive illness, some of the signs of depression among the very young, aged one to three, may be clues of which you should take note as your child develops. Principal among these are inadequate weight gain according to established pediatric guidelines, feeding and sleeping problems, tantrums, and lack of playfulness and responsiveness. A little later, between the ages of three and five, add phobias—an unreasonable fear or dislike of specific situations or objects—and a tendency to be accident-prone.

Preschoolers exhibit the same signs of depression as even younger children. Unable to verbalize how they feel, they offer no overt evidence of sadness, but their feelings of guilt and inadequacy may manifest themselves in other ways, such as unexpected and unnecessary apologies for knocking over a glass of milk, spilling food, or for messy rooms and other run-of-the-mill transgressions over which few normal youngsters feel much remorse. Unlike their non-depressed peers, they may often criticize and chastise themselves.

School-aged children from six to twelve exhibit signs of depression that are easier to read, but they certainly won't use words like *depressed* or *hopeless* to describe their feelings. They'll look like shy children who haven't many friends and are perhaps lonely and dissatisfied, as if they're dealing with what many parents think of as standard developmental issues. A child's natural mood, however, is one of exuberance; chronic boredom, listlessness, and lack of enthusiasm are signs that something is wrong.

Adolescents who suffer from depression look and behave similarly to depressed adults, but their behavior is cloaked in the vicissitudes of puberty. Like undepressed teenagers, they experiment with making their own decisions without the experience to judge what is good for them and what is damaging, all the while tossing about in a turbulent sea of hormones. To an extent, all of this is perfectly normal; however, depression changes the balance, tipping it into the abnormal. Many parents fail to recognize this shift, attributing it to so-called adolescent angst.

We expect teenagers to be a handful, to push boundaries, and to attempt, as all children must, to establish themselves as people in their own right. But we should not expect them to display delinquent behavior, extreme moodiness, continual and rude outbursts of temper, extended periods of despair, a lot of trouble making friends in school, or suicidal fantasies. Not only does this add up to aberrant behavior; it indicates that a depressive disorder may be present.

Among the clues parents should look out for and distinguish from normal adolescent behavior are the following symptoms, which constitute the American Psychiatric Association's guidelines for diagnosing childhood depression:

- *Loss of interest in previously enjoyed activities,* just as in adults, is a sign that something is wrong. In adolescents, this symptom manifests itself in sudden declines in academic interest and performance, or in a loss of enthusiasm for sports or making friends.

- *Sleeping and eating disturbances* are classic symptoms, but not always evident ones, unless they develop into anorexia or bulimia, or severe insomnia or oversleeping beyond even teenage limits.

- *Low self-esteem* is another symptom sometimes discounted by parents as a normal teenage experience. If your teenager begins to express constant self-doubt and self-criticism, if he or she feels ugly, unloved, unwanted, always on the outside and on the outs with everyone, and dwells on trivial defeats, these are reasons to suspect that depression rather than teenage volatility is driving his or her feelings.

- *Irritability and aggressive behavior* are two more hallmarks of adolescent behavior that parents often accept as inevitable, but when carried to extremes they are atypical, and provide further clues to a depressive disorder. It is *not* typical for children to exhibit antisocial traits, to get into endless hassles with parents and peers, to abuse drugs and alcohol, or to be in trouble with the law.

- *Lack of energy* is the flip side of aggression, and it, too, is unusual in teenagers, especially if they have previously been active and energetic. If your teenager suddenly falls below his or her usual energy level for no apparent reason, add this to your list of clues.

- *Physical complaints* that a doctor can't pin down are a signal, just as they are in adults. Experts theorize that these are somatic problems, a way for children to express feelings they cannot verbalize.

- *Thoughts of death and suicide,* whether voiced directly or indirectly, are danger signals. Being extremely moody, irritable, volatile, and antisocial, abusing drugs and alcohol, and getting in trouble in school or with the law are common among young suicides, a topic covered more fully later in this chapter.

Reading the above places parents in a situation analogous to the classic dilemma of the third-year medical student who believes himself afflicted with every disease studied thus far. If your child exhibits a symptom here and there, don't leap to the alarmist conclusion that he or she is suffering from depression. Children are complicated individuals who already show strong signs of the adult personality into which they are growing. No single mode of behavior is an indication of anything other than the creation and formation of yet another unique human being. Instead, view these symptomatic behaviors as a cluster of clues, a collective signpost that may or may not indicate the presence of depressive illness. If your child has never exhibited much interest in school and homework, perhaps he or she is a late developer, but if school, sports, and social activities have been a big part of life and no longer are, this may be a cause for action on your part.

On the other hand, recognize that adolescence does not in itself guarantee either particularly sad or particularly aggressive actions and feelings. While it is true that puberty brings with it distinct changes in how your child views the world and his or her place in it, such changes should not show themselves in extreme departures from their usual behavior. Way too much, way too little, or both at the same time are all signals that should concern you.

It bears repeating that parents often shy away from the possibility that their child has abnormal reactions and feelings. When we observe uncharacteristic behavior, we reassure ourselves by looking around for similar behavior in other kids, and so put off the day of reckoning not because we are poor parents, but because we cannot bear the thought of mental illness in our children. It's easy to do this, because the depressed child isn't sending clear messages. Like many adults, children have no idea what's at the root of their feelings. If they perceive themselves as inadequate and unable to fit in, they may just say they feel lousy. When pressed for an answer, more often than not they will deny feeling depressed and reply instead that they just aren't interested in much of anything, or that they have no friends.

In all this, parental guilt loiters in the wings. Such thoughts as "What have I done wrong?" and "It must be my fault" are common but unwelcome. Unless you abuse your child, or reject, neglect, or ignore his or her wants and needs, the depression, if it exists, is not of your making.

Manic Depression in Young People

For a long time, experts didn't believe bipolar illness set in until young adulthood, in part because there is a major difference between the way mania is expressed in bipolar children and in adults. Manic children are rarely euphoric and grandiose; instead they tend toward tearful irritability or prolonged and aggressive temper outbursts. More-recent research on adult manic-depressives, however, indicates that often the illness has been present for some time, just not labeled as such. It appears that manic depression may have a long incubation period, with a time lag of five, ten, or even more years between the first appearance of symptoms and a display of the disorder serious enough to be recognized and treated. Because initial symptoms in children are so different from those in adults, and may, for instance, be mislabeled as hyperactivity or attention deficit disorder, there still remains uncertainty among diagnosticians, and so some early onset bipolar illness goes undetected.

The principal difference between early and later bipolar illness is that in young people the onset of symptoms may be very sudden, and changes in the cycle of ups and downs, called rapid cycling, are more prevalent than in adults. So are psychotic symptoms. The latest edition of the *Diagnostic and Statistical Manual of Mental Disorders* does not offer different criteria for diagnosis of the illness in young people and adults other than to note associations of bipolar illness in adolescence with antisocial behavior, failure in school and school truancy, and substance abuse.

Paula's daughter, Meredith, was one of those children who showed none of the tendencies mentioned above. On the contrary, her only departure from ordinary childhood had been a precocious intelligence and a determination to be good at everything she undertook, whether it was perfecting her cursive script or ice skating. When she was twenty-three she moved from her mother's home in Phoenix to New York City, where she found a job immediately, but she was unhappy in it from the start. She began to call her mother more and more frequently, complaining that her co-workers treated her like a servant.

One day Meredith called Paula and reeled off a bizarre, overexcited monologue full of fantasy. After rattling on rapidly and disjointedly, she suddenly began to outline an idea for a book. "I can't remember exactly what it was about, but she sounded brilliant and clear-headed, very articulate," said Paula. "But then she started speaking in riddles with religious and political overtones, something about a conspiracy against our family." Paula knew something was terribly wrong, and when she called the family doctor he agreed, telling her to go to New York immediately, which she did.

When she arrived, it was an icy January day. Meredith had on a little summer dress and was rubbing Noxzema into her arms. She seemed pleased to see her mother, but not surprised. "She had put everything she owned on the floor, all her dishes, her books, her clothes. I started crying right away, and I told her we were going home as soon as we could get everything packed up." But while she was trying to put things in order, she suddenly realized Meredith was no longer in the apartment. Panicking, Paula called the police, who found her daughter wandering the winter streets, still wearing nothing but her little summer dress. They brought her back— violently resistant, ranting, terrified, and accusing her mother of being Satan—and managed eventually to coax her into an ambulance, which took her to a city hospital, still screaming. A doctor there gave her lithium and antipsychotic drugs, and discharged her after four days.

Paula, who knew next to nothing about manic depression, took her daughter home to Phoenix. Within a month, Meredith was bored and hostile, and insisted on returning to New York. A doctor in Phoenix had simply said that Meredith should continue taking her medications, offering no further elaboration or cautions. Meredith left. Within five days the phone calls resumed, this time tearful, anxious, and with periods of silence during which her daughter was unable to speak. Paula immediately flew east again and moved into her daughter's tiny apartment.

"I knew then for the first time what depression really meant. I found it unbearable to watch. She lay in bed all day, hardly moving. When she spoke she was irritable, sullen, and insulting. I kept thinking, 'Where is my daughter? Who is this clone they're showing me?' The *person* wasn't there anymore." Since then a year has passed, during which Meredith has very slowly improved, but while improvement has brought hope to both mother and daughter, their lives have been greatly altered. "There are many times," says Paula, "when it's all too much to bear, when I think I'm at the point of not being able to stand it anymore, but I have to, just as she has to. The changes for the better are so small. Finally, after months, I looked at Meredith one morning and knew she felt a little better because her eyes were blue again where they had been gray, as though there had been clouds in her head. I use them as a barometer now, to know how she's feeling on any given day." On that first day of blue, Meredith went out and bought bagels and cigarettes, her first venture outside on her own in two months.

But along with the creeping improvement have come other problems born of Meredith's illness and the changes it has wrought in her. The stress with which mother and daughter are forced to live is nipping away at the closeness and ease that had always before existed between them. Paula has long since quit her job in Phoenix, and now works in New York, where she shares a small apartment with her daughter. One year after Meredith's manic episode, she has not had another, but her depression is severe with its attendant lethargy, hopelessness, and helplessness. She is still unable to work. Although she goes on job interviews, anxiety overwhelms her and she becomes tongue-tied and confused. A weight gain of twenty pounds, a side effect of the drugs she takes, makes her feel ugly and self-conscious.

On a recent Friday night, Paula arrived at the friends and family group shattered by yet another scene born of tension at home.

"The other day we had a big fight. Meredith announced she was moving out, that she hated being dependent on me for everything, having to ask my permission for everything. How can she move out? She has no money, no job, nothing. She said she was too old to be living with her mother and she hated it, hated having to live with me. It was just ridiculous, and I got angry. I knew what she hated, and I said it. It was that whatever she had, I was paying for it and she couldn't possibly change that.

"So I said, 'Fine. Cut off the air conditioning, because that's my money that's paying for it. And turn off the lights and sit there in the dark because my money is paying for that, too. And when you go to the refrigerator, stop and think, and then close that door because you should remember that that's my food in there. I bought and paid for it.' It hurt me so much that she didn't see how bad I felt, how much effort I was making, too. Then I told her that she'd have to apologize to me, and that I wouldn't speak to her until she did, no matter how long it took. After about an hour she did apologize. And then I said to her, 'I want you to do one thing for me every day.' I was thinking of things like making her bed, maybe, or putting the roll of toilet paper on its proper gadget instead of just leaving it wherever. I wasn't expecting or asking her to do anything she wasn't capable of. I know she's ill. I know it's hard for her. But it's really hard for me, too. And that's what I wanted her to recognize.

"If Meredith's manipulation of me could help her get well," Paula added, "then she could manipulate me day in and day out, and that would be just fine with me. But it won't, and we both have to be clear on that. I have to have some boundaries, and she has to learn to live within them."

This confrontation and all the other events and emotions experienced by Paula in the aftermath of Meredith's manic episode are textbook examples of depression fallout. Having passed through confusion and guilty self-doubt in the early stages of her daughter's illness, Paula then settled into demoralization, with constant forays into stages four and five: anger and the desire to escape from the situation that has absorbed her entire life. Paula is a survivor—intelligent, determined, and strong in her resolve to emerge on the far side of her pain—but Meredith's illness has upended both their lives and will continue to do so for the foreseeable future.

When I first joined the friends and family group, Meredith's illness was six months old. A year and a half later, Paula has learned everything there is to know about coping with the situation. Back then she told us what Meredith had said one day: "I'm mentally ill, and you don't want to believe that." She was right at the time, Paula admits, but now, with knowledge has come acceptance. "Understanding is the key; each atom of it is like an epiphany. Of course, sometimes in my life I've felt down and stayed in bed because I didn't want to get up, but that's not like being unable to get up. When you see something like that day after day, you really feel the difference. That's where the professionals can't help you at all. They've never been depressed."

Paula has also learned that verbal abuse and manipulation often go hand-in-hand with depressive illness, and she has experienced more than her share of both. Often they cause her to lose her temper, as she did when she read Meredith the riot act that day. She probably could have made her point without losing her temper, but the fact is that what she said worked. Meredith has made an effort, undertaking each day to do one thing, no matter how small, to help her mother: putting magazines and newspapers into piles instead of throwing them about their small apartment, helping with the shopping, making coffee for her mother, and apologizing when she has been rude and ill-tempered. Paula, too, has learned to apologize for what she admits is frequent bitchiness in their interactions.

She also has come to understand that the Friday night support group is critical to her well-being. "I can't admit to my friends or co-workers that I'm hell on wheels at home sometimes. I don't even want to talk to them about what's happening. I'm embarrassed. I don't want pity. It diminishes me. And they really cannot understand the pressures. You have to live through them to do that." Having a place to blow off steam has helped to steady Paula and make it easier for her to express to her daughter how much she loves her. This is undeniably difficult when one is angry. The love is there, but it doesn't come out sounding much like love. "In twelve-step programs like AA, they seem to have it all figured out with rules and regulations about what you can do and say, what boundaries you can set, and so forth. But with this illness we know nothing. We have to figure it out for ourselves."

The levels of anger to which Paula has occasionally risen have been matched, in their ability to cause her pain, by her need on two occasions to have her daughter hospitalized. Sometimes psychotic mania or a suicidal down makes commitment necessary because in both of these states the sufferer may do harm to him- or herself. Psychiatric wards are no fun. The doctors and nurses often appear uncaring and even hard-hearted, in part because to them your child is just one of many patients. They are usually busy and harried, and have little interest in or time for family members, and often fail to explain to them what is going on and why.

But hospitalization serves an important purpose: to stabilize the illness under close professional supervision until the depressive or manic-depressive is well enough to return home. If a child needs to be hospitalized, then you must accept this need. Try not to feel guilty and as though you were consigning him or her to some dreadful fate. No matter how distressing the decision is for you, make it in the knowledge that in the hospital your child is safe. That's why he or she is there. You have done the right and the loving thing, even if it hurts.

A Primary Coping Strategy

Depressive illness is never self-contained. It occurs within a family, not in a vacuum, and the entire family will feel its ripple effects. The initial shock of the diagnosis leaves many parents perpetually angry at the turn of fate that has struck them such a blow. Unless they can work through and out of their anger, they risk becoming overemotional and even antagonistic toward their child. Moving into acceptance helps control and channel angry energy into positive action, and permits a constructive coping strategy.

Doing this is neither automatic nor easy. Most parents know little about depressive illness, and doctors and other professionals with whom they speak often fail to cover what they need to know. While the physician may have briefly outlined the characteristics of the illness and its possible course, he's probably done so in the remote and impatient manner of busy practitioners today, without directly addressing the problems parents will face on a day-to-day basis. Confusion in this regard will sooner or later stretch both family and spousal bonds to the breaking point. Many mothers and fathers arrive for their first evening at the friends and family group in a state of shocked despair and disharmony. Often denial, guilt, and anger have led each to place blame for their child's illness on the other's poor parenting or on a crazy aunt's gene. Knowing little about treatment, they disagree about what should be done. Instead of putting their energies into their child's welfare, they bicker together and grieve apart, and are ill-prepared to meet the task of seeing to their child's best interests.

If you suspect that your child may suffer from depressive illness, or if the diagnosis has already been made, you and your spouse need to jointly educate yourselves about the disorder and to recognize that only if you act as a team will you be able to help your child. As Paula notes, parents have to figure things out for themselves, not just from books but also, if possible, through talking to other parents who share their problem. If no support group specifically concerned with depressive illness exists in your area, look for one that helps parents of children suffering from other severe illnesses such as schizophrenia. Even though the medical facts may not pertain to your child, coping strategies will certainly be a part of the group's discussion, and they will serve you well.

Information and cooperation will go a long way toward overcoming denial and other negative feelings, and clear the way to getting your child well. If you haven't already done so, you need to schedule a visit with a professional who is well versed in the diagnosis and treatment of young depressives. Delay can be dangerous because— as previously noted—this increases the risk of more severe episodes at a later time. Children whose depressive illness goes untreated also develop other ancillary problems that will outlive their episodes. They will experience difficulty in making and keeping friends, thus delaying social development, and lapses in academic performance will be hard to make up. In both instances, their self-esteem will come in for a beating. Far better to be safe than sorry and consult an expert as soon as you feel something may be amiss with your child. If you have assumed depression where none exists, you have lost nothing and gained peace of mind.

The Treatment of Child and Adolescent Depression: Medication, Psychotherapy, or Both?

Just as in adult depression, there are two sides to the treatment debate in juvenile depression. Dr. Harold S. Koplewicz, professor of clinical psychiatry at New York University Medical Center and director of the Child and Adolescent Psychiatry Department there, has written a book titled *It's Nobody's Fault* (Times Books, 1996) that deals with a range of mental disorders in young people. His thesis is that both unipolar and bipolar depression, as well as attention deficit hyperactivity disorder (ADHD), obsessive-compulsive disorder, eating, conduct, and anxiety disorders are all what he and others term no-fault illnesses. They are simply accidents of fate or genetics, and his treatment of choice is medication. On the other side of the fence is Laura Mufson, a psychologist at the Columbia University Medical School and coauthor of *Interpersonal Psychotherapy for Depressed Adolescents* (Guilford Press, 1993). Her treatment of choice is psychotherapy, more specifically interpersonal therapy.

"Sure, a depressed kid can pass his exams and get himself through college with depression and without medication, but it will be a terrible slog," says Koplewicz. "I've known students who took six years to do it. But I want them to have more than just a degree. I want them to have a boyfriend or girlfriend. I want my kids having a love life and a sex life, and hobbies and interests. Depression kills all that so they won't ever be able to get the full benefit of their school and college experience."

Koplewicz says that because the genetic component of depressive illness is so strong, early onset is of serious concern. "If the mean age of onset for depression is twenty-eight to thirty years old, but a kid starts showing symptoms at ten or twelve, that means he has a very potent gene. The answer is quick intervention with medication. Why wait until the gene digs in, and as a result the disorder endures and is harder to treat later on in life?"

He highlighted the fact that many parents do wait, sometimes for a long time. "Parents can't believe their kids are depressed. They want them to have everything," says Koplewicz, "and that includes happiness. When their kids are unhappy, they figure they must have done something wrong." Many parents simply can't figure out what their child has to be depressed about, so "they sit on their hands and wait for the problem to pass because they think it's just a phase." He adds that parents, like their depressed child, often resist the idea of medication for a mental illness because they feel this brands their child as "crazy."

"If a child's symptoms aren't causing him or his parents distress or dysfunction we watch and wait. . . . The first line of attack should be and is psychosocial intervention." I asked Koplewicz whether this statement, which appears in his book in the chapter on depression, means that he favors psychotherapy before meds; his answer was no. Teenage depression is different from adult depression, he explained. The mood changes are much more rapid and the symptoms very intense. The clinical picture can change extremely rapidly, literally in front of the physician's eyes. "When parents send a kid to my office, a certain percentage of the time he'll lose some of his symptoms before he leaves. Often symptoms of depression can mimic deep distress over something that's going on in his life, and after a talk they'll ease or even disappear. For example, perhaps his divorced mother is dating, and telling him too much about it. In that case it may be as simple as suggesting to the mother that she stop discussing her social life with her child. Or he might be upset about a move from one town to another, or a big school failure, or a divorce; just talking to him and his parents about that may help a lot. I call that 'environmental manipulation.'" But if Koplewicz judges the child's distress to be an indication of real depression, he prescribes an anti-depressant.

Koplewicz believes that once medication has stabilized the disorder, it's a good idea for the child to see a therapist for a few months. "But it should be very goal-directed and specific," he noted. "It should address the crisis that triggered the depression, the divorce or school failure or whatever, or it should deal with the crisis that came about as the result of the depression, the failed social life or the poor grades. It should address targeted problems." Of the two psychotherapies most often prescribed for depressed kids, he prefers behavioral over interpersonal. Behavioral therapy deals with negative thoughts about oneself that lead to self-defeating attitudes such as always anticipating failure and ignoring the times when things go well, and being pessimistic about oneself and the world in general. If a child has failed an exam, for instance, the therapist would encourage him or her to think, "I didn't study hard enough," instead of "I'm stupid."

Dr. Mufson's specialty is interpersonal therapy, which focuses on interactions between the depressed child and parents, teachers, and peers. A fifteen-year-old might, for instance, be getting into constant noisy arguments with her mother over whether or not she's old enough to go out on dates. The job of the interpersonal therapist is to help the girl recognize and understand her mother's point of view and at the same time learn how to express her own in a calmer, more logical way. The outcome might be a compromise whereby the girl could invite a boy to the house rather than going out with him.

Unlike Dr. Koplewicz, Dr. Mufson firmly believes that childhood depression comes about as the result of life events, and that talk therapy is the best treatment. "There is no data," she states, "to support medication for depressed kids as an effective treatment," citing fourteen clinical trials that failed to demonstrate any difference between medication and placebos in lifting childhood and adolescent depression. Nor, she admits, are there as yet any published research studies measuring the impact of psychotherapy versus medication for young people. "But remember that we have no information on the long-term physiological effects of medication on them. The field is still in its infancy, and there's a lot of work to be done." It is true, as Mufson rightly cautions, that we don't yet know what effects antidepressant medications started in childhood or early adolescence will have in later life, but it is equally true that no studies have shown that long-term use of antidepressants in adults is either damaging or dangerous. The clinical trials to which Dr. Mufson refers were conducted using tricyclics, with all their attendant unpleasant side effects; none have yet been carried out with SSRIs or with MAOIs. Many adolescents suffer from atypical depression, which responds best to the MAOIs, but doctors shy away from prescribing them for young people because of their dietary restrictions. One can only hope that eventually the reversible MAOIs will be available in this country as they are in Canada and Europe.

Until more conclusive evidence is available, Mufson and many of her therapist peers are extremely reluctant to suggest medication unless after at least four months of talk therapy a child still looks severely depressed, his or her functioning has dramatically deteriorated, or he or she has had to be hospitalized. "Then I'd start them on medication, but always with therapy at the same time.

"Psychotherapy is beneficial for troubled kids," says Mufson. "If you want, you can say that depression is biological, but their social functioning is still impaired. They still have social deficits. It affects them and their friends, their school achievement, and how they cope with their life. When things go wrong for them, kids get depressed. When they get depressed, things go worse and deepen the depression. It's a vicious circle in which we psychotherapists can intervene. Who cares whether the depression was brought on by environmental problems or whether the source of the problem is biological? There may indeed be a genetic component to depression, but who's to say? If a child is problem-free, maybe it's because he has the right parents and the right environment. Perhaps if that child had been born into a different family, if his life circumstances had been different, he might have become depressed."

Mufson also noted, as did Koplewicz, that kids don't like to take medication, and by and large are poor compliers, so it's extremely difficult to measure accurately what the medication is or is not accomplishing. "When the depression is severe and we think there's a possibility that it will return, then we teach them how to live with their depression, how to know when they are getting depressed again." This is done by identifying what a child's specific symptoms are, and then teaching them how to monitor those symptoms. Are they having problems sleeping, or concentrating? Are they more irritable? Do they have problems at school? Are they spending less time with their friends? "These are the changes that herald the return of their depression. They learn to recognize and to deal with them."

Dr. Mufson is strongly in favor of psychotherapy because, she says, it works. "Even with kids who have severe psychotic symptoms, seeing or hearing things and voices which don't exist in reality, I've seen those symptoms disappear after four sessions of interpersonal therapy."

Dr. Koplewicz's long-term approach differs. "We usually keep them on meds for six months, starting very slowly and increasing the dosage until the depression lifts, and we take them off equally gradually. About 50 percent to 60 percent will probably be depression-free for quite a long time, maybe years." If and when the depression does come back, he suggests to the kids that they restart meds and stay on for two more years. "You can't tell a child they may have to be on meds for life. If it does keep coming back, I explain that depression is their Achilles' heel, that everyone has one. For some it's acne, for others it's diarrhea or headaches or whatever. Everyone gets something when they have a lot of problems. So I make sure they know their symptoms and their reactions well. They need to keep an eye on the signs and symptoms, just as women feel for lumps to get an early jump on breast cancer."

The dilemma for parents is choosing between psychotherapy and medication, or using both simultaneously as the treatment for their child. With such widely divergent ideas held by practitioners who are well thought of in their respective fields, this is an extremely difficult decision. One factor seems of critical importance: Is there any evidence of depressive illness in the family tree? This may mean looking at aberrant behavior of family members in a new way.

Many parents grew up in an era when depressive illness was neither recognized nor treated as such, so perhaps relatives who were thought "eccentric" should now retrospectively be considered as possibly suffering from the illness. What about Great-aunt Mary, who quarreled with everyone in the family and always took to her bed when she didn't get her own way? Or Grandfather Hal, who spent his wife's money and his own as well, and suffered the occasional "nervous breakdown"? Or maybe there's a workaholic uncle who drinks heavily and is generally impossible to get along with, or an aunt who from time to time decides to be an astrophysicist or an airline pilot, despite neither talent nor training? Perhaps you or your spouse have periodically fallen into downs lasting two weeks or more, lost your sense of joy, and felt hopeless and helpless to change your outlook.

According to a report in the *Harvard Mental Health Letter,* 25 percent of mothers of depressed children and 8 percent of fathers have been seriously depressed. The rate of depression rises with the number of depressed family members: it is twice the average if one parent has been depressed, and four times the average if both have been. Depression tends to start at an earlier age in these cases as well.

To prepare for this decision, you as the parent must mobilize yourself into information-gatherer and assessor of practitioners. What are the credentials of the professional who is recommending with such authority one treatment or the other? Where did he receive his training? How long has he been practicing? How many kids has he treated, and with what results? This means not just accepting without question what he tells you, but asking if he has published results in scientific journals, or participated in major trials. Is he considered by his peers to have achieved expert status? I personally would not want someone treating my child with either psychotherapy or medication unless they were affiliated with a well-recognized institution such as a major hospital or a university medical school, or had been recommended by at least two professionals in these or similar institutions.

Dr. Mufson says that if four months of interpersonal therapy by a trained therapist don't bring results, then she would consider recommending medication. This seems an eminently balanced view—what significant difference could four months make? But the disorder may have already existed for several years; Dr. Mufson says many of the children brought to her, for instance, have already spent time with an insight-oriented psychotherapist of the Freudian persuasion. In some cases those four months may represent a critical period for a disorder already well advanced. And what about recurrent episodes: should these, too, be treated with psychotherapy rather than medication? Once again, it may be important to consider the family tree. If one buys the prevailing argument in favor of an important genetic component, it does matter if one sits and waits to see what will happen next. If the child is a member of the lucky 25 percent who may not have further episodes, then perhaps psychotherapy is indeed the most judicious decision. No one at the present time can accurately predict what pattern or path the illness will take in any given person.

The issue for parents is one of severity as well as genetics. If your child suddenly starts manifesting a lot of the symptoms cited earlier—most particularly strident irritability and crankiness—and if those symptoms represent a distinct departure from your child's "norm"—in short, if there is, as Dr. Koplewicz puts it, "a dramatic qualitative change in their behavior," even without a depressed mood—then the moment of decision is at hand. He also cautions that young depressives frequently exhibit signs of other problems, such as ADHD, eating disorders, and anxiety, as well. These disorders are co-morbid, or coexist, with depression approximately 50 percent of the time, so if one is present, there's a good chance that depression is lurking in the wings.

Dr. Koplewicz and Dr. Mufson have two areas of complete agreement: the first is that schools should spend less time warning their students of the dangers of such diseases as tuberculosis and more on the possibility of depression at some point in their lives. "A girl should be aware that one in every four of her female classmates will suffer a major depressive episode during her lifetime, with the boys not that far behind," Koplewicz says. "Both should know what the disorder is and how it manifests itself as the first line of protection."

They also agree on treatment strategies for manic depression. "Bipolar depression," Mufson says, "is definitely a biological illness. I'd send a bipolar kid to a doctor immediately, and expect lithium to be prescribed. This is a very serious illness and a heavy-duty diagnosis for a kid to accept. They'll have to live with it for their entire life, so of course they need therapy to help them do that. But meds immediately is the answer here."

Keeping a United Front

Key elements of every family strategy must include spousal teamwork. That problems centering upon a child can drive a wedge between parents is a recognized phenomenon, and spousal disagreements arising from a depressive illness are no exception. In an article from *The Women's League Outlook,* a mother whose child cycled several times from home to hospital and back again shared her hard-earned wisdom:

> A contemplative parent soon begins the process of self-questioning. Did I do too little or too much? Was I too permissive or too restrictive? These are questions which have no answers. For my husband and myself, the unarticulated dialogue becomes deafening. During our son's hospitaliza-

tions and other crises, we speak the language of silence. We do this unconsciously. We cannot bear to make eye contact with one another, for if we were to look into each other's eyes we would be forced to acknowledge the scorching sadness enveloping us. It is this despair which consumes and divides us.

Parents who come to the group as couples often show signs of spousal dissent, one sitting cross and grim-lipped as the other speaks, waiting for the opportunity to set the record straight as he or she sees it. One of those parents, with whom I subsequently spoke privately, told me of the difference in the way she and her husband deal with the emotional stress: "When I came to understand that this was a life-long illness, that it was going to go on and on into the future, I was devastated, and I was deeply angry. Although I never showed it in front of our child, I gave my anger full rein in the presence of my husband. Ten and twenty times a day I would obsess about our daughter and how her illness was going to ruin my life. 'If this is living,' I would scream, 'then I hate my life.' And that made *him* angry. We grew apart when we needed to be closer than ever." Her answer was to make a career of helping other parents in similar situations, and she has gone back to school for a degree in social work. She credits this as having saved her marriage as well as her sanity.

Parents who jointly face a problem about their child are far more likely to arrive at solutions than those who separate it into battle sectors labeled "His" and "Hers." Men and women are equal, but they are not the same. When faced with a problem, a man's usual first instinct is to solve it; a woman's initial response is normally to talk about how it makes her feel. Each finds the other's approach lacking. Men are often uncomfortable with verbally expressed intimacy; women thrive on it and resent its withholding. Spouses need to be aware of these differences, and to accommodate each other's needs. Managing a child's illness demands both emotional understanding and problem-solving. Most important of all, the child needs parents who act in harmony and speak with one voice. Conflicting parental messages are upsetting for all children, and especially so for depressed ones. Moreover, like all unhappy, fractious, or troubled children, young depressives often deliberately or unconsciously put parents at odds with each other in a nonmalicious, attention-grabbing way. To avoid this, it's best to settle on a united course of action and to deliver clearly the same messages, whether in expressing love or laying out boundaries for acceptable behavior. You should not abandon this basic child-rearing advice just because your child is depressed.

You've already read, in chapter 9, the story of Jim and Audrey's manic-depressive daughter, who falls into a worst-case category all her own. It is as painful to contemplate Susan's parents' position as it is to think of Susan herself. Both parents are teachers, but in spite of years of experience in dealing with disadvantaged and difficult kids, nothing prepared them for Susan. For the first year they perpetually went in opposite directions, one pulling for Susan to be allowed to move herself, her addict boyfriend, and his dog into the family's apartment, the other advocating twice-daily emergency runs with food and clothing to the homeless site where their daughter was camping out. Each was seeing a psychotherapist, seeking some way to live with the pain, to get up and go to work each day, and to live with each other. It was Jim's therapist who suggested, when Susan became pregnant, that they also see a marriage counselor together, which they did, with good results.

I have known Jim and Audrey for two years through the friends and family group, and am always amazed by their ability not only to cope with their ordeal, but to do so with dignity and compassion, and still to find energy and interest to offer support and advice to other members. "We have dedicated so much time and energy to dealing as a team with what's going on that now we automatically take the same approach without even having to consult each other," Jim told me recently. "The other day Susan called us to say she was worried about her clothes, wasn't sure she had the right ones for her new job. I called her at the end of the day to ask her how things were going and if she wanted to meet me for shopping and supper, and she told me Audrey had already taken her to lunch and brought along a present of a new skirt and sweater."

Jim and Audrey's united front is working not only for them but for their daughter, too. They have managed to persuade her to see a therapist and are hopeful he will be able to convince her to seek the medical help she requires. "Not long ago we would probably have been sending her mixed messages because there was so much tension and conflicting emotions and feelings between us. We were all over the place. I'm sure Susan feels more secure because of that. And it's really helped Audrey and me to stay in one piece and still be hopeful."

Few parents will ever have to face such a dire situation, but this couple's solution can help in far less drastic circumstances as well. Marital therapy may help you meet your twin goals: to stay together and provide your child with a united and loving front. If you allow your child's illness to tear you apart, everyone will be harmed and no one, least of all the child, will be helped.

How Should You Treat Your Depressed Child?

A family strategy needs also to address how you and your spouse will treat your child. You should be constant in demonstrating your love and understanding, but avoid a kid-gloves approach, as though your child were breakable or lacking in intelligence and antennae. Your child needs to know that your love isn't related to the fact that he or she is ill. If you make a point of singling the child out as a "different" person just because he or she is depressed, you will find it difficult to communicate this. Try to urge your son or daughter into a normal routine of activities, but don't push by telling him to cheer up, or by insisting that she can do anything if she just puts her mind to it. Depressives do not respond well to this sort of platitude, and may interpret it as a putdown rather than as a piece of parental advice.

Avoid instructions the child is unable to follow, such as "Stop feeling sorry for yourself." This will only make him or her feel even more inadequate and guilty. Encourage, don't instruct; there is a big difference. Lying about in solitude is bad for all depressives, kids included. If they can't get up steam on their own, suggest doing something or going somewhere together. Instead of insisting on attendance at basketball practice when the child obviously doesn't feel up to it, take him or her to a game, to a movie, or for a walk.

Good, easy communication can make a telling difference here. If you are able to encourage your child to express his or her feelings and to identify their cause, then you are already far ahead of the parent who isn't comfortable discussing emotional issues or doesn't listen. Many children have trouble putting their feelings into words—even more so if they are depressed. Sometimes it helps to speak about your own emotions and feelings, because then the child will know you trust him or her and so may be more willing to trust you in return. Depressed kids often feel alone and misunderstood, and it's up to you to convince them that they have your respect as well as your sympathetic attention.

Avoid responses like "You don't really mean that," or "You don't really feel that way, you have so much going for you." Let them say their piece without criticism and don't leap in immediately with your advice on how to fix what they think is wrong. If you interrupt them with constant reassurances to the contrary, or tell them it's all in their imagination, you will defeat the purpose of listening, which is, more than anything else, supportive, a way to show that what they have to say is important to you.

Your most productive course is to be sympathetic and to acknowledge that they are feeling awful and having a lot of problems, to reasure them that time, the doctor, the psychotherapist, or a combination of all three will help them get through a difficult period, and that the bad feelings will eventually disappear. Depressed children, like depressives of all ages, need some hope to hang on to. You are in a better position than anyone else to provide that until the moment when hope becomes reality thanks to effective treatment.

Depression in young people often manifests itself as crankiness, touchiness, sullen irritability, and violent spurts of unreasonable anger, rather than in lethargy and sadness. This is exactly the sort of behavior that leaves parents cross and impatient. During the four to six weeks until treatment takes hold, you need to rein in your temper and also set some solid boundaries that will restrict the behavior. With psychotherapy, the passage of time will be longer. In the interim, don't just sit about and wait for good things to happen. Be vigilant and firm, loving but not permissive. Let your child know that although the behavior is the result of their depression, that does not make it excusable or tolerable.

Depressed young people are capable of reining themselves in. Choose your control issues selectively; don't try to fix everything at once, and don't waste parental currency arguing about lesser issues. Pick important ones first. For example, laying down the law on drugs and drinking while letting minor transgressions go undisciplined for the moment.

Should your child have occasional outbursts of anger, muster your patience and don't make a big issue of it. But should he or she be constantly rude and confrontational, let them know that verbal abuse or disruptive behavior is unacceptable to you. The trick is to set boundaries that are meaningful and enforceable. Avoid making threats like "Do that again and I'll punish you," without having an appropriate punishment in mind or the means to enforce it. Instead, substitute a strategy of trade-offs. For example, "I know it's not your fault you're depressed and it's hard for you, but let's both make an effort here. If you can get through one week without insulting me, we'll go out for dinner Saturday night at your favorite restaurant."

There is no trade-off insofar as taking medications is concerned. Following the doctor's orders on meds is not a rule, it's a law, and you have the authority, the responsibility, and the right to impose it. Children are like grown-ups in that many don't like the idea of "putting that stuff in my body" (even though they may be simultaneously getting drunk and smoking pot), and they may complain of side effects, which can indeed be annoying and uncomfortable, particularly in the beginning. Nonetheless, this is not an issue for negotiation. If you suspect your child is not taking the medication, put it on the breakfast table and make clear that taking it in front of you is a precondition to leaving the house. Similarly, don't allow the child to skip psychotherapy sessions; they are just as much a part of treatment as any meds that may have been prescribed.

While you can and should enlist the medicating doctor, the psychotherapist, and also teachers as allies and sources of information and help, remember that ultimately you are in charge. Not only do you know your offspring better than anyone else, but you are living together. You see behavior the doctor and therapist never see. Make yourself heard. Set a good precedent by insisting on sitting in on the first session with your child and the doctor, and on subsequent ones when you have relevant information that your child may not be reporting. Where psychotherapists are concerned, make it abundantly clear that while you have no right to seek access to what the therapist and your child discuss in privacy, you insist on being alerted immediately to any situation in which the child may be a danger to himself or herself or to others. All reputable talk therapists make these exemptions from their rules governing patient confidentiality. As a twenty-four-hour parent and observer, you are an early-warning system, and unless you make your position clear, the therapist will be reluctant to accept important information you may possess. One such piece of information could be any knowledge you have of your child's suicidal thoughts and intentions.

Suicide Among Teenagers

Teenage suicide rates are soaring. According to the Centers for Disease Control and Prevention, the incidence of suicide among teenagers and young adults in the United States nearly tripled from 1952 to 1992. Some estimates set the number of attempted suicides by young people as high as 500,000 a year, but no one has accurate figures, because families often remain silent about such a tragic event. If no hospitalization is required following the attempt, it may easily go unreported. According to Dr. David Shaffer, professor of child psychiatry and of pediatrics at Columbia University and an expert on young suicide, an estimated two thousand teenagers kill themselves every year, a figure that leaps to more than five thousand if the age bracket is extended to twenty-four. This makes it the leading cause of death after accidents and homicide, claiming more young lives than asthma, cancer, and heart and kidney disease combined. Approximately 90 percent of these teenagers suffered from some form of depression or other related psychiatric disorder; many also had drug and alcohol problems.

A high proportion of suicides and attempters have had a close family member (sibling, parent, grandparent, aunt, or uncle) or a friend who committed or attempted suicide. Whether this indicates a genetic predisposition to mental illness, or whether it is a case of imitation, no one knows. Follow-up interviews with parents and friends indicate that most young suicides had given some indication of their intentions. Some of these were overt, such as talking and reading about death and dying, or specific threats to harm themselves. Whatever the origin of the myth that talking about suicide somehow defuses the possibility of action, be assured that it is indeed a myth. Even if your teenager is not "ideating" (as the professionals call it) about suicide, he or she may be giving you other clues, such as giving away prized possessions or expressing unreasonable frustration over the inability to reach self-imposed, unrealizable goals at school or in sports.

In Maine, in the fall of 1995, a popular, high-achieving seventeen-year-old named Scott left his family's house one night, went into the woods, and shot himself with a gun his father had bought for self-defense and long since forgotten. In a *New York Times* account of the event, Dr. Thomas Jensen, head of the adolescent psychiatric unit of St. Mary's Hospital in Lewiston, Maine, observed that "When you are depressed, you could have a million things going for you but if one thing is wrong, the depressed person completely loses perspective. He focuses on that one negative thing, and he convinces himself that suicide is the only option." Jensen reported that several of the young patients he was treating at the time came to him after Scott's suicide to say they could identify with the boy, that they had themselves at some point felt tempted by suicide. One told him, "My God, I was so distorted. It was scary. I look back now and think, 'How could I have even thought of killing myself?' But I thought it was the only option. I know better now."

Suicide prevention programs for teenagers are one response to the galloping increase, but many experts find them lacking in effectiveness. Most such programs ignore depression as a possible cause, preferring instead to focus on environmental stress such as warring parents or problems in school. They also assume that all teenagers share a potential vulnerability to suicide, which is not true. If stress is given as the predominant cause, that may actually remove the protective taboos against suicide. Ignoring depression will only confuse and further isolate youngsters, instead of raising useful questions in their minds.

Dr. Shaffer has developed a brief, two-step screening process for high school students that protects confidentiality and identifies those at risk. First a questionnaire is given out that takes only ten minutes to complete, asking about mood, alcohol, and other potential areas of concern, with the replies leading to further questions about how severe the problem is and whether the student feels in need of help. Any student who has had thoughts about suicide in the past three months, as well as those who may have attempted it in the past, who have severe mood problems, or who abuse drugs and alcohol, then go on to a second questionnaire. These questionnaires, which can be administered quickly in a classroom, yield a diagnostic profile that is passed along to a school psychologist or psychiatrist, who then interviews the student in person.

Dr. Shaffer has found this two-step approach to be a sensitive indicator; it has identified students known to be at risk, as well as some who were not perceived as such by school psychologists or social workers. "The process," says Shaffer, "has been shown to be as reliable as using a clinician, and it is probably a safer, much more valuable procedure for schools than lecturing to teens about suicide and its risks."

If you have any suspicion at all that your teenager may be harboring ideas of suicide, the best thing is to address him or her directly on the subject by asking, for instance, "Have you ever felt so low that life seemed not worth living?" Adolescents who do not feel suicidal will say so; those who are ambivalent or who respond positively to such questions should immediately talk to a psychotherapist, who will probably suggest that the child and family meet together and work out some ground rules. These may include agreement that the child immediately enter therapy, and that he or she promise to report to the parents any suicidal thoughts that may arise between therapy sessions.

Parents should never attempt to deal with a suicidal child entirely on their own. Call in the experts, but before you do, seek out the best, because not all practitioners are equally proficient. A child psychiatrist or psychotherapist can usually be found with the help of a pediatrician, a family doctor, a school psychologist, a guidance counselor, or the department of child psychiatry at a hospital associated with a university. Given the importance of this selection, it would be a good idea to call several of these sources and to compare their recommendations before making a final selection. There are lemons out there; try to make sure you find a peach. That means not only checking out practitioners' credentials, but asking if they have dealt with other suicidal kids. It's a bad sign if they speak in hard-to-understand textbook terms; they should be able to relate to you in everyday language, and to show some sympathy or at least sympathetic awareness of the way you feel about your child's problems.

Siblings Need Attention, Too

Whenever parental attention shifts toward one sibling, it's going to disturb the others. This is as true for depressive illness as it is for the birth of a new baby. Never sacrifice the family to the illness of one member. Never make that member's illness the axis around which the entire family revolves. Certainly parents and siblings should not ignore the child's illness, either. The healthiest response is for the family to recognize it, acknowledge that it has affected one of them, and deal with it as a unit—not, as so often happens, for each member to sweep it under his or her own private rug and react in isolation.

When depression visits one child, the others will display their recognition of the change in some fashion. They may somehow feel themselves to be the cause of the depression, particularly when they lack all knowledge of the illness; or they may be jealous of the attention given to the depressed child, and even try to emulate the behavior that is securing that attention. Many will experience feelings of loss and abandonment, thinking that the depressed sibling has stolen their parents' affection from them. At school they will almost assuredly feel anxious about the risk of being teased or singled out in some unpleasant fashion by their peers. Too much overt sympathy from well-meaning teachers may backfire, causing them unwanted "special treatment."

Parents need to be alert to all these possibilities, and to effect damage control before problems arise, not after. Common sense is your best guide. Tell siblings the truth. Make sure they understand that depression is an illness, not bad behavior or a bunch of psychological issues, and that it's not anybody's fault. Use the information in this book to explain how the illness is making their brother or sister feel, and hammer home the point that for a while the depression may cause their sibling to seem cross or tired, unsure or discouraged. Explain to them about medication and its possible side effects, especially those such as weight gain, and be honest about how long medication takes to work. Most important, reassure them that you love them as much as ever, even though you may have less time for them right now.

Siblings will deal far better with the facts than with the fantasies and misinterpretations they will cook up if the problem goes unnamed. They will be less troubled and more supportive of their sibling if they are informed and involved in the family strategy and treated as responsible beings, rather than shut out from an adult situation.

Siblings are always affected in a manner consonant with their own personalities and ways of viewing the world. Since you know them better than anyone else, you'll be able to see subtle changes in their behavior if you are on the lookout for them. As a parent you can't and shouldn't try to shield them from their sibling's illness, but you can make sure it doesn't take on too much importance in their lives. One group parent noticed that her nine-year-old was creeping about the house and stifling his natural inclination toward boisterous giggles because he thought it wrong to appear happy in front of his depressed sister. His smart mother set him straight by explaining that laughter was always good medicine as long as it was never at his sister's expense. You should strive toward normalcy in the household. Make sure the other children know it is you and your spouse, not they, who are responsible for dealing with the depressed child's problems.

Many parents who attend the friends and family group initially give the impression they have only one child—the one with the illness—acknowledging the existence of another only when someone asks a direct question. Though this is understandable in times of crisis, it can be a warning that brothers and sisters are perhaps being lost in the shuffle.

I raised this issue privately with some parents, all of whom acknowledged it as troublesome. "It's so hard for me to see beyond my daughter's illness," admitted one whose son was acting up in school. "My husband and I have divvied up responsibility for our two kids. I spend so much time and energy on Anna that I have little left over to give my son, so my husband concentrates on him. We share the burden, but in different ways." This is one strategy, and it works for this family because each parent is doing what he or she does best. There is no perfect way to deal with the problem, and each family must seek its own solutions. Not seeking one, but simply allowing events to unfold and reacting to them without forethought and deliberation is what parents should avoid.

When Adult Children Have a Depressive Illness

Ten years ago, when I emerged from my own descent into the depths, I warned my daughter that depression might one day find its way to her. Her lack of interest in this information was phenomenal, eliciting simply an "uh-huh." Since she and her grandmother had gotten on famously, and since she was already on her own and living in another city when my depression had its way with me, she had been untouched by evidence of its presence in either of us, and had never dealt with depression fallout.

My daughter and I are lucky in the quality of our relationship, and we know it, often citing ourselves as the world's greatest example of mother-daughter congeniality. When she comes to town or I visit her, we routinely sit up late into the night, talking amiably and intimately. Although I would occasionally refer to my own experience during these years, we never progressed beyond the "uh-huh" stage.

Six months ago she broke with a man she had been seeing for some time. My daughter has wonderful social skills, among them patience, discretion, and tolerance, so the inner workings of their relationship as it deteriorated were unknown to me. I was aware only of an increasing reluctance on her part to talk about her friend, and a gradual damping of her enthusiasm for that and other parts of her usually crowded and busy life. She did not tell me she felt depressed, but her voice lacked enthusiasm and variety when we spoke. She loves her job, which is both demanding and time-consuming, yet what she chose to tell me about now was always negative: the office politics, the irrationality of those with whom she dealt on a daily basis, what a drag it had all become, how exhausted she was. She began to wonder if she shouldn't switch fields, shed responsibilities, and try to lead what she referred to, crossly, as a "normal" existence. I listened with a sympathetic ear; a combination of boyfriend and office problems is enough to get even my special and talented daughter down. Two months passed without either of us waking up to what was going on, despite all the evidence.

One morning she phoned me from her car, en route to see her doctor about some minor but troublesome ailment. Her voice was a monotone; she sounded dazed and close to tears. At last realization dawned. I told her to tell the doctor how she felt, for how long, and about her family history. "You're depressed," I said, "and you need an antidepressant. Call me when you get home." She did, and said she had a prescription. It took four days of urging from me for her to get it filled, not because she resisted doing so, but because the effort of going to the drugstore seemed immense to her.

After that we spoke every day, sometimes twice. My daughter has an office at home, but normally she spends most of the day visiting clients. I would ask if she had been out; the answer was always "Not yet." "Get on your bicycle and ride around the garden outside your building," I told her. Sometimes she managed it, more often not. Often she couldn't speak at all except to worry about her work. I suggested she tackle whatever business matters were most pressing, and leave the others. "You'll deal with them when things are better, in three or four weeks," I explained. I held her hand by long distance, did what I could to reduce her anxiety level, and went on urging her to leave the house at least once every day. Almost exactly three weeks later my phone rang one morning and a bright and animated voice came through the wires. "I'm back!" she crowed. "I'm me again." And so she has remained ever since.

When your child is young and still living with you, you are in a position to deal with the illness in a hands-on fashion, monitoring both behavior and adherence to treatment on a continuing basis. Depressed or manic adult children, out from under your nose and your guidance, present a problem even when they live in the same town or city as you. Grown up and on their own, they are beyond the bounds of close parental supervision, and most likely will not welcome interference in their affairs. If they become severely depressed, as my daughter did, they will perhaps be more amenable to your help, but if they are manic they most assuredly will not. During my attendance at the friends and family group there has been a steady parade of parents whose grown manic child has caused them unceasing pain and despair. This usually endures until the depression which eventually follows at last kicks in, rendering the sufferer more malleable and cooperative about seeking or sticking to treatment for a while.

Seth, the thirty-year-old son of Eileen and Larry, was diagnosed as manic-depressive five years ago, and takes his medications when he feels like it which, judging from his parents' reporting, is not very often. "He has no conscience, no values, no morals. He's behaving like some sort of con man," says Larry. "I don't know anyone like him. I don't know him anymore." Seth is a high-rolling stockbroker, pulling in hefty sums of money from his various jobs. He is also a prototypical manic-depressive on a long high, full of grandiose notions, tricky and extremely bright. He's given up his own apartment, which proved too expensive during one of his brief down times, and now lives with various friends, moving from one to another each time he wears out his welcome. His parents can't understand why anyone would voluntarily invite Seth to stay, but more likely than not, the verbal abuse and unconcerned arrogance that Seth regularly heaps upon his parents is not displayed in full force to others. As Howard often observes, depressives may be sick but they're not stupid, and so confine their worst behavior to their intimates. "Our son," says Larry, "treats us like little people beneath his notice."

But Seth owes his parents several thousand dollars. One day when he came to see them, he announced that he'd had his best earning week ever, about ten thousand dollars, which as usual he was busy dissipating on expensive suits and dinners. "I asked him to repay us what he owed, and he said why should he, we could afford it, plus a lot of other things I don't care to repeat here." His father's view is that brokerage firms will accept without question almost any behavior in their brokers, as long as they produce. Whether or not that is true, Seth's chosen profession does allow him to earn a great deal of money on a sporadic basis, to quit when he feels like it, and to pick up another job with ease.

Eileen and Larry are nearly at their wits' end. "What can we do?" they asked helplessly at a recent meeting. First, suggested the group, stop handing Seth sixty dollars or more for food when he's out of work and comes running home for a handout. Money, Howard explained, is one of the few leverages parents have to protect themselves and to get their child back on track. "Use it. Tie him down with it." Seth's generous friends are running out, fed up with his cavalier behavior. Soon he will have only his parents to turn to for a bed, food, and care. "When that happens," said Howard, "tell him there are two conditions attached to being allowed to return home: you will not allow him to treat you as he does, and he must remain on his medication, checking in with his doctor on a regular basis."

Like many manics, Seth is a poor complier, often taking himself off his medication because he misses the highs that give his professional and social life a risky and exhilarating edge. A good psychotherapist could be helpful here; unfortunately, like many long-term nonpsychotic manics, Seth is superbly good at conning his therapists, of whom he has had three or four thus far. Once a week he effortlessly persuades the therapist that he has his life and his illness in firm control. In desperation Eileen and Larry bought fifty minutes of Seth's most recent therapist's time to set the record straight. "Can you believe it?" Larry exploded. "She says Seth has readjusted well to his illness, that we have nothing to worry about. I asked her how it was possible to say he's okay, that we could see how he was behaving. The other day he barged into our house at two in the morning, woke us up, and told us to give him five hundred dollars. We are practically living with him, and his therapist says he's just fine on the basis of one hour a week."

The only solution is for Seth's medicating psychiatrist to use his influence to persuade the psychotherapist to take a closer look. But the doctor, whom Seth visits infrequently and only when he is temporarily taking his medication, is not amenable to that. So the parents can only wait for Seth to crash. In the meantime, they must stop all the handouts and refuse to take the abuse, even if this means barring Seth from the house. Eileen and Larry have to protect themselves as best they can, calling upon whatever reserves of patience are left to them.

Grace's thirty-year-old son, Alex, is also a diagnosed manic-depressive, but since one brief manic episode eight months ago, he has sunk into an anxious, dependent state of gloom. He had been a respected teacher in a city high school, a job to which he still hopes to return, but his depression is stubborn, and so far his doctor has been unable to treat it successfully. Although he is intent upon keeping his tenure, whenever he focuses on going back to work he is overcome with anxiety. "He can't be alone," says Grace, explaining that she and her husband have become what feels uncomfortably like baby-sitters. "He wants us with him all the time. He often comes over and spends the entire day with us, speaking little, never smiling. It's heartbreaking. And when it's time to go home, he begs us to come with him and spend the night at his place, which we often do. Then the next day we start all over again."

Alex's psychotherapist wants the parents to spend less time with their son, and believes he would be better off in a day program that will give him a reason to get out and generate a little energy. Day programs are halfway houses for many who suffer from severe depressive illness, places where self-isolating depressives can find companionship free of the exigencies of a normal social life, yet still live on their own. The problem with day programs is that among the attendees are many who still lack hope, leading many recovering depressives to opt out because of what they describe as an atmosphere imbued with negativism and despair. Manic-depressives are often exceptionally bright and achievement-oriented; they, in particular, tend to find the day program company below their level, composed as it often is of people who have not worked in years.

The group agreed the day program would be good for both Alex and his parents, and suggested they present the idea to Alex as just what it is intended to be: a temporary pause between complete dependency upon his parents and a return to teaching, as well as a place to practice rusty social skills. Alex's psychotherapist has explained to him that continued reliance on his parents as his sole social contact will inhibit his recovery. All three are now working together to encourage Alex to give the program a try for a month, to set himself the goal of finding one or two other participants who also expect to return to their former lives in the near future, and to begin seeing them socially outside of the program.

To the psychotherapist's suggestion, the group added another of their own: that Alex attend a support group for depressives. Though it is true that support groups also include depressives full of lassitude and hopelessness, there are also present others who are on the way up and out into the active world again. Identification with them will be another source of hope and encouragement for Alex. Those who have returned to work but continue to come to the group will be the best role models of all.

The group also asked many questions about Alex's medicating doctor, and arrived at the opinion that a consultation with a psychopharmacologist is a must. When anxiety joins with depression, the illness becomes more recalcitrant and harder to treat. As the foremost experts in treating the illness with medication, psychopharmacologists may prescribe a combination of medications of which another doctor might not have read or heard. In Alex's case he has been seeing the same doctor since the beginning of his illness, a doctor who lacks interest in communicating with either the parents or the psychotherapist. Now, eight months later and without much improvement, it may even be time to skip a consultation and instead seek out another, one with a solid reputation for excellence. It bears repeating that our tendency to accept the decisions of medical people as definitive is a mistake. Professionals do err, especially in a field as new as the treatment of depressive illness, still more of an art than a science. Depression often goes hand in hand with dependency, and it is up to family members to become the depressive's advocate, since he or she lacks the will and energy to be their own. That means accumulating knowledge and information to create a base from which questions and challenges are both permissible and possible.

When Adult Children with Depressive Illness Come Home to Roost

The only thing worse than having an unmedicated manic-depressive adult child who does not live with you is one who has flown the coop and then comes home to roost. Most parents see their children off on their own with a somewhat guilty sense of relief. Plans for vacations with friends or a spouse alone, freedom from the economic burden of tuition, the expectation of grandchildren, and other such delights go a long way toward making up for the empty nest.

Just such a parent is Martha, who is divorced, living on her own since her daughter moved to Chicago several years ago, and enjoying her freedom. She told her story her first night at the group with such ladylike civility and dignity that at first we failed to hear the desperation behind her words. "I have a lovely daughter just turned thirty. Some days she's wonderful and some days she's the Wicked Witch of the East. I have the privilege of living with this person, and most of the time it's not fun." Just how unamusing this cohabitation had become was difficult for Martha to express. Like her quiet anger, the tale came out in dribs and drabs over two or three evenings, each time told with less restraint.

Christina had left home a bright and ambitious young woman determined to become a writer; she had supported herself with many other jobs, only occasionally turning to her mother for money. Although they enjoyed each other's company, they exchanged visits only once or twice a year, keeping in touch by telephone, until one day, two years ago, Christina turned up on her mother's doorstep, drastically in debt and not in the least apologetic. She simply announced she was moving in.

Much has transpired in the meantime. Christina's initial manic phase has long since passed with the help of medication, which she takes most of the time. Creditors are no longer calling daily, but two months ago Christina spent her thirtieth birthday sobbing helplessly. Unfortunately, sobbing is not her total repertoire. She frequently characterizes her mother as stingy, mean, evil, selfish, stupid, conniving, manipulative, and a bitch, and that makes Martha very angry. Like many other attendees, the group is the only place she feels safe venting her anger. "I am in a state of rage much of the time, and totally isolated from my friends. I drag myself to work every morning and crawl back home at the end of the day, only to find someone who says she hates me." One newcomer, whose depressive husband is of the sticky-flypaper sort, piped up in distress, saying Martha shouldn't be angry because "it's not Christina's fault, it's the depression." "But I'm human," snapped Martha in reply, and most of the room nodded in agreement.

It soon became evident that neither the therapist nor the psychiatrist in charge had been well chosen and needed to be jettisoned, since neither Christina's behavior nor her symptoms had budged in six months. Prying anyone away from a therapist presents a problem, but Christina's mother told us a previous therapist had apparently made unwelcome sexual advances, a lever she could use to suggest to Christina that one can be wrong twice in choosing a professional helping hand. As for the medicating psychiatrist, the fault lay with Martha, who had selected him without looking into his background. While he hasn't a poor reputation, he is not among the top thirty in the city. Nor had Martha established any channel of communication with him, so although she had read copiously about the illness and was knowledgeable, she had never posed questions or attempted to communicate to him her own version of what was going on, surely quite a different one from that provided by her daughter. Poor communication and an unknown professional in charge of a sometimes recalcitrant and backsliding manic-depressive are a chancy combination.

The therapist believed Christina should return to work, and Martha agreed with her suggestion. Finances were tight, and she welcomed the possibility of another source of income, as well as some diversion, any diversion, that might lessen Christina's animosity toward her. One group member reminded Martha that the therapist had not been present at Christina's weepy thirtieth birthday, nor had Christina seen fit to tell her. Had she known, she might have hesitated in recommending that her patient seek employment. Changing the cast of treatment providers will probably help Christina, and also relieve somewhat the stress to which Martha has so long been subject.

Like drill sergeants, the other members instructed her to look to her own needs and wishes by doling out small sums of money, but only in response to improved behavior, including a cessation of insults, and by setting a boundary on time spent in gloomy rumination. When Christina sobs in despair, Martha should, of course, be sympathetic and responsive; but she should keep in mind that depressives have an even greater talent for manipulation than most human beings, and her daughter may be using tears as a ploy to get her own way. There have been many reports in the group from parents who, scarcely able to concentrate in the office because of concern for a grown child who was sad and tearful when they left, some genuinely so, have telephoned later in the day for reassurance that all is well. When their calls went unanswered they feared the worst and rushed home in a panic, only to find no one there because their son or daughter had decided to hang out with friends.

This is not to suggest that vigilance is wasted or that there is never any cause for alarm, but only that appearances can sometimes be misleading. Depressives do have a bad time of it, but they may exaggerate just how bad. Parents who agonize over having to be away during the day are usually worrying needlessly; and it is not normally necessary that they return directly from their office and stay in every evening. You need to keep your antennae out. After gauging the situation for a month or so, you will begin to know if and when your absence presents a danger to the depressive.

Protecting Yourself Against Distress

Unrelieved stress is bad for the body and for the spirit; when both are depleted, you will have nothing to support you and, equally important, nothing left over to support your child. In times of crisis, adrenaline takes over. It is the aftermath that takes the toll, the daily struggle to muster strength for two. You owe it to yourself as well as to the person with the illness to make a concerted effort to remain stable. Few among us are able to do so unless we learn to satisfy our own needs.

More and more, it becomes clear to me as I attend the group every Friday evening that there is a two-step reaction to the appearance of the illness in someone you love. The first step is all about them: how you can help them, what you can learn, how you can become a bastion of love and support and an effective advocate for them. You are so confused, so challenged by what is happening, that it's difficult to maintain a connection with anything other than the illness. Your child's needs are paramount. Then an unwelcome awareness of what this means for your own life kicks in. No matter how much you love this person, you realize that his or her illness now holds you hostage, too. So begins your journey along the depression fallout continuum, proceeding from confusion, self-guilt, and demoralization to resentment, anger, and the desire to escape. Parents, for whom escape is unthinkable, cycle back again and again to anger painted with guilt.

There are a number of ways to deal with such feelings. One is to join a support group organized for others in the same situation. Venting resentment and guilt is a healthy way to deal with both, but is best done among those who are intimately familiar with the syndrome. Friends, no matter how sympathetic, cannot understand. If you decide on psychotherapy, use your therapist as your advocate, as the best friend your best friend cannot be in such a situation, no matter how willing.

I write this book as a divorced parent, but one who did not have to deal with a daughter's depression until she was an adult. I am ever mindful on Friday evenings of all the other divorced parents, most of whom bear full responsibility, both emotionally and operationally, for a child with the illness. Some have managed to involve the absent father or mother, especially if their child has been hospitalized, but mostly they cope on a solo basis. The very fact that the other parent is no longer living with the child creates a barrier to understanding. The only advice I have is to try to involve the absent parent by, for instance, inviting him or her to attend sessions with the child's medicating psychiatrist, and to encourage him or her to acquire some insight and understanding of the illness by reading about it and by listening to what you have to say. If you succeed, you will gain a much-needed ally. If not, know you are not alone and do the best you can.

One divorced mother in the group presented a strong case for seeking therapy:

> My daughter's illness was running my life, was indeed ruining my life. I finally went to a shrink. She asked me what was the matter, and I told her about Clara's illness. For a long time that was all I could talk about, all the details of how it began and the problems she had, about the hospitalization, about how, when she finally could go back to school, the teachers called to tell me she was huddled in a corner and wouldn't or couldn't talk. All about her medication and the problems she had with it, the side effects and how wretched they made her feel.
>
> The shrink finally said to me one day, "I want you to repeat after me: Clara has an illness; I have a life," and I said to her, "Clara has an illness; maybe one day I'll have a life of my own back." And she said, "No, repeat after me: Clara has an illness; I have a life." It was incredible how hard it was for me to say that. I kept hedging. Then finally I could say it, in the sense of repeating it, using the same words. Once I did, I suddenly realized it was true, and that if I didn't have a life, well then, I wouldn't be able to help my daughter anyway.
>
> So I started thinking about myself, and my need to stay healthy, my need not to follow Clara through all her ups and downs. I learned that unless I had a little distance between myself and her, there was nothing in the world that I could give her that would be of help.

These are wise words from an insightful therapist and a mother who has escaped her anger. If you can take them to heart and act upon them, you will be doing the right thing both for your child and for yourself.

12

INNOCENT VICTIMS:
CHILDREN OF A DEPRESSED
PARENT

THE MORE ONE LEARNS ABOUT depressed parents, their spouses, and their children, the more one appreciates why the nature-versus-nurture conundrum is still unsolved. There are so many factors at play in addition to a parent's depression: genes, the personal histories of both spouses, stress, human nature, and human needs all lie in a jumble that is impossible to assemble in one orderly design. But while no one has yet found a way to untangle all these inputs, the outcome is abundantly clear: children of a depressed parent are in for a lot of unhappiness.

This is because virtually all the attributes of good parenting are inconsistent with the feelings and behavior associated with depression. Like other depressives, parents with this disorder feel miserable, insecure, cross, and dissatisfied, unable to cope in the present and overcome with hopelessness when they look to the future. Thus encumbered, parenting for them becomes a taxing chore, and their children become increasingly unhappy and difficult to handle.

Children of depressed parents are more likely than children of non-depressed parents to have behavioral and academic problems, exhibit depressive symptomology, and be at greater risk for depression. They are more self-critical and less skilled in their interactions with people, and have more difficulty dealing with their emotions. As a result, they're apt to encounter rejection from others, which undermines their self-esteem, causing them to become withdrawn, so that their social and emotional development falls behind that of their peers. While other kids whose parents have a serious psychiatric or medical illness also suffer stress and disruption, depression is the single diagnosable condition for which kids of depressed parents show a significantly higher risk, with rates of major depressive disorder six times higher than that of children of non-depressed parents.

One researcher, James Coyne, summarizes the results of a large number of diverse studies in a chapter in *Development Perspectives on Depression* (University of Rochester Press, 1992). There are plenty of poor marriages and poor parents, but it's apparent that depression in families acts as a wild card, changing the family game plan in unexpected and unpleasant ways. One of these, called assortative mating, actually precedes the marriage. It appears that depressives may have a predilection for choosing a troubled spouse. One study found that more than 50 percent of the depressed women surveyed had husbands with a history of psychiatric disturbances that predated the marriage—often depression—and another found that approximately 50 percent of depressed women experienced marital violence. Assuredly, a far higher number are subject to verbal abuse and intimidation.

A majority of depressed persons have serious marital difficulties and judge their marriages disappointing and unfulfilling. Interactions with their mates reveal a pattern of mutual hostility and anger, or of inhibition, avoidance, and withdrawal. Their relationship lacks the intimacy that helps alleviate the feelings of depression. Anecdotal evidence from support groups bears out research that husbands do indeed become critical and unsupportive of their depressed wives, and are often fed up and thinking of leaving them.

Although a depressed parent of either sex creates problems for a child, the bulk of the research on parental depression and its effects on children has zeroed in on the mother, because she is the center of a young child's existence: the primary nurturer, teacher, and emotional and social contact. Ideally, a mother is a good listener, communicator, and problem solver; authoritative without being authoritarian; warm and consistent; and tolerant and patient. Mothers in the grip of depression are often just the opposite: harsh, critical, impatient, irritable, and unaffectionate. These deficits exact a high price from their children. And because one in every four women will suffer serious depression at some time in her life—more often than not, right in the middle of her prime childbearing years of twenty-five to thirty-five—the research findings are applicable to a very substantial number of children.

All the family members become enmeshed in the web of the mother's depression. The child may become first a pawn between the warring parents, and then a participant in the battle. The depressed parent may, for instance, try to enlist the child as a source of comfort or as an ally, and then cut the child off when he or she proves disappointing in this respect. In this way the unhappy child unwittingly validates the depressed parent's feelings of ineptitude and worthlessness and opens the way to criticism of parenting failures by the non-depressed parent. As the child becomes increasingly upset, he or she is more difficult to handle and is more openly critical of the mother. The negative feedback loops among all three family members are reinforced, and the patterns of behavior become ingrained. It's almost impossible for any of them to break out of the negative maze, says Coyne, because the depressed mother, despite her deficits, keeps trying to fill her role of caring parent and family problem-solver. Because she has committed her own sense of self-worth to the quality of her family's life, and because she judges herself according to the opinions of the other members, she feels increasingly bad: besieged, helpless, angry, and racked with guilt.

The difference in the ways depressed and non-depressed mothers interact with their children show up even when the child is an infant. Instead of constantly hovering over the crib and making kitchy-kitchy-coo noises and faces, the depressed mother is aloof and speaks without animation. The baby reacts to this detachment by turning its head and averting its gaze, and will soon learn to do this with other adults as well. These infants offer few smiles and are unresponsive, fussy, and fretful.

Toddlers of depressed parents are often super-argumentative, prone to temper tantrums, and unusually resentful of boundaries and punishment, behavior a depressed parent is ill-equipped to handle. This often results in pitched battles, with the child kicking and screaming, "I hate you!", and the mother feeling increasingly miserable and inept. Neither punishment, indulgence, nor withdrawal on the mother's part calms the child or resolves the situation. When children are older, depressed mothers are often overly angry and antagonistic toward them, and less apt to encourage their independence and individuality. Throughout their dealings with their children, their inability to cope is manifested in either aggressive hostility or avoidant withdrawal.

This behavior was amply demonstrated in a study conducted by psychologist Constance Hammen at UCLA. Hammen assembled pairs of depressed and non-depressed mothers and their children and asked each pair to choose a typical source of contention between them—curfew, chores, or allowance, for instance—and to spend five minutes together trying to resolve the issue. She observed that unipolar mothers in particular were significantly more negative and critical in their interactions, inclined to get off-track and to throw in lots of irrelevant, contentious blather. Their children responded in kind by becoming increasingly negative. While the non-depressed mothers were able to negotiate a settlement, depressed moms were more apt to throw up their hands and say something like, "You're impossible to deal with," or "You'll do what I say, or else."

Hammen's observations indicate that it's difficult for these children to acquire problem-solving skills because they aren't learning them at home. Instead of negotiating or reaching solutions, they make demands or throw up their hands and walk away, just as their mothers do. Friendships with peers can buffer maternal negativity, but these kids don't know how to make or keep them, perhaps because they are too needy or too ready to attract the attention they lack at home by throwing their weight around in school. They often do poorly academically, don't respond well to teachers' encouragement, and may be mislabeled "bad" or "stupid," in part because their chaotic and disruptive home environments preclude good homework and study habits.

Perhaps most damaging of all is the poor opinion these children have of themselves. The experts used to think that this was a copycat phenomena, that they were simply mirroring their mothers' low self-esteem. But now it appears that these kids aren't mimicking what they see; they're taking to heart what their fault-finding mothers tell them. This infuses all their social interactions, and negatively affects their academic performance as well. They come to anticipate failure and rejection, and often carry these perceptions into adulthood.

About one-fourth of children with a depressed mother exhibit symptoms of depression. This is not the same thing as being depressed; the former is what the child *does* and the latter what the child *is;* the two just look alike. Exhibiting the symptoms without having the illness is classic depression fallout, and children who grow up in a family with a depressed parent travel through all five stages: confusion, self-guilt, demoralization, resentment and anger, and avoidant or escapist behavior. As noted, a substantial number of these children do go on to become clinically depressed.

How much of this subsequent depression is genetic and how much is influenced by environmental factors, no one is sure at the moment. Whichever is the case, the statistics tell a tale that parents should heed. If a child does begin to show signs of depression—especially if there is depression in the family—parents should tell the pediatrician so that he will be prepared for the possibility if it arises.

Postpartum Depression

Mothers and fathers, too, should be alert to the possibility of postpartum depression. A case of the "baby blues" hits between 50 percent and 90 percent of all women within three or four days of giving birth, but it's not impairing and lasts only two weeks or less. A more severe version of postpartum depression typically appears between six weeks and four months later, and may endure anywhere from six months to a year. The approximately 10 percent of young mothers who develop the latter may already have been genetically vulnerable to depression, or their bodies may be responding adversely to the hormonal changes associated with childbirth; the facts aren't yet in on this. Some experts have observed that psychological problems, as well as unipolar and bipolar illness, also increase for men around the pregnancy and delivery of their partners, so the mental stress surrounding childbirth may also contribute to postpartum depression.

Baby blues typically produce crying spells, changes in eating and sleeping patterns, and general anxiety related to taking good care of the new arrival, all of which are normal and should disappear in short order. The real thing, however, can be dangerous, and should be treated in the same manner as any severe depression. Failure to do so can occasionally have disastrous results, as in a case reported in early 1997 in the newspapers. One month after the birth of her second baby, a young mother left the house at dawn one morning after feeding her child, and was discovered dead a few days later, an apparent suicide by drowning. While the report quotes the police as saying she had no previous history of psychiatric illness, her family said they had no doubts that her death was a suicide rather than misadventure, so they must have noticed that she had not been herself since the baby's arrival.

While suicide is extremely rare in even the most severe postpartum depression, the impact of a mother's untreated illness is at least temporary bad news for the child. Researchers note that many infants continue to behave as though the mother were depressed for as long as a year after the depression spontaneously remits or is successfully treated. Timely intervention may prevent a tragedy.

The Aftermath of Parental Depression

When I began this book, my ideas about the long-term effects of my mother's depression on me were private and subjective. The only psychotherapist I ever consulted favored my father as the pivotal parent in my psychology. His early departure from my life, she insisted, explained my poor opinion of myself and my miserable record of maintaining intimacy with men. I yielded to what I believed was her infallible expertise and accepted her interpretation, even though it felt like wearing a dress several sizes too small. Deep down, however, I never relinquished my certainty that my mother was the real villain in my life, and continued to hold her responsible in some indistinct way for my shaky adult self. In addition to her genes, she gave me clear messages about life: I was inadequate and unlovable, and men were bad and not to be trusted. By the time I was grown, these instructions were as much a part of me as my DNA.

My thesis of depression fallout clarified for me the influence of my mother's depression, but I still harbored a gnawing suspicion that I had tailored my own experience and that of a handful of other adult children of similar mothers to fit my theory. As I delved more deeply into the research about the hostility and criticism typical of many depressed mothers, however, my suspicions abated. While most of the research done in this country has focused principally on interactions between depressed mothers and their young children, now some English researchers are looking at how such children fare in adulthood. *Parental Psychiatric Disorder* (Cambridge University Press, 1996), edited by Michael Göpfert, presents evidence that parental depression does leave an imprint that persists through the years.

Full of observations such as the need for adult psychiatrists to start worrying about the welfare of their clients' children "whether they like it or not," the book includes the personal account of Denise Roberts, who grew up in the presence of a mother's severe depressive illness. Titled "On Being and Becoming Mindless," it traces the connection between her mother's illness and her own problems, first in childhood, then in adolescence and adulthood. The author is now working in the mental health field, where, she says, she often encounters children who are struggling unnoticed with a parent's illness.

Denise writes that in telling her story at last, she has been attacked by guilt, as if she were telling tales to seek attention and will not be believed. She remembers constant fights in her parents' bedroom, with her father trying to console or calm her mother, who was often violent. "She would scream that she could not go on anymore . . . that she'd had enough. She would go into a rage and throw objects around the room, completely clear the entire surface of the dressing table with one sweep of her arm." Unable to comprehend or rationalize this behavior, young Denise was constantly frightened, wondering when the violence would ever stop and what would happen next. "I was preoccupied and startled with the chaos in our home and wondering if it would be safe. Not telling anyone about what was happening, just performing as if it were not happening . . . it feels as if the terror became encapsulated and stored inside, hidden and not addressed. This left me with the sense of floating on the outside, interacting but not really feeling part of things."

It was her eleven-year-old sister who accompanied their father to the hospital on visits, leaving the younger Denise a bewildered observer of her mother's alternate rage and despair. One night a "Dr. Brown" arrived at their house because her mother had had a relapse. "My father and mother were upstairs while Dr. Brown waited downstairs to see my mother. . . . I recall being dressed in a baby-doll nightsuit and going into the lounge where Dr. Brown was seated. . . . I hoped he would speak to me . . . that he might at least think that I looked nice enough to talk to. I waited and waited. I thought to myself that he might ask me something, about me, how I was, what did I think? He never asked me anything . . . only sat in the chair in silence with a pleasant enough smile on his face."

Denise began to get into difficulties at elementary school. "My friendships with peers seemed to be more fragile. I was argumentative and I was being tormented by children who previously had been my friends but were now going around saying that my mother was 'mental.'" She took to stealing pennies and other coins at home and from her teacher, hiding them in her blazer pockets until they made such a bulky weight that she was discovered and punished. "I began to feel isolated, like a misfit and somehow contaminated by all this madness and badness."

When her mother returned home from the hospital, the violent scenes continued and Denise and her sibling were often beaten for minor transgressions. While their father was away at work, the sisters were expected to control their mother, but they were unequal to the task, often giving in to her demands in order to avoid her angry rages. As a result, they faced their father's blame and anger; sometimes he would not speak to them for a week. It was, she says, like living in a vacuum.

Her answer was to overdose—she does not say on what—not once but twice; she considers herself lucky to be alive. "I wanted to be out of the terrorizing world that I felt I was living in and I also felt tremendous feelings of responsibility and guilt. . . . I don't think I had a real concept of wanting to be dead but a sense of wanting to stop dead, to go no further." At seventeen she left school and home. Now an adult, she is, with the help of long-term psychotherapy, beginning to find herself and to feel for herself, but the lack of adult attention when she was young has left her feeling she isn't deserving of help or care.

Denise's account highlights the guilt that she and others in her situation feel: guilt for trying to seek her parents' attention for herself when it was all focused on her mother; guilt for being somehow contaminated by proximity to her mother's illness; guilt for often being the trigger of her parents' terrible tantrums and relapses; and guilt for wishing to be free of the responsibilities forced upon her. But how could she feel otherwise, when everyone shut her out from explanations and understanding, leaving her unnoticed, helpless, and scared?

Recollections of the Past

Of the seven adult children of a seriously depressed or manic-depressive parent with whom I have spoken, all had reached the fifth stage of depression fallout—the desire to escape the source of their pain—and all had acted upon it in varying ways. None remained close to their parent. Two, like Denise, attempted suicide; three became alcoholics or drug abusers. Only two have managed to maintain a lasting intimate relationship with a partner. All but one—who grew up in the company of several older siblings—have sought psychotherapeutic help to address the long-term consequences of their troubled childhoods.

While the experience of a few does not make a scientific case, it does raise serious questions about the emotional risks of growing up with parental depression. The tales that follow illustrate two particular dangers such children face—too much responsibility and too little love—that have continued to cause problems into adulthood.

Isobel was only seven when her mother's manic depression burst into her life. Her father had just moved out, perhaps because the illness had been long brewing and he was unable to cope with its effects on their marriage. But Isobel, viewing the two events from a young child's perspective, assumed she was the cause of both. "I felt it was my responsibility to look after Mom," she told me, "and I took that responsibility very seriously." Her mother's moods were wildly erratic, swinging from paralytic despair to psychotic mania. "I was ever-present at all those extremes. I knew where she was every minute. I listened and I could hear, could sense what was going on in her." Sometimes she crept out of bed at night and slept outside her mother's door, ready to assume her role as sole protector and ally.

Isobel's mother is fiercely intelligent; when occasionally she pauses at normal in her travels up and down the manic-depressive scale, she is witty and warm, and fully cognizant of her plight. "Mania isn't all bad, you know," Isobel observes. "In some stages Mom was charming—seductive and exciting, too. Looking back, I have the sense of having been in some kind of adventure where everything was very high-risk, extremely dramatic. I felt entirely reckless."

What she recollects most clearly from those years was not so much unhappiness as feeling immensely powerful because she saw herself as in control of her mother's life, and for that she received rewards.

"I got a lot of compliments for being able to cope with Mom's illness with strength and responsibility. Being strong got me Dad's love because I knew I was freeing him up, and of course it brought me Mom's as well. And the admiration of all those adults who told me how wonderful I was. None of it, none of what I was or tried to be then, had anything to do with my heart or my body. It was all in my head."

Through the ensuing years, Isobel remained profoundly attached to her mother despite the chaos and craziness. "Some part of my life with Mom must have been stable and loving. I think she was sometimes aware that I had shouldered her burden, but her need for me was greater than her awareness. I think perhaps Mom found an identity for herself in me."

As Isobel grew older, however, she developed what she describes as a "murderous rage" toward her mother, and by the time she was eleven or twelve, she couldn't wait to get away. "I used to think to myself, 'If I don't get out of here I won't survive.' When I did leave, I felt profoundly guilty about abandoning my mother. The fact that I left seemed brutal to me, and the realization that I was capable of such profound brutality added to the guilt."

At fourteen, Isobel went off to boarding school, where she discovered alcohol and, not long after, heroin. "I liked it a lot," she says calmly, "because it gave me what I was looking for: oblivion. I started doing all that stuff to save myself, but now it occurs to me that I was looking for a way to kill myself. Of course, I didn't see it that way at the time. I still think it something of a miracle I survived."

Survive she did, and on her twenty-seventh birthday she gave up both drugs and alcohol, but after less than two years a doctor prescribed Percodan, an addictive painkiller, for severe back pain. Isobel says one of the effects of the drug, which she enthusiastically abused because it was "legal," was that for six months she slept hardly at all. Although she has never been diagnosed as manic-depressive, she appears to have experienced something akin to psychosis, which she describes as "going through the looking glass" and living "in an archetypal universe." She soon began drinking again, and in little more than a year ended up in Bellevue in a true psychotic state. That episode ended Isobel's drinking and drug abuse; she's been free of both for ten years, takes no medications, and has been through no more looking glasses.

Those who study the impact of parental depressive illness on children have little to say about bipolar as opposed to unipolar mothers except to note, with surprise, that their children develop fewer problems. Had the researchers come to observe Isobel when she was still living at home, seemingly able to cope and enjoying the admiration of her father and other adults for doing so, perhaps they would have marked her down in their charts as a child relatively free of the repercussions of her mother's illness. But had they followed her into the future, they would have seen the shattering impact it had upon her development.

Isobel retained, during those years, a sense of her mother's love for her—achieved, perhaps, during those periods when her mother hovered between normality and the upper reaches of mania—that protected her somewhat from the down periods, making them seem less final in the way they removed her "real" mother from her. Nonetheless, she certainly did not emerge unscathed. Although attractive and possessed of a lively mind and a sense of humor, she has not married, nor has she yet, at thirty-six, had a lasting relationship with a man. Isobel says that those qualities which enabled her to survive her early life inhibit her now as an adult. "I have to work very hard on my instinct to deny truth and to control everyone and everything around me. Providing it doesn't kill you, I do think an experience like mine can act as a catalytic force, that it's possible to gain from it and create." But she admits she is only now beginning to think of herself and her own needs. "All that time I thought only of my mother and her needs. I never managed to properly separate from Mom, and I guess I missed some key developmental phases. I've been dealing with all that ever since."

More than a full year elapsed after my conversation with Isobel until I spoke with Sam—which makes a comparison between them even more startling. Their cultural and social backgrounds are at opposite poles: Raised in New York City, Isobel was the only child of a banker father and a mother who, before her illness, was a successful literary agent; when she left home it was to go to a private school. Sam, the middle of three brothers, grew up on the edge of genteel poverty in a small town in northern California; his mother was a profoundly religious woman trained as a social worker, although she was rarely well enough to practice her profession, and his father was the local chemist. When Sam left home at seventeen, he headed for a small community college a few miles away. Yet both suffered depression fallout as children and have felt its effects well into adulthood.

All three boys in Sam's family grew up in the shadow of their mother's enduring deep depression, but it was he who became the principal recipient of her attentions. His earliest recollections are of his mother confiding in him about her unhappy life and marriage to a cold, abusive husband—who was also a cold and abusive father. "I could understand, really understand, not just what happened to her and how she felt about it, but her process of feeling. It was important to me to listen, to take care of her. We were one, I was like a live-in therapist. My job was to listen and absorb what she said, and then explain things to her."

Like Isobel, Sam narrates his story in a matter-of-fact style, without self-pity or regret. "I didn't seem to matter a great deal to anyone except when I was taking care of my mother. I realized that whatever she felt, I should feel it too—all her anxiety, her doomsday approach to life. If I did anything that displeased her, she withdrew, became unavailable. I felt abandoned more than sad. I learned that I wasn't important, that my real role was not to think about myself but to take care of others. If you grow up with that, it lasts. Even now, when things are going well, I get nervous. Seeing to my own needs still feels to me like walking through fear—if I do it I'll be abandoned or shut out."

Sam says that he was never allowed to do the normal things that teenagers do when they're growing up: he was never permitted to be assertive or rebellious. When he was, he was punished. If he showed anger, his father beat him and his mother emotionally withdrew from him, so he learned to suppress it. "I had to be an entirely safe person for my mother to allow me to be around her, to be close to her. Did you ever read that poem by Emily Dickinson," he asked me, "the one where she wonders, 'Why did they shut me out of heaven? Did I sing too loud?' "

When he was about fifteen, Sam fell into his own black hole of depression. His mother, as always when there was disturbance in the family, took to her bed; his father turned away. "I fell apart," says Sam, "couldn't sleep for what seems an eternity. I prayed for sleep as a way not to have to think. My mind was like a dust storm. I had a video game at the time that involved shooting down asteroids, and in order not to go crazy in those long black nights, I began to shoot down the infinite dust in my mind as though each particle was one of those asteroids. And suddenly I realized I didn't have to stay in my mother's doomsday world. That's when my anger came. I lived with that anger for three years, without expressing it to anyone."

A year after Sam left home for college, he fell into another depression and decided to kill himself. When he called his parents to tell them, his mother wept and said he couldn't do that to her; his father said go ahead and do it, he had two normal sons and that was enough for him. After Sam had hung up, he wrapped tourniquets around his forearms to make his veins pop up, and climbed into the bathtub. "I had the knife ready, but then I looked up and saw myself in the mirror, and I was amazed because I saw a beautiful person, and I knew I couldn't kill that person. I thought to myself, 'It's her or me,' and I knew then it wasn't going to be me."

Sam's brush with suicide sent him to a talk therapist for the first time in his life. "I learned that everything was always about my mother, and that she addressed her own issues only through me. It's as if she saw herself as having carte blanche to do as she liked with me and to get what she wanted. My parents fought their own battles through me, too. So I seemed always to be in the middle." Sam says that through therapy he discovered that he hadn't ever been loved, that what he had been receiving from his mother was an imitation, a kind of pseudo-intimacy to meet her needs, not his. "I realized then I had to give myself the kind of love I wanted. My next step is to find out how to receive love from others." These are processes that most people take for granted, not as skills that have to be acquired.

Fathers and the Parenting Gap

It would be comforting to imagine non-depressed fathers as stepping briskly in to fill the parenting gap when mothers are depressed, but they don't. A researcher with the appropriate name of M. R. Dadds is one of the few to draw attention to this fact. Dadds's view is that as interactions between depressed mothers and their children deteriorate, causing both to become more difficult to handle and less rewarding to be with, fathers remove themselves from both. Nor do they feel particularly guilty about their withdrawal, instead assigning blame to the mother for being a poor parent or to the child for not being responsive to their own fathering efforts.

This behavior may in part be explained by traditional gender roles. Although society and personal attitudes are changing, the major child-rearing burden continues to fall on the mother; many fathers still don't see themselves as responsible in this regard. Another contributing factor is the phenomenon of assortative mating: spouses who bring mental health problems of their own to the marriage may find it difficult to perform well as fathers, particularly when they are in a troubled marriage and dysfunctional family.

One study that compared the problems of children in a family with a depressed or manic-depressive mother to others in which both parents were unipolar or bipolar found there were no more problems in the latter than in the former—causing at least one layperson to suspect that fathers living with a depressed spouse do so little parenting that it doesn't make much difference whether they are ill or not. The researchers, too, were surprised by their finding, and wondered if perhaps in such situations other family members or social support systems stepped in to close the gap. Yet anecdotal evidence from the friends and family group indicates that other family members also tend to distance themselves. Whatever the explanation, the parenting gap exists, and although substantiating research evidence is lacking, non-depressed mothers may also be guilty in this respect, as you will see below.

When the Depressed Parent is the Father

In reading the literature on depressive parents, it's hard to avoid the impression that all their children are the products of immaculate conception. Even in those journal articles that contain the words "Depressive Parents" in their titles, the word *father* rarely appears. Mothers dominate the researchers' interest, with the rationale that they, not fathers, do the essential nurturing. While the rate of depression in women is presumed to be twice that in men, you can bet your life there are depressive fathers out there, and that they, too, are causing problems for their kids.

While they aren't the primary nurturers, fathers do play a significant role in a child's life: they help shape the marital relationship and the environment it creates for the kids; they are or should be role models; and they are also a source of love, support, and companionship. When fathers are absent because of abandonment, separation, divorce, or death, children are invariably distressed. It is unreasonable, therefore, to expect that a father abducted by his depressive illness should cause a child any less distress than one removed by other reasons. In short, fathers count for a great deal in a child's life, and when they suffer from this illness the family equation is going to be thrown out of whack just as it is when mothers are depressed.

Judith, whose story in chapter 2 illustrates the self-doubt stage of depression fallout, is a child whose father's depression infused her upbringing. What makes Judith's experience of particular interest here is that not only did her father have the illness, but her mother did little to mitigate its impact on the four children and appears to have been only peripherally involved in the business of parenting. Judith's impression is that she viewed her mother's primary role as protector of her husband, rather than of her four children. As Judith notes, in her family it was the kids who were always at fault, not the parents. She says all four siblings lack self-esteem, and all but one have or had serious problems with alcohol and overweight; she is herself a recovering alcoholic. When Judith left home, she left not just her father but "them," and the self-enforced exile she maintained for several years was from both her parents.

Judith remains uncertain about the nature of her father's depressive illness, since her parents never openly acknowledged, confronted or discussed it as a family. Because of this, the children grew up believing their father's criticism and coolness was a sign he did not love them, or that they were too flawed to merit his love and approval. Judith says her opinion and confidence in herself, despite psychotherapy and her own best efforts, remains shaky and ungrounded. Much of our conversation was oblique because she still slides away from discussing what clearly was a difficult and unhappy childhood. What she does choose to remember and discuss reveals anger not only toward her father but toward her mother as well. Listening to the story, terms such as *enabler* and *co-dependent* come to mind, suggesting a mother who, instead of actively grasping the parental role with both hands, opted for, or was maneuvered into, a passive, subsidiary stance, one that inclined her to go along with the ill parent. If, as the literature suggests, depressive women tend to choose husbands with problematic backgrounds, depressive men presumably do the same. The net result is not much different, especially as far as the children are concerned.

Parenting Strategies for the Non-depressed Parent

So what are you to do if your parenting partner is depressed and falling down on the job? Confront the problem; if you duck it, it will grow and your spouse, your marriage, and your children will suffer. Talk with your depressed wife or husband about what's happening within the family. Choose a time when he or she is relatively unstressed, not just as you are leaving for the school play or the baseball championship that your depressed spouse has reneged on. Focus on the child's well-being, not your own. Make every effort not to be accusatory and critical, no matter how clear it is to you that the other is culpable. Refer to the research evidence—"Experts say that sometimes parenting is harder when one parent is depressed"— instead of complaining that your partner isn't doing his or her job properly. Remember, they have no self-esteem and will be all too ready to assume you are out to reduce it even further by saying, "You're a bad parent."

Children miss their depressed parent in the same way the caregivers described in chapter 3 grieve because their ill family members are no longer the same people they were before their illness. While you don't have to teach your children all that you now know about depression, they are quite capable of being told that Mom or Dad isn't well right now, but is taking medicine to feel better soon. Older children should be informed on a more specific level. Whatever you choose to tell them, the purpose is to allay their fears about the "changed" parent, and to assure them that in a while everything will be back to normal again. Consult the section of the preceding chapter on creating a family strategy.

If your parenting partner is in denial and refusing to take medication, explain to him or her the problems this may be causing for the kids. Depressed people don't stop loving their children; they just have a great deal more trouble showing it. The parental instinct remains alive, even though it may look moribund. You need to find a way to cajole it into action, which is, in this case, seeking treatment.

Fathers whose wives are depressed may need to rethink their own role vis-à-vis the children. Their kids will be more of a handful than usual, but pulling away from them will only increase their unhappiness and bad temper, and reinforce the cycle of familial distress. The non-depressed fathers described in this chapter did everything wrong. Denise Roberts's father was so selfishly miserable and worn out that he went days without even speaking to his daughters, having laid upon them much of the responsibility for coping with their mother, and punishing them when they did not measure up to his demands. Sam's father was cold and insulting, and conducted his battles with his wife through their son. Judith's mother added to her daughter's belief that she was unloved. Isobel's father moved out. All of the children fared badly.

More parenting by fathers doesn't necessarily mean staying home during the day or spending Sundays washing the kids' T-shirts. It does mean joining them at the dinner table, listening to what they have to say, taking a greater interest in their homework and other tasks, calling them occasionally from the office when they are home from school, or bringing home special treats from the local take-out joint. Show affection more demonstrably by offering hugs and kisses; this isn't time-consuming, but it's extremely reassuring for kids whose mother may be showing a lot less affection than normal. Take the children out of the house. Invite them to come along when you run errands, arrange play dates at a friend's house, take them for a walk on the beach or in the woods, or go for a drive and a hamburger. Your children need some breathing space and distraction to compensate for the tension at home.

Many in the friends and family group have complained that grandparents, aunts and uncles, and in-laws are reluctant to get involved when depression moves into the house, sometimes because of denial, and sometimes because they really don't understand how bad things are. While they may not be of much help in sorting out your problems, they can help with the children. Instead of going into chapter and verse about how impossible your spouse is these days, just ask them to help you cheer up and distract the kids. You can tell them your wife or husband is feeling very down and exhausted and it would be a big help if they'd lend a hand.

Non-depressed parents can also help by speaking with teachers and school psychologists. Since children of a depressed parent often have problems in school and become disruptive and difficult to handle, teachers may treat them accordingly. This will result in even more adverse behavior on the part of the children. Youngsters who are referred to the school counselor or psychologist may be unwilling to admit the source of their distress, either out of loyalty or lest they, like Denise Roberts, be identified as having a "mental" mother. When the school functionary is in the dark, the purpose of the intervention is defeated.

The salient message for parents is that while depressive illness is an impediment to good parenting, it should not excuse abdication of parental responsibilities. Being depressed does not correlate with being blind and stupid. Being married to a depressive does not correlate with being irresponsible. Both make constructive action difficult, but not impossible.

A Broader Agenda

The group of British researchers who are the collective voice of *Parental Psychiatric Disorder* make a strong contribution to the area of solutions. At the heart of the book is their conviction that those professionals—whether psychiatrists, psychologists, social workers, or others—whose primary responsibility is working with mentally ill parents, or whose job it is to promote the health and development of children, need to operate from a base of shared assumptions and common goals for families. Many of their concerns and suggestions are directed at individuals and agencies who serve families in need of public assistance, but the premise on which they are based applies to the private sector as well. Noting in the introduction that the book attempts to cover uncharted territory, they acknowledge that dealing with the combination of mental illness, couple relationships, and parenting issues is enormously complex. Furthermore, thinking about children and parents is often kept artificially separate because services are organized to help individuals, not families.

The program of several innovative groups that succeed in linking together all these elements is described in the book, but The Network—started by Jane Marlowe, whose mother's depression laid waste to her childhood—holds particular interest for depression fallout sufferers. The organization is an informal and loosely organized support group that enables young people and adults whose childhoods are similar to Marlowe's to address the heavy emotional burden of a parent's mental illness.

Marlowe started her organization in 1989 by the simple expedient of sending a press release to ten publications in the fields of health, social science, and women's issues. In it she asked anyone who had grown up with a parent suffering from mental illness and wanted to exchange experiences to get in touch. Soon she had enough enthusiastic responses to organize a self-help group that met for ten weeks; most who attended had never met anyone else who shared their problems, nor had they ever talked about how their past affected their present. The Network continues to grow, and now has members throughout England. Members communicate by telephone and letter, and everyone receives The Network's newsletter. Its address is listed in Appendix 1, "Information Resources."

Most of Marlowe's childhood memories revolve around her mother's illness. When she was not in the hospital, her husband and two daughters—Jane and her younger sister—were entirely responsible for her care, the only alternative being abandonment. Jane became the family's diplomat and "tried to communicate between family members who could no longer live in harmony and were bottling up acute stress because there was nowhere to take it." She felt as though she were constantly failing. "I missed [my mother's] presence as a person who took interest in what I did. That loss and watching her like a person close to death hurt very deeply. I thought she didn't care for me."

Like so many other children in her circumstances, she had a bumpy adolescence: "Alcohol, late nights, no homework, skipping school, not eating properly, too much too soon and no one noticing or taking an interest. I . . . used anger to survive. Ambition left me and I grew to hate my life. . . . I knew I had to leave home or I would kill myself." Only many years later was she able to experience a release, of sorts, from "so much unexpressed resentment, sadness, anger, grief, confusion, and fear," as do the other "Young Carers" who are members of The Network.

Marlowe put together a list of Young Carers' rights, which she offers as guidelines for public policy, at the same time pointing out the dichotomy that exists in her country and in ours as well: "In this society children are generally seen as 'cared for,' and this right is protected in social policy. It follows from this that children cannot be the carers. But in reality some children are. So policy and attitudes need to change."

Whether children are forced into a caregiving role by economic or other factors, or whether they are simply the recipients of faulty parenting caused by a depressive illness, they need help. Right now such help is not forthcoming, in large measure because the information researchers are gathering has not yet been applied by either clinicians or parents.

These children are more than passively unhappy. Many of them get into trouble; they abuse alcohol and drugs, fight, skip school or drop out, and have run-ins with the law. They have a higher rate of physical illness than do children of non-depressed parents, and a far higher rate of psychiatric illness. They have lower academic achievement rates, and that means they have more difficulty finding jobs that can support them and their own families. Having learned far fewer social skills than other children, they are often isolated and inept, and so have difficulty finding and soliciting help. The lucky ones will receive psychotherapeutic help, either privately or through city or state services if they cannot afford to pay for their own. One way or another, many will become what society calls a burden.

In addition to what mothers and fathers can do to help these children, professionals who care for the depressive or manic-depressive parent should make it their responsibility to take into consideration the probable effects of the illness upon children at home. Their excuses for failing to do so are that their patient is their prime responsibility and that they must preserve confidentiality. A more honest explanation is probably that they do not see such interventions as within their purview. Were they to speak up without being invited to do so, their efforts might be misinterpreted as meddling, a job they are not paid to do.

The notion that the family is somehow a private, sacrosanct unit, beyond the prying eyes of outsiders, has a firm hold on our collective democratic psyche. This point of view has allowed some alarming family business to be conducted behind closed doors. But studies have shown beyond doubt that depressive illness within a family can destroy the entire unit, as well as the individual members of it. Unlike child molesters and spousal abusers, about one-third of those who suffer from depressive illness do seek help for what ails them, putting professionals in a position to do something beyond medicating or psychotherapeutically assisting the parent. If even a fraction of them were to open their eyes a little wider and devote some portion of their time and attention to the ripple effects, a great deal of unhappiness could be avoided.

In the meantime, every depressive or manic-depressive parent and his or her spouse should take responsibility in the following ways:

- Any parent who suspects he or she suffers from a depressive illness should immediately seek help for it, inform the helper that there are children at home, and stick to whatever course of treatment is prescribed; if treatment is going badly, seek a second opinion.

- A spouse who suspects that his or her mate has the illness should persuade them to seek help, using the possible ill effects on the children as a principal arguing point.

- Fathers should be aware that a mother's depression particularly endangers effective parenting, and should accept responsibility for increasing their own parenting role to compensate.

- Both parents should initiate a policy of openness and collaboration in dealing with the illness and its effects, and devise a family strategy for coping with them.

- Children should be included in family deliberations to the extent they are able to understand; older children may be enlisted as full participants in the strategy, while younger ones may simply be given an explanation of what the illness is and how it may affect their parent's response to them.

- Children should be told that depression temporarily changes people; they need to be assured that the affected parent still loves them, although the parent may have difficulty demonstrating that love as long as he or she is ill.

- Children should be given a sufficient understanding of the illness and the effects of medication to allow them a sense of the future, of expectation that medication and other treatment will return their parent to them.

- Both parents should be aware that the effects of parental depression upon children do not disappear as soon as the medication takes effect; they persist. The mother and father should not expect the children immediately to snap out of whatever behavior they have adopted during the illness.

- If children start acting up in reaction to the parent's depression, the well parent should inform school officials of the other parent's illness as a probable cause. These children may need extra help and support, time with the school psychologist, or tutoring. Take advantage of parent-teacher conferences to see if there are signs of trouble at school.

- Children in such a situation need some fun, since they probably aren't getting it at home. The non-depressed parent and other family members should make extra efforts to distract and entertain them.

- Make sure these children get an extra helping of love. This is even more important if they are having problems at school or with their friends.

13

AGAINST STIGMA, FOR

SUPPORT

WHY DOES A COMMON TREATABLE illness carry a stigma strong enough not only to cause millions of people to hide what is wrong with them, but also to make their friends and families go along with the cover-up? Why is it so shameful to be a depressive or manic-depressive? Why do so many people still give no more than lip service to the fact that the illness is biological and involuntary? And why do they persist in suspecting that those who suffer from it are really malingerers and layabouts with good reason to feel guilty and ashamed?

I believe the answer is rooted in the American system of values. We are a nation founded on principles of self-determination, where—we are told—anyone can succeed if he or she simply tries hard enough. We are strong adherents of the bootstrap approach, which dictates that adversity can be overcome by the application of character and willpower. Because the mentally ill don't *look* sick, many people suspect them of making excuses for their shortcomings and as lacking in gumption.

The National Alliance for the Mentally Ill, which fights against stigmatization of people with mental illness, conducted a survey in a typical shopping mall. Asked to select causes of depression from a list, only 10 percent of those polled believed that mental disorders had a biological basis involving the brain. 71 percent said that mental illness was caused by "emotional weakness"; 65 percent said "bad parenting" was at fault; 35 percent noted "sinful behavior"; and 45 percent said that people "bring on their own illnesses." It's easy—and correct—to say these views are uneducated, but what makes them so difficult to dislodge is that they reflect the values of our society.

Stigma has been around for a very long time. In colonial America, when their families were unable or unwilling to provide care, those with mental illness were shackled and jailed. These were not new treatments; they were brought here by settlers from England and elsewhere who perpetuated a tradition that considered the mentally ill shameful and at fault, based on the values of the societies they came from.

During the nineteenth century and well into the twentieth, English views of mental illness, for instance, were shaped by a need to preserve the class system and the supremacy of the British Empire. In *All That Summer She Was Mad* (Continuum, 1981), Stephen Trombley follows the course of the writer Virginia Woolf's persistent mental disorder—probably recurrent bouts of deep depression—and the treatment prescribed for her by the three leading experts of her day: Dr. George Henry Savage, Sir Maurice Craig, and Dr. T. B. Hyslop. The views of these physicians, although expressed far more boldly, are remarkably similar to those of the mall shoppers. According to Trombley, to these doctors insanity was nothing more or less than nonconformance with the beliefs and wishes of the ruling elite. Savage bears him out by calling it "a disorder of mental balance which renders the person alien—that is, out of relationship with the surroundings into which he has been born, educated, and has hitherto fitted."

Dr. Savage, who did little for his patient other than prescribe potentially fatal sleeping drugs along with prolonged rest and a prohibition on thinking and writing, was followed by Dr. Craig, who offered the same prescription and was motivated by the same convictions. "The degree of education and the social status of a person whose conduct is under consideration are also important facts," he wrote, "for habits which would be regarded as decidedly eccentric in educated members of the upper class, might pass unregarded in the lower grades of society." (Both men saw social climbing as a form of insanity.) Nevertheless, many members of the latter suffered the rigorous horrors of Bethlam Royal Hospital (popularly known as Bedlam); the rich, like Woolf, were sent to private clinics.

Such views drew on the growing knowledge of genetics, which enabled their proponents to claim scientific validity for them. Branding the mentally ill not only as aliens and troublemakers but also as biological degenerates, they promoted eugenics in "the hope that the collective wisdom of [the Medico-Psychological Association of Great Britain] might evolve a practical scheme whereby a polluting stream might be dammed and great good thus accrue to the national health," as Savage put it in addressing that body.

Dr. Hyslop, called in to consult on whether or not Woolf should have a child, was, of the three, the most rampageous in condemning nonconformity as a sign of insanity. His "insane" targets included the Post-Impressionists, the Cubists, and promoters of women's suffrage and education for the lower classes. So convinced was he of the dangers posed by those who failed to behave according to the prevailing standards that he recommended that the insane forfeit their citizenship. His targets for statelessness were all those "who are incapable of aiding in their own survival, or of adding to the vigour of the race, and those who by reason of mental hebetude or other psychological factors are unable to support either themselves or their progeny, and who fall into the category of the 'unemployed' or 'unemployable.' "

No one seems to have criticized Hyslop's pronouncements except a former student who wrote in an obituary that "his latter days were saddened by something in the nature of a neurosis," owing to "an anxiety state in consequence of air raids during the war." But during his long career he was all the rage; far from being rated suspect or extreme, his ideas were welcomed and supported by those in power.

About the time Savage began to practice his trade in England, Freud was igniting the flame of psychoanalysis in Vienna. Although Hogarth Press, founded by Virginia and Leonard Woolf, published Freud's work in England, Virginia was never treated with psychotherapy. Had she lived in the United States, she surely would have been its recipient.

From the beginning, the American love affair with Freud was hot and heavy. Although in 1937 he mused about the possibility of chemical substances that might one day exert influence over the mind, his followers on this side of the Atlantic didn't share his speculative interest. Instead, they cleaved to psychoanalysis and its offshoots as the sole remedy. Freud's theory—that only a deep excavation of the unconscious could affect positive changes in one's feelings and behavior—was embraced here with a tenacity unmatched elsewhere.

So enthralled were we Americans with the psychoanalytic approach that we ignored the mounting evidence from other parts of the world that there was a biochemical aspect to depressive illness: the discovery in 1949 by an Australian psychiatrist that lithium could counter the effects of manic depression; another in 1951 by a pair of French psychiatrists that chlorpromazine controlled psychotic agitation; and a Swiss pharmaceutical company's claim in the mid-1950s that imipramine was an effective antidepressant.

Even earlier, a nineteenth-century German doctor, Emil Kraepelin, studied manic-depressives and schizophrenics—he termed the latter condition *dementia praecox*—and came up with two different sets of symptoms and the course of each, thus laying the foundation for modern psychiatry. Yet as recently as twenty years ago American psychiatrists were still routinely misdiagnosing manic depression as schizophrenia, and blaming the mothers of schizophrenics for having caused the illness by bad parenting. Only in 1980, with the publication of the third edition of the *Diagnostic and Statistical Manual of Mental Disorders*—the standard diagnostic reference work of the psychiatric profession—did a medical view of mental illness officially take precedence over Freudian theory.

Even within some circles of the medical profession, however, the biological explanation of mental illness is not universally accepted. Trombley states the issue as it was seen in Virginia Woolf's time: "[T]he insane are always guilty—of some transgression against society and the prevailing codes of that society. The behaviour that these doctors describe is, from their point of view, shameful—that is how they regard their patients." Depressive Kathy Cronkite, in her book *On the Edge of Darkness* (Doubleday, 1994), brings it up to date by quoting a distinguished contemporary expert on depression, Dr. A. John Rush, professor and vice-chairman for research in the Department of Psychiatry at the University of Texas Southwestern Medical Center. Rush acknowledges that "doctors are still reluctant to make the diagnosis [of depression] because they, too, feel like, 'Oh, you must have done something wrong. How did you get yourself in this pickle?' which sort of means that the patient is to blame."

Talcott Parsons proposed a social-contract theory that Dr. Donald Klein has updated; it provides a useful model for understanding the stigma against mental illness in our culture. Parsons's premise is that all societies expect their members to make contributions to and receive benefits from society in more or less equal balance. Society willingly suspends this contract in periods of illness and agrees to carry a disabled member until he or she is able to resume a productive role; helping people get well is a good investment.

This contract works well, says Klein, providing there's proof of illness. But people with a depressive disorder don't look as though they're sick and can't produce any evidence—a limb in a plaster cast, a hacking cough, a suspect X ray—to substantiate their claim to exemption. This makes society suspicious that the depressive is trying to get something for nothing. Feeling exploited, it tears up the contract and feels morally justified in doing so. If a claimant lands in the hospital in full-blown mania or with a stomach full of sleeping pills, this is acceptable evidence, and the contract is reinstated, but its terms aren't open-ended. Lacking such proof, depressives and manic-depressives are taken for malingerers and layabouts, and society stamps their claims Denied.

Had psychiatrists been able earlier to locate the cause of depressive disorders in the brain's chemistry, everyone would by now have accepted depression and manic depression as no-fault illnesses responsive to medication. Had psychotherapists been less in love with Freud, they might have been less resistant to the medical evidence when it finally did emerge. Instead, the two are in opposing camps. With the false dichotomy so precisely drawn, the general public's suspicion remains that if a talk therapist can "fix" it, then the problem must be with the sufferer, not with an involuntary illness. The persistent belief that this is a personal fault rather than a medical, correctable mishap stigmatizes the illness and causes those who suffer from it to go into hiding.

The cover-up is costing the U.S. economy an estimated $43.7 billion annually. The MIT Sloan School of Management, together with the Analysis Group, Inc., broke this figure down into workplace, mortality, and direct costs. In 1990, they found, workplace costs— based on lost productivity and 88 million days of absenteeism— totaled $23 billion; mortality costs—loss of lifetime earnings by the 15,000 men and about 3,400 women who that year took their own lives as a consequence of depression—were $7.5 billion; and direct costs— inpatient and outpatient care including the cost of medication— were $12.4 billion. Their study made no attempt to estimate the cost of substance abuse and physical violence—both associated with depressive illness—or of broken marriages, imperfectly cared-for children, and personal unhappiness; these are, indeed, beyond measurement. Despite medical evidence, backed up by the economic facts and personal testimony, the view that depressives are shamming is widely held. Current discussions in Congress, the insurance industry, and the business community on the issue of attaining insurance parity for mental illness are a case in point. No physical evidence to offer? No money.

A growing number of distinguished Americans have courageously broken ranks by publicly acknowledging their depression or manic depression, offering proof that this illness can coexist with talent and productivity. But even among the "outed," many continue to see themselves as lacking will, showing how deeply this stigma is rooted in our culture. Dr. Kay Jamison holds "an absolute belief that I should be able to handle my own problems." For years she hid her manic depression from all but a handful of close associates and friends, and, with the publication of her memoir, worries that her peers will judge her work as suspect because she suffers from the disorder she is researching.

In *The Beast* (Penguin, 1996), Tracy Thompson, an award-winning journalist with *The Washington Post*, traces her long-term secret depression through a near suicide to its eventual harnessing by medication. She writes that she often felt shame and still finds it almost impossible to stop thinking of her depression as a personal defect that she should be able to correct herself, without the aid of an antidepressant. Her journalist colleagues, she says, warned her not to write the book because "revealing I had suffered a mental illness would harm my career."

When Senator Thomas Eagleton revealed he had been hospitalized three times for depression, and had been given electroshock treatments, it caused an uproar and his eventual removal as George McGovern's vice-presidential running mate. Depression as the explanation for Vince Foster's suicide has been resisted by many who prefer a blacker scenario, in part because Foster revealed his illness to only a few intimates and asked they remain silent because he feared for his job in the White House.

In his book *Moodswing*, Dr. Ronald Fieve identifies as manic-depressive or hypomanic a cluster of business tycoons who hid their illness, including Harold Geneen of ITT, Charles Bluhdorn of Gulf and Western, Jack Dreyfus of the Dreyfus Fund, and Charles Zeckendorf and Ivan Boesky. Contemporary legend Ted Turner is a diagnosed manic-depressive, but while his illness is no secret to those closest to him, he has never publicly outed himself despite the protection his spectacular success affords him.

There are no cures for depressive illness, but only ways of controlling it. This means that once the stigmatic label is applied, it sticks. Depression and mania can sometimes leak through the protective barrier of medication. Serious depressives and manic-depressives can't pop a pill and forget about their problem. They deal with its stubborn residue on a daily basis, are used to its demands, and mobilize their characters to fight it. Until they feel spectacularly in control, most will remain silent and feel safer as a result.

Enclosed in that silence are their families and close friends, a monolithically reticent group. The easy answer to why intimates close ranks is loyalty. Loyalty does play a part, but so does stigma. Were this not the case, we would be as open about depression as we are about cancer or heart disease. Bruce Link of the New York State Psychiatric Institute is one of the researchers now investigating stigma and its effects upon the mentally ill. Link says most people have negative opinions about people with mental illness. When they themselves fall prey to it, they personalize those opinions and as a result anticipate rejection. In an attempt to minimize or avoid it, they become more withdrawn and their ability to function diminishes. Family members and close friends do the same because they, too, fear adverse reactions from others. Feeling guilt by association, they hide the other's illness as well as its effects upon themselves.

Many depression fallout sufferers also feel that their emotional turmoil and poor coping skills are signs of personal weakness. They're afraid that if they speak the first piece of truth, they'll open up Pandora's box and reveal their own inadequacies. Far safer to keep that box shut and throw away the key. But this only seals them in with the depressive, and ensures an even more damaging case of depression fallout.

The way out is to put loyalty to the depressive aside and talk, but this will bring only partial release if you turn to the uninitiated for understanding. You need empathy, not sympathy, and the most likely place to find it is from others who also live in close proximity to this illness. I began attending the friends and family support group for research purposes, and found what I was looking for. But I also found something I had not been seeking: a way to assuage and then erase the pain and anger I had accumulated in all those years of growing up with my depressive mother. This provided an unexpected joy and a source of confidence in myself that had been previously out of reach. I am lighter, stronger, and freer, no longer the carrier of guilt, shame, resentment, or anger. I am a true believer in support groups.

Starting Your Own Support Group

Howard Smith, whose wisdom and advice inhabits every nook and cranny of this book, is this section's sole authority. He has never met a support group that didn't love him. The next best thing to having him in charge of yours is to heed what he has to say here about how to start and run one. He's one expert you'll never have to second-guess.

One of Howard's potent tools is his sense of humor. Though you may find it hard to imagine, our group is quite often convulsed with noisy laughter. We don't take one another's problems lightly, nor do we laugh at others' burdens. But Howard has the knack of finding the absurd in a manic-depressive's ability to persuade her spouse that she needs twenty pairs of sneakers, or in a depressive's fifth call to his wife's office to ask where his red sweater is hidden. Allow some humor into yours. It's a great healer.

There will be little laughter and even fewer insights if you just sit around and chew the fat with two or three other depression fallout sufferers. Cataloging a jeremaid of complaints may get rid of some tension and relieve your isolation, but it won't help you to find specific solutions. There's a difference between a gripe session and a support group; you need a real support group. Your first step is to see if a suitable one exists in your area. Both the National Depressive and Manic-Depressive Association (NDMDA) and the National Alliance for the Mentally Ill (NAMI) have chapters throughout the United States. You can get a list of them by calling or writing their respective national headquarters, the addresses and phone numbers of which appear in Appendix 1. Although most of the groups they sponsor are organized for depressives and manic-depressives, some chapters have one for family members and friends as well.

If you do locate a group and find it serves your purpose, you have had a stroke of good luck. If, however, the group is poorly organized, meeting only sporadically and operating without guidelines, it won't be the answer. Attend only long enough to learn what *not* to do and then go start one of your own. Sitting in on an Al-anon group (a

Twelve Step program for relatives and friends of alcoholics) may also give you some useful pointers in this respect, but, as I'll explain, you shouldn't use a Twelve Step program as your model. Though these work for their members, they won't be as effective for your purposes.

Assembling a Core Group

You need a core group of three to get going. The most obvious place to look for core members is within your group of friends. Reading this book should have provided you with a sixth sense capable of sniffing out fellow depression fallout sufferers. Go trolling as I did and you, too, are sure to get a bite or two. When you're out fishing, remember that all volunteer entities entail teamwork. Often those with the energy and vision to help launch groups end up sinking them by making unilateral decisions without soliciting the input of others. Look for good communicators who are also good listeners and who will approach the task as a team. Pick people who are down to earth and focused, not those who are hysterical or scattered, no matter how eager to help. They will become members later, when the group is up and running.

As soon as you have chosen your fellow founding members, sit down together and think about how you're going to proceed. A support group is more than a casual gathering of like-minded people. To accomplish its purpose the group needs structure, and that means some standards and rules to give it cohesion and continuity of purpose. While you are working on that, you may begin sharing some common concerns, checking out what this book has to say about them, and trying some of the solutions offered. This will give you a feeling for how problems are voiced and how they can be addressed before you rush to recruit others to join you. Think of these initial meetings as dress rehearsals, and rotate leadership so that all three of you have a chance to try your wings.

Who and Where

Recruiting others is your next job. Start by making a list of places with bulletin boards on which you can post a notice that might read as follows: "A group is being formed to share problems common to family members and close friends of someone who is seriously depressed or manic-depressive. Please call [insert a member's phone number] if you are interested in learning more." Unless you want to, there's no reason to include a name.

Possible locales for posting your notice include laundromats, copy shops, libraries, health-food stores, supermarkets, and churches. If NAMI or NDMA has a local chapter that serves people with the illness, ask if you can drop off copies so their members can share them with families or partners. Ask the local PTA if you can do the same at its meetings. Similarly, you might post notices where AA or Al-anon groups meet, because alcoholism often goes hand-in-hand with depression.

Ask your family doctor if he will allow flyers to be placed in his office. He may be reluctant to do this if you are just getting started, because he can't be sure the group will be on track and helpful; once you are well established he will probably agree. You can take the same approach at the local clinic or hospital. Psychiatric nurses and social workers will probably make referrals because they, more than doctors, have contact with the families of patients.

Be prepared with a date, time, and place for the first meeting. It will probably take place in someone's living room, but in the long run that isn't the optimal choice. As soon as your group expands to ten or more members, hold meetings in a neutral location. That way there won't be a host or hostess who can't resist displaying their talent for entertaining. Support groups that turn into coffee klatches or cocktail parties are doomed to failure. My group offers only candy contributed by members and tossed onto a table within everyone's reach. Caffeine addicts bring their own takeout coffee or tea.

Possible sites include a local school after class time, a church basement, a member's office, or any similarly impersonal yet private place that's available. If this means paying a small rental fee, divide the costs and make them payable in advance by all members on a monthly or longer basis. Start off by holding meetings on a semimonthly basis. It's better to have ten people once every two weeks than a handful once a week. Make the switch to weekly meetings when the size of your population warrants it. Choose a time that accommodates people who work. Each meeting should last about two hours. Whatever place, date, and time you pick, try to make them consistent. Last-minute changes confuse and discourage attendees, and they'll stop coming. Never cancel a meeting if only a few people turn up. If a change is inevitable, inform members well in advance.

When people begin to call in response to your notice, resist any temptation to screen them, unless of course they sound like certified weirdos—"I bet you're cute, will there be any booze?" or "Trashing crazies is right up my alley"—of which there may be a few. Deal with them by saying your plans aren't yet finalized; take their phone numbers and tell them you'll contact them at some future time. Don't try to keep the group homogeneous, composed only of people from your own social milieu. Variety will make for a much richer and more absorbing group. Urge parents to come as a team, and to bring older siblings with them. Never allow anyone to bring their own depressive or manic-depressive; they will be an inhibiting presence. Be firm about this, and take Howard's word that there should be no exceptions to this rule.

Whichever member is taking the calls needs to remind him- or herself that the phone number is not a hot line but a source of information about the group's purpose, time, date, and place. If someone phones in distress because a friend or relative is suicidal or out of hand, suggest calling the presiding doctor or 911. Don't attempt to solve problems over the phone. Later on, when the group has become a living, breathing organism, it can function as an informal network to help members through crisis, as my group once helped Clarence when Lina went off the deep end. He was so upset by her crazy behavior—she had a pot of water boiling on every burner of the stove and was ready to heave them at him—that he forgot all the right things to do. We reminded him of them and held his hand by telephone for a few days until things, and he himself, calmed down.

Standards and Rules

A support group should be like a nonexclusive club with a small board of directors. Like any club, it needs to maintain standards, and its members need to follow rules. Your core group is responsible for deciding what they'll be. I've already mentioned a few basics: Anyone (except those weirdos) can be a member. The friend or family member who has the illness may not attend. No drinks or meals are served. Meet at the same place, time, and day of the week for every meeting, preferably not in one member's house.

In addition, there are three other essential standards to establish.

- *Confidentiality is imperative.* No one *ever* has the right to repeat what is said and heard within the confines of the group. One way to ram this point home is by pointing out the obvious: How would you feel if a private concern of your own were to become common knowledge? How would your spouse, lover, parent, or child feel if his or her behavior became fodder for gossip? Repeat the need for confidentiality both at the opening and closing of every session.

    While neither depressives nor manic-depressives have any reason to feel ashamed of their illness, they might not be pleased if this information was broadcast in either their social or professional milieu. Tell your partner or family member about the group and its purpose, but emphasize that everything said within the confines of the group remains there. When you circulate notices of meetings or other information pertinent to the group, mail them in blank envelopes so that snoopers have no way of knowing their contents. Although this may seem a minor matter, it isn't.

- *Everyone should be allowed a chance to speak.* Don't set arbitrary time limits, but do be careful that a few stories don't dominate the session. As a loose rule, fifteen minutes is usually long enough for someone to say what he or she needs to say; after that most begin repeating themselves. There are several ways to cut someone off painlessly. A leader can wait for a pause and then say, "This is a really interesting discussion. Let's come back to it when others have had a chance to speak." An alternative is to pick up on one of the speaker's themes, such as, "He criticizes me all the time," or "She's stopped taking her medication," throwing the topic out for open discussion by saying, "That's a very common problem. Is anyone else having trouble in this area?"

- *Interruptions are allowed* and should be encouraged. By interruption I mean cross-talk, that is, asking questions and interjecting a helpful piece of advice or a word of sympathy. Twelve Step programs don't allow this; members of those groups are permitted to speak only after they have raised a hand and been recognized by the person in charge. Howard considers this too authoritarian. Some of the best sessions in my group have been dominated by so much cross-talk that Howard hardly has to say a word. That way, members have far more chances to interact, and the session is more dynamic and productive for everyone.

Rules are really a matter of good manners. People who always come late, for instance, must wait until prompt members have had their say. I've never been in the group when someone was tossed out, but Howard says he's done it on occasion, usually when a member has been consistently rude to others or disruptive. I have certainly heard him let a member know he or she is hogging the limelight, but he does it with skill, not with rules. If you try to subject communication to a whole pile of petty regulations, you won't get much of it. Use common sense when deciding what your rules should be.

Who Should Be the Group Leader?

This is a matter for the core group to decide. Some people don't want to be the leader; others aren't cut out for it. Whoever has the job should know that *group leader* is not a synonym for *dictator*. The job requires tact and patience. Leaders should, for instance, hold off telling their own stories until later in the evening to ensure that they don't dominate the meeting.

You may want to assign the role of leader on a rotating basis. Howard gets one Friday off in every six, and the three facilitators who sit in for him all have very different styles. Although we're always glad to have Howard back again because of our affection for him, his subs serve a good purpose. Some members respond well to one style; others respond better to another. But try to ensure that leaders come to every group so they're on top of stories. If one of a rotating group of leaders comes only on his or her designated day, they risk repetitious renditions of tales already told and retold in prior sessions. Many attendees simply can't resist a virgin audience, and even less a virgin leader. When a leader runs a group after several weeks' absence, previous leaders should bring him or her up to date on what's been going on so that no time is wasted.

Always decide who will lead in advance of the meeting, so as to avoid an Alphonse-and-Gaston routine.

Calling the Group to Order

The leader should open the group by stating its purpose. He or she might say something like this: "We're all here to get support and help for our common problem, and to learn more about this illness and its treatment. Try not to be judgmental about what you hear, but to share experiences. I'm the group leader for today. Think of me as a guide. You may speak without raising your hand, but I have overall responsibility for making sure we all stay focused and on track. Everything you hear in the group is confidential. That's our most important rule."

It's helpful if everyone has a stick-on label with his or her first name. Don't use last names; they contribute nothing, and asking for them will make many people nervous. The members of the core group should, however, ask for the full names, addresses, and phone numbers of all members so they can communicate any change of plans and check up on very distressed members between sessions. If some prefer not to provide them, that is their privilege.

Getting the Discussion Going

When Howard has finished his opening remarks, he then asks each member to state briefly why he or she is present by saying, "My name is ———, and my [husband, wife, son, mother, etc.] is a depressive [or a manic-depressive]." After this initial identification, he asks if anyone has something that needs saying right away, thus allowing super-distressed members a chance to go first. If no one responds, he does one of two things. He may choose someone who knows the ropes and ask him or her to begin, by saying, for example, "Joe, I know you've been having trouble with Betty's irritability. How have things been going this past week?" If that opening fizzles, he suggests one of the topics most apt to emerge in every group. These include denial, compliance with medication, and the usefulness of therapy, or such questions as, "How can a lethargic depressive be so angry?" and "How do I encourage my manic-depressive to see a doctor?"

How to Deal with Medical Questions

Questions are frequently asked about medical issues. Since you and your fellow members lack the training that Howard and his facilitators receive, you won't be able to address authoritatively such problems as dosage, side effects, drug choices, and new treatments. The present work gives you a lot of information, but also repeatedly reminds you that you aren't an expert on diagnosis and treatment. You have sufficient information to pose knowledgeable questions to the experts, but not to answer them. There are a number of ways to address this problem.

First, raise the level of amateur expertise by asking all group members to collect books and articles about depressive illness from newspapers, magazines, and medical journals. Articles should be photocopied and made available at each meeting for ten or fifteen cents a page. That allows everyone to begin building their own files. Appendix 1 includes some helpful references in this respect.

Second, consider the possibility of occasionally inviting a knowledgeable professional to whom everyone can pose questions that are specific to their own family member or friend. Depending on where you live and whom you select as your expert, the cost will range from $100 to $400, so be sure members know well in advance and can prepare their questions and present them clearly. If ten members pay $40 apiece, they'll get their money's worth if you have chosen your expert well.

Before you invite a professional sage, check his or her credentials thoroughly. If you fail to do so, you're risking far more than money. Newcomers, especially, will take every word uttered as gospel even if it's not, and more knowledgeable members shouldn't end up challenging or dueling with the so-called authority. You may want to sound out potential experts by explaining what their role will be. Then take a question that you or another member might pose, and see how the expert deals with it. If the answer is unspecific or hard to understand, thank them for their time and try someone else.

Stay clear of inviting someone's family doctor. Unless he breaks the mold, he probably knows more about ulcers and heart disease than he does about depressive illness. A better candidate, if you can't find an established expert in the field, is an intern at the local hospital or clinic who specializes in psychiatry. Psychiatric nurses and social workers, though they haven't been to medical school, often know a great deal and are accustomed to dealing with a patient's family and friends.

If you don't invite an expert, you can still help members pose the right questions to the professional in charge of their depressive or manic-depressive. If members offer medical information to the group, be sure they are repeating accurately what they have been told by a doctor, not what they sort of think he might have meant. You can always rely on the accuracy of information in this book, but you cannot be sure a given piece of medical lore is relevant to your own sufferer. Every case of depression or manic depression is different; what may help one person will not necessarily help another.

Group Dynamics

A group soon develops a life and personality of its own, and that's desirable. Don't try to squeeze and pull it to fit a precise shape. Leaders do, however, need to be aware of the group's flow and how to keep it alive and directed toward the members' needs. Not every attendee comes for the same purpose. Some look for hope or information; others have a need to vent or are seeking support and validation. In my group, Howard's proclivity is for providing information and solutions. "What can we do to help you tonight?" is his typical intervention. My inclination is to give people a chance to talk about how they feel, so my interjections often start with a sympathetic shove—"I bet that made you feel just awful"—or a reminder that they shouldn't feel guilty because they blew up at their depressive or can't cure their illness. Most people need both approaches. Newcomers, especially, tend to focus almost entirely upon their depressive's illness and never on themselves. Let them get a feeling for how the group operates before calling on them; they rarely volunteer their first time. Should their first meeting be one that sticks close to the informational side of the problem, encourage them to express their own feelings, if they so wish, by asking them a question like mine.

Expressing feelings doesn't mean that people should leap up and hug each other. In Howard's group we never intrude in that manner. When members become very emotional, or break down and

cry, we allow them time to proceed in their own way without interruption other than a few words of encouragement. In the end they'll
say what they need to say. Group tears and hand-holding really
aren't useful, and sometimes they rob a speaker of dignity. If, however, a member comes week after week without expressing his or her
feelings, that doesn't mean he or she has none. It may mean he is a
stiff-upper-lip type like James, or that she is embarrassed or fearful
of breaking down. Give them an opportunity to speak, but don't
push them to emote. When a member, as has happened in my group
on several occasions, asks why everyone talks about their depressives,
not about themselves, use this as an opening to encourage a discussion about the strong negative feelings that are characteristic of
depression fallout.

One of the advantages of allowing people to interject questions
and comments is that bores and egotists can't dominate the proceedings. After four or five meetings it will be fairly easy to identify
them. One woman in my group repeatedly told the same story and
each time received excellent advice. She always responded to the
advice by saying, "Yes, but . . ." For several meetings, other members
just squirmed in their chairs and allowed her to get away with this,
but finally, fed up, they drowned her out: "There are no buts here.
Why don't you listen to what is being said?" She never did listen, and
we were thrilled when she stopped coming.

Sometimes speakers repeat themselves because they're so upset.
When they do, try to slow them down and break their problem into
parts, making it more manageable and amenable to solutions.

Closing the Meeting

Try to end every meeting on a hopeful note, not with someone sobbing in discouragement. People need to leave the meeting feeling
better than when they arrived. Orchestrating this is a matter of skill,
which good leaders develop over time. You'll learn not to leave the
most difficult cases for the tail end, and you'll also learn how to turn
a downer into an upper by saying, for instance, "You'll come to realize that your problem is manageable and that it does have a solution." Someone else is bound to chime in and agree. Or the leader
might compare the member's seemingly hopeless story to a similar
one now under control.

Repeat the confidentiality dictum, but encourage members to exchange telephone numbers and to go out for a drink or coffee together. Everyone with depression fallout needs to know as many fellow sufferers as possible. They are a source not only of mutual support, but of a lot of information and advice about personal matters not fully explored during the meeting. The more opportunities they have to listen to one another, the more positives they will discover in what previously appeared to be an annihilating negative.

There is almost always a solution if one plugs away at it. Of course, sometimes the solution takes time to work. In the two years during which I have attended the friends and family group, every difficult situation in which its members have been caught up has improved. Clarence doesn't even come anymore, except to drop in occasionally as a sort of elder statesman who offers a piece of sage advice here and there. James's wife, Ursula, hasn't been to a rehab clinic, but her multiple medications have been reduced to three—thanks to an expert second opinion—and now keeps a far more civil tongue in her head because James has learned to assert his rights. The Sofa Mother's daughter has a firm therapist who doesn't let her get away with skipping her medication, and Paula's Meredith has a job. I have made peace with my memories of my mother. Every case of depression fallout has become less severe and less isolating than when it was first presented to the group, and all but a few members who were present when I first came have left the group and are now living a far less troubled existence.

Mental illness seems suddenly to have at last captured the public's attention in a constructive fashion. Almost every week brings another movie, book, or television program about it, both fiction and nonfiction. The fallacious myths that sustain stigma are being dispelled both on a personal level and in the realm of public policy. Only this morning, as I prepared to tackle these final paragraphs, *The New York Times* reported on its first page that the government has issued clear guidelines for employers on how to accommodate the mentally ill, just as in the past it had issued similar guidelines for accommodating physically disabled workers. This is a big step toward parity, and others will surely follow soon. Bit by bit, stigma and discrimination are beating a retreat. With them will go the undeserved shame and guilt carried by depressives and manic-depressives, and by their families as well.

In the meantime you now possess all the ammunition you need

to do battle with your own depression fallout. I have employed the terminology of battle throughout this book, because depression fallout doesn't just fade away. It needs to be conquered. If you fail to take action against it, you will be its prisoner. This is not a time for negotiation or truce. Better by far to be the outright victor. Go win the war.

Appendix 1

Information Resources

The following organizations can provide printed material and information about depressive illness as well as addresses of state and local chapters and support groups:

American Psychological Association
202-336-5700

American Psychiatric Association
212-682-6069

National Alliance for the Mentally Ill
1-800-950-NAMI

National Depressive and Manic-Depressive Association
1-800-82-NDMDA

National Foundation for Depressive Illness
1-800-248-4344

National Mental Health Association
1-800-969-6642

National Institute of Mental Health Depression Awareness, Recognition, and Treatment (D/ART)
1-800-421-4211

U.S. Department of Health and Human Services
1-800-358-9295

Dr. Ivan Goldberg (for detailed information about depressive illness and treatment)
E-mail: Psydoc@PsyCom.Net
http://www.psycom.net/depression.central.html

The Network, based in England, is a self-help organization for depression fallout sufferers. It has members throughout that country, and publishes a newsletter. Write to The Network, P.O. Box 558, London SW2 2EL, England.

Appendix 2

Medications Used in Treating Mental Disorders

Notes: Trade (brand) names are capitalized. When there is more than one brand name for a drug, they are listed in alphabetical order. Following the list of medications are some commonly used medical abbreviations.

Generic and Trade (Brand) Names		Use(s) of Medication
Adapin	doxepin	antidepressant
amantadine	Symmetrel	side-effect control
amitriptyline	Elavil	antidepressant
Anafranil	clomipramine	antidepressant
Antabuse	disulfiram	blocks alcohol metabolism
Artane	trihexyphenidyl	side-effect control
atenolol	Tenormin	side-effect control
Ativan	Lorazepam	antianxiety agent
Aventyl	nortriptyline	antidepressant
bethanechol	Urecholine	side-effect control
bupropion	Wellbutrin	antidepressant
Buspar	buspirone	antianxiety agent
buspirone	Buspar	antianxiety agent
carbamazepine	Tegretol	mood stabilizer
Catapres	clonidine	anti-ADD/antianxiety agent
Centrax	prazepam	antianxiety agent

Medications Used in Treating Mental Disorders (cont.)

Generic and Trade (Brand) Names		Use(s) of Medication
chlorpromazine	Thorazine	antipsychotic
chlordiazepoxide	Librium	antianxiety agent
Cibalith-S	lithium citrate	mood stabilizer
clomipramine	Anafranil	antidepressant/anti-OCD
clonazepam	Klonopin/Rivotril (Canada)	antianxiety agent
clonidine	Catapres	anti-ADD/antianxiety agent
clorazepate	Tranxene	antianxiety agent
clozapine	Clozaril	antipsychotic
Cylert	Pemoline	psychostimulant/potentiates antidepressants
cyproheptadine	Periactin	side-effect control
Cytomel	liothyronine	potentiates antidepressants
Decadron	dexamethasone	diagnostic test for depression
Depakene	valproic acid/ Valproate	mood stabilizer
Depakote	divalproex/Valproate	mood stabilizer
deprenyl	*see* selegiline	antidepressant
desipramine	Norpramin	antidepressant
Desoxyn	methamphetamine	psychostimulant
Desyrel	trazodone	antidepressant/hypnotic
dexamethasone	Decadron	diagnostic test for depression
Dexedrine	dextroamphetamine	psychostimulant/potentiates antidepressants
dextroamphetamine	Dexedrine	psychostimulant/potentiates antidepressants

diazepam	Valium	antianxiety agent
disulfiram	Antabuse	blocks alcohol metabolism
divalproex	Depakote	mood stabilizer
doxepin	Sinequan/Adapin	antidepressant
Effexor	venlafaxine	antidepressant
Elavil	amitriptyline	antidepressant
Eskalith	lithium carbonate	mood stabilizer
ethchlorvynol	Placidyl	hypnotic
felbamate	Felbatol	mood stabilizer
Felbatol	felbamate	mood stabilizer
fluoxetine	Prozac	antidepressant/anti-OCD
fluphenazine	Prolixin	antipsychotic
fluvoxamine	Luvox	antidepressant/anti-OCD
gabapentin	Neurontin	mood stabilizer
Haldol	haloperidol	antipsychotic
haloperidol	Haldol	antipsychotic
imipramine	Tofranil	antidepressant
Inderal	propranolol	side-effect control
isocarboxazid	Marplan	antidepressant
Klonopin	clonazepam	antianxiety agent/mood stabilizer
Lamictal	lamotrigine	mood stabilizer
lamotrigine	Lamictal	mood stabilizer
levothyroxine	Synthroid	potentiates antidepressants/mood stabilizer
Librium	chlordiazepoxide	antianxiety agent
liothyronine	Cytomel	potentiates antidepressants/mood stabilizer
lithium carbonate	Eskalith	mood stabilizer
lithium carbonate	Lithane/Lithonate/Lithotabs	potentiates antidepressants

Medications Used in Treating Mental Disorders (cont.)

Generic and Trade (Brand) Names		Use(s) of Medication
lithium citrate	Cibalith-S	mood stabilizer/potentiates antidepressants
Lithonate	lithium carbonate	mood stabilizer/potentiates antidepressants
Lithotabs	lithium carbonate	mood stabilizer/potentiates antidepressants
lorazepam	Ativan	antianxiety agent
loxapine	Loxitane	antipsychotic
Loxitane	loxapine	antipsychotic
Ludiomil	maprotoline	antidepressant
Luvox	fluvoxamine	antidepressant
Manerix (Canada)	moclobemide	antidepressant
maprotoline	Ludiomil	antidepressant
Marplan	isocarboxazid	antidepressant
meprobamate	Miltown	antianxiety agent
mesoridazine	Serentil	antipsychotic
methamphetamine	Desoxyn	psychostimulant
Miltown	meprobamate	antianxiety agent
mirtazapine	Remeron	antidepressant
Moban	molindone	antipsychotic
moclobemide	Manerix (Canada)	antidepressant
molindone	Moban	antipsychotic
Nardil	phenelzine	antidepressant
Neurontin	gabapentin	mood stabilizer
Norpramin	desipramine	antidepressant
nortriptyline	Aventyl/Pamelor	antidepressant
olanzapine	Zypreza	antipsychotic
Orap	pimozide	antipsychotic

oxazepam	Serax	antianxiety
Pamelor	nortriptyline	antidepressant
Parnate	tranylcypromine	antidepressant
paroxetine	Paxil	antidepressant
Paxil	paroxetine	antidepressant
pemoline	Cylert	psychostimulant/potentiates antidepressants
Periactin	cyproheptadine	side-effect control
perphenazine	Trilafon	antipsychotic
phenelzine	Nardil	antidepressant
pimozide	Orap	antipsychotic
pindolol	Visken	potentiates antidepressants
Placidyl	ethchlorvynol	hypnotic
prazepam	Centrax	antianxiety
Prolixin	fluphenazine	antipsychotic
propranolol	Inderal	side-effect control
protriptyline	Vivactil	antidepressant
Prozac	fluoxetine	antidepressant
Remeron	mirtazapine	antidepressant
Risperdal	risperidone	antipsychotic
risperidone	Risperdal	antipsychotic
Ritalin	methylphenidate	psychostimulant/potentiates antidepressants
selegiline	Eldepryl	antidepressant
Serax	oxazepam	antianxiety
sertraline	Zoloft	antidepressant
Stelazine	trifluoperazine	antipsychotic
Surmontil	trimipramine	antidepressant
Symmetrel	amantadine	side-effect control
Synthroid	levothyroxine	potentiates antidepressants/mood stabilizer

Medications Used in Treating Mental Disorders (cont.)

Generic and Trade (Brand) Names		Use(s) of Medication
Tegretol	carbamazepine	mood stabilizer
temazepam	Restoril	hypnotic
Tenormin	atenolol	side-effect control
thioridazine	Mellaril	antipsychotic
Thorazine	chlorpromazine	antipsychotic
Tofranil	imipramine	antidepressant
Tranxene	clorazepate	antianxiety agent
tranylcypromine	Parnate	antidepressant
trazodone	Desyrel	antidepressant/hypnotic
triazolam	Halcion	hypnotic
trihexyphenidyl	Artane	side-effect control
Trilafon	perphenazine	antipsychotic
trimipramine	Surmontil	antidepressant
Urecholine	bethanechol	side-effect control
Valium	diazepam	antianxiety agent
valproic acid	Depakene	mood stabilizer
Valproate	Depakote/Depakene	mood stabilizer
venlafaxine	Effexor	antidepressant
Vivactil	protriptyline	antidepressant
Wellbutrin	bupropion	antidepressant
Zoloft	sertraline	antidepressant
Zyprexa	olanzapine	antipsychotic

Abbreviations

bid	twice a day
BP	bipolar
BPD	borderline personality disorder

CPZ	chlorpromazine (Thorazine)
DMI	desipramine (Norpramin)
hs	at bedtime
IMI	imipramine (Tofranil)
IV	intravenous
MAOI	monoamine oxidase inhibitor
od	once a day
PBO	placebo
po	by mouth
prn	as needed
SSRI	selective serotonin reuptake blocker
q4h	every four hours
qd	once a day
qid	four times a day
RIS	Risperidone
TCA	tricyclic antidepressant
tid	three times a day
UP	unipolar
VA	valproic acid

Compiled by and reprinted with permission of Ivan Goldberg, M.D.
Psydoc@PsyCom.Net

Bibliography

Anderson, C. A., and C. L. Hammen. "Psychosocial Outcomes of Children of Unipolar Depressed, Bipolar, Medically Ill, and Normal Women: A Longitudinal Study." *Journal of Consulting and Clinical Psychology* 61, no. 3 (1993).

Breggin, Peter. *Toxic Psychiatry*. New York: St. Martin's Press, 1991.

Coyne, James C., G. Downey, and J. Boergers. "Depression in Families: A Systems Perspective." In *Developmental Perspectives on Depression*. Rochester, N.Y.: University of Rochester Press, 1992.

Coyne, James C., R. C. Kessler, M. Tal, J. Turnbill, C. B. Wortman, and J. F. Greden. "Living With a Depressed Person." *Journal of Consulting and Clinical Psychology* 55, no. 3 (1987).

Cronkite, Kathy. *On the Edge of Darkness*. Garden City, N.Y.: Doubleday, 1994.

Dyer, J. G., and D. E. Giles. "Familial Influence in Unipolar Depression: Effects of Parental Cognitions and Social Adjustment on Adult Offspring." *Comprehensive Psychiatry* 35(4) (1994).

Fieve, Ronald R. *Moodswing*. New York: Bantam Books, 1989.

Gelfand, Donna M., and Douglas M. Teti. "How Does Maternal Depression Affect Children?" *Harvard Mental Health Newsletter*, November 1995.

Goleman, Daniel. *Vital Lies, Simple Truths*. New York: Simon and Schuster, 1986.

Graham, Katharine. *Personal History*. New York: Alfred A. Knopf, 1997.

Hammen, Constance. "The Family-Environmental Context of Depression: A Perspective on Children's Risk." In *Developmental Perspectives on Depression*. Rochester, N.Y.: University of Rochester Press, 1992.

Hirschfield, Robert M. A. "Guidelines for the Long-Term Treatment of Depression." *Journal of Clinical Psychology* 55:12 suppl. (December 1994).

Jamison, Kay Redfield. *An Unquiet Mind*. New York: Alfred A. Knopf, 1995.

Kahn, Jana, James C. Coyne, and Gayla Margolin. "Depression and Marital Disagreement: The Social Construction of Despair." *Journal of Social and Personal Relationships* 2 (1985).

Keitner, Gabor I., and Ivan W. Miller. "Family Functioning and Major Depression: An Overview." *American Journal of Psychiatry* 147 (1990).

Keitner, Gabor I., I. W. Miller, and C. E. Ryan. "The Role of the Family in Major Depressive Illness." *Psychiatric Annals* 23:9 (September 1993).

Kingsbury, Steven J. "Where Does Research on the Effectiveness of Psychotherapy Stand Today?" *Harvard Mental Health Newsletter,* September 1995.

Klein, Donald F. "Depression and Anhedonia." In *Anhedonia and Affect Deficit States.* Edited by D. C. Clark and J. Fawcett. New York: PMA Publishing Corp., 1987.

———. "A Proposed Definition of Mental Illness." In *Critical Issues in Psychiatric Diagnosis.* Edited by Robert L. Spitzer and Donald F. Klein. New York: Raven Press, 1978.

Klein, Donald F., and Donald C. Ross. "Reanalysis of the National Institute of Mental Health Treatment of Depression Collaborative Research Program General Effectiveness Report." *Neuropsychopharmacology* 8, no. 3 (1993).

Klein, Donald F., and Paul Wender. *Understanding Depression.* New York: Oxford University Press, 1993.

Koplewicz, Harold S. *It's Nobody's Fault.* New York: Times Books, 1996.

Kramer, Peter D. *Listening to Prozac.* New York: Viking, 1993.

Link, Bruce G., F. T. Cullen, J. Mirotznik, and E. Struening. "The Consequences of Stigma for Persons with Mental Illness: Evidence from the Social Sciences," in *Stigma and Mental Illness.* Edited by Paul J. Fink and A. Tasman. Washington, D.C.: American Psychiatric Press, 1992.

Ludwig, Arnold M. "Mental Disturbance and Creative Achievement." *Harvard Mental Health Newsletter,* March 1996.

Manning, Martha. *Undercurrents.* San Francisco: HarperSanFrancisco, 1994.

Marlowe, Jane. "'Shaping the Silence': a personal account," in *Parental Psychiatric Disorder.* Edited by Michael Göpfert, Jeno Webster, and Mary V. Seeman. Cambridge, England: Cambridge University Press, 1996.

Mufson, Laura, D. Moreau, M M. Weissman, and G. L. Klerman. *Interpersonal Psychotherapy for Depressed Adolescents.* New York: Guilford Press, 1993.

National Institutes of Health Consensus Conference, "Diagnosis and Treatment of Depression in Late Life." *Journal of the American Medical Association* 268, no. 8 (1992).

Papolos, Demetri F., and Janice Papolos. *Overcoming Depression.* Harper & Row, 1987 (revised 1992).

Radke-Yarrow, M., E. Nottelman, P. Martinez, M. B. Fox, and B. Belmont.

"Young Children of Affectively Ill Parents: A Longitudinal Study of Psychosocial Development." *Journal of the American Academy of Child and Adolescent Psychiatry* 31:1 (January 1992).

Real, Terrence. *I Don't Want to Talk About It*. New York: Scribner's, 1997.

Roberts, Denise. "'On Being and Becoming Mindless': A Personal Account." In *Parental Psychiatric Disorder*. Edited by M. Göpfert, J. Webster, and M. V. Seeman. Cambridge, England: Cambridge University Press, 1996.

Sacks, Oliver. *An Anthropologist on Mars*. New York: Vintage, 1996.

Struening, Elmer L., A. Stueve, P. Vine, D. E. Kreisman, B. G. Link, and D. B. Herman. "Factors Associated with Grief and Depressive Symptoms in Caregivers of People with Serious Mental Illness." In *Research in Community and Mental Health* vol. 8, Greenwich, CT: JAI Press, 1995.

Sturn, Roland, and Kenneth B. Wells. "How Can Care for Depression Become More Cost-Effective?" *Journal of the American Medical Association* 273 (1995).

Styron, William. *Darkness Visible*. New York: Vintage, 1990.

Thompson, Tracy. *The Beast*. New York: Penguin, 1996.

Trombley, Stephen. *All That Summer She Was Mad*. New York: Continuum, 1981.

Weissman, Myrna M. "Depression: Current Understanding and Changing Trends." *The Annual Review of Public Health* 13 (1992).

Wells, Kenneth B., R. D. Hays, M. A. Burnam, W. Rogers, S. Greenfield, and J. E. Ware, Jr. "Detection of Depressive Disorder for Patients Receiving Prepaid or Fee-For-Service Care." *Journal of the American Medical Association* 262, 23 (1989).

Women and Depression. Edited by Ellen McGraph, G. P. Keita, B. R. Strickland, and N. F. Russo. Washington, D.C.: American Psychological Association, 1990.

Index